Jerrold R. Brandell, PhD
Editor

MW00723287

Psychoanalytic Approaches to the Treatment of Children and Adolescents: Tradition and Transformation

Psychoanalytic Approaches to the Treatment of Children and Adolescents: Tradition and Transformation has been co-published simultaneously as *Psychoanalytic Social Work,* Volume 8, Numbers 3/4 2001

Pre-publication
REVIEWS,
COMMENTARIES,
EVALUATIONS . . .

"**R**ICH AND DETAILED. . . . This book is vivid evidence of the continued power of psychoanalytic therapy for children and adolescents. Here are new findings in child development, new meanings of familiar symptoms, and creative new therapeutic techniques."

Scott Dowling, MD
Training & Supervising Analyst
Cleveland Psychoanalytic Institute
Ohio

The Haworth Press, Inc.

Psychoanalytic Approaches to the Treatment of Children and Adolescents: Tradition and Transformation

Psychoanalytic Approaches to the Treatment of Children and Adolescents: Tradition and Transformation has been co-published simultaneously as *Psychoanalytic Social Work*, Volume 8, Numbers 3/4 2001.

The *Psychoanalytic Social Work*™ Monographic "Separates"

Below is a list of " separates," which in serials librarianship means a special issue simultaneously published as a special journal issue or double-issue *and* as a "separate" hardbound monograph. (This is a format which we also call a "DocuSerial.")

"Separates" are published because specialized libraries or professionals may wish to purchase a specific thematic issue by itself in a format which can be separately cataloged and shelved, as opposed to purchasing the journal on an on-going basis. Faculty members may also more easily consider a "separate" for classroom adoption.

"Separates" are carefully classified separately with the major book jobbers so that the journal tie-in can be noted on new book order slips to avoid duplicate purchasing.

You may wish to visit Haworth's Website at . . .

http://www.HaworthPress.com

. . . to search our online catalog for complete tables of contents of these separates and related publications.

You may also call 1-800-HAWORTH (outside US/Canada: 607-722-5857), or Fax 1-800-895-0582 (outside US/Canada: 607-771-0012), or e-mail at:

getinfo@haworthpressinc.com

Psychoanalytic Approaches to the Treatment of Children and Adolescents: Tradition and Transformation, *edited by Jerrold R. Brandell, PhD, BCD (Vol. 8, No. 3/4 2001). "Outstanding . . . The case material is beautifully presented and affords readers the experience of witnessing master clinicians at work. This book is timely and profound, a valuable addition to the libraries of all mental health professionals who work with children, adolescents, and their parents. It is equally useful for those in the field who teach and supervise." (Diane Siskind, MSW, BCD, Author,* A Primer for Child Psychotherapists*; Faculty, New York School for the Study of Psychotherapy and Psychoanalysis)*

Comparative Approaches in Brief Dynamic Psychotherapy, edited by William Borden, PhD (Vol. 6, No. 3/4 1999). *Provides an introduction to contemporary models of brief dynamic psychotherapy and describes fundamental tasks and methods in time-limited intervention.*

Narration and Therapeutic Action: The Construction of Meaning in Psychoanalytic Social Work, edited by Jerrold R. Brandell, PhD, BCD* (Vol. 3, No. 2/3 1996). *Nine contributors examine various aspects of narrative theory and its relationship to psychoanalysis and clinical social work.*

*Published under the title *Journal of Analytic Social Work*

Psychoanalytic Approaches to the Treatment of Children and Adolescents: Tradition and Transformation

Jerrold R. Brandell, PhD, BCD
Editor

Psychoanalytic Approaches to the Treatment of Children and Adolescents: Tradition and Transformation has been co-published simultaneously as *Psychoanalytic Social Work*, Volume 8, Numbers 3/4 2001.

The Haworth Press, Inc.
New York • London • Oxford

Published by

The Haworth Press, 10 Alice Street, Binghamton, NY 13904-1580 USA

The Haworth Press is an imprint of The Haworth Press, Inc., 10 Alice Street, Binghamton, NY 13904-1580 USA.

Psychoanalytic Approaches to the Treatment of Children and Adolescents: Tradition and Transformation has been co-published simultaneously as *Psychoanalytic Social Work,* Volume 8, Numbers 3/4 2001.

The development, preparation, and publication of this work has been undertaken with great care. However, the publisher, employees, editors, and agents of The Haworth Press and all imprints of The Haworth Press, Inc., including The Haworth Medical Press® and The Pharmaceutical Products Press®, are not responsible for any errors contained herein or for consequences that may ensue from use of materials or information contained in this work. Opinions expressed by the author(s) are not necessarily those of The Haworth Press, Inc. With regard to case studies, identities and circumstances of individuals discussed herein have been changed to protect confidentiality. Any resemblance to actual persons, living or dead, is entirely coincidental.

Cover design by Thomas J. Mayshock Jr.

Library of Congress Cataloging-in-Publication Data

Brandell, Jerrold R.
Psychoanalytic Approaches to the Treatment of Children and Adolescents: Tradition and Transformation / Jerrold R. Brandell.
     p. cm.
    "Co-published simultaneously as Psychoanalytic Social Work, volume 8, numbers 3/4 2001."
    Includes bibliographical references and index.
    ISBN 0-7890-1726-1 (hard : alk. paper) – ISBN 0-7890-1727-X (pbk : alk. paper)
    1. Child psychotherapy. 2. Adolescent psychotherapy. 3. Child analysis. 4. Adolescent analysis. I. Psychanalytic social work. II. Title.

RJ504.B73 2002
618.92′8917–dc21
                                                    2001059417

Psychoanalytic Approaches to the Treatment of Children and Adolescents: Tradition and Transformation

CONTENTS

Introduction

In the nearly one hundred years that have elapsed since Freud's publication of his pioneering work with "Little Hans," psychoanalysis has transformed not only our clinical work with children, but also has immeasurably enriched our understanding of normal child and adolescent development as well as developmental deviations and derailments. We have gradually come to understand childhood and adolescence as a complex tapestry of developmental themes, conflicts, and crises–sometimes discontinuous or discrete, at other times, harmonious and integrated, yet always occurring within a transactional matrix of environmental influences and internal experience.

Although libido theory and the Oedipus complex and its various resolutions, pathological and adaptive, once represented the overarching framework for understanding both developmental and clinical processes with children, contemporary psychoanalytic approaches to children and adolescents reflect theoretical and clinical heterogeneity. The development of the ego and of the self now command as much attention as the distribution of the libido once did; attachment theory and direct observational studies of infants and young children have augmented and, in some cases, supplanted earlier classical psychoanalytic notions about pre-oedipal experience. Similarly, ideas derived from object relations theory, such as containment and projective identification, have gradually gained currency for the contribution they make both to the clinical situation and to psychoanalytic developmental theory.

In this transdisciplinary anthology, eight authors explore the changing terrain of child and adolescent psychoanalysis and psychoanalytic therapy. The contributions are both innovative and varied, ranging from the highly abstract and theoretical to those which consider very specific dimensions of clinical process. Collectively, they make a compelling case for the continued relevance of psychoanalytic ideas in the treatment of children and adolescents, and this in a practice climate transformed by the dicta of managed care, biological psychiatry, and aggressive marketing by pharmaceutical companies to consumers, a sort of *managed care-psychiatric-pharmaceutical complex*. In such an envi-

[Haworth co-indexing entry note]: "Introduction." Co-published simultaneously in *Psychoanalytic Social Work* (The Haworth Press, Inc.) Vol. 8, No. 3/4, 2001, pp. 1-8; and: *Psychoanalytic Approaches to the Treatment of Children and Adolescents: Tradition and Transformation* (ed: Jerrold R. Brandell) The Haworth Press, Inc., 2001, pp. 1-8. Single or multiple copies of this article are available for a fee from The Haworth Document Delivery Service [1-800-342-9678, 9:00 a.m. - 5:00 p.m. (EST). E-mail address: getinfo@haworthpressinc.com].

1

ronment, one in which physical illness has become the root metaphor for psychological problems and conflicts, the significance imputed to descriptive diagnosis often far exceeds any attention to etiology and intercurrent dynamics. Interventions are typically symptom-based, time-limited, and only minimally focused on the therapeutic relationship and clinical process. Particular behaviors may be "targeted" for intervention, and novel solutions to a client's problems may be proposed in the first hour or in the absence of any therapeutic relationship. Truly, psychoanalytic treatments now compete in a marketplace saturated with alternative therapies, single session solutions, and biological agents; and yet, as the following essays demonstrate, psychoanalytic ideas continue to offer something unique and enduring.

The first essay, "The Play Relationship and the Therapeutic Alliance," is written by Morton Chethik and examines the function of play in normal development and within the treatment relationship in both child and adult psychotherapy Noting its developmental function and the natural role that play has as a mode of communication with children, Chethik proceeds to emphasize its centrality in the construction of the therapeutic alliance. He also suggests that play is an essential element in the transference. Two detailed clinical vignettes furnish illustrations of the ways in which play themes and scenarios develop in therapy and of how their association to the therapeutic alliance and transference relationship may be understood and interpreted.

Interestingly, as child analysts have focused increasingly on the developmental function of play in the context of child treatment, some have concluded that play as a process independent of interpretation may *itself* promote change and growth (Abrams, 1993; Cohen & Solnit, 1993; Neubauer, 1993, 1994; Yanof, 1996). This idea is, of course, not a novel one; it has its modern origins in the pioneering work of developmentalist and child analyst Erik Erikson (1959, 1977) and was recognized by the poets long before that.[*] Play, these authors contend, may be both mutative and sufficient *without* interpretation in work with developmentally arrested or ego-impaired children (Yanof, 1996; Cohen & Solnit, 1993; Neubauer, 1993). Although in Chethik's clinical illustrations the interpretive work is revealed as an important ingredient in his therapeutic efforts to create meaning through play, his article, nevertheless, redefines play in a manner that elevates its importance for the clinical encounter. This seems particularly true of his characterization of the alliance as a libidinal attachment, a new object relationship through which developmental experiences involving play may be revivified and which, ultimately, lead to the forging of more enduring and successful adaptations.

In the second article, "Discovering the Inner Life of a Child: Exploration, Illumination, and Elaboration of Play Space," Brenda Lovegrove Lepisto focuses on play as a potential space in child psychoanalysis. Many children referred for psychoanalytic treatment, she suggests, have for various reasons failed to develop the capacity of *mentalization*–the ability to make sense of one's inner experience and of the actions of others. In consequence, they are incapable of reflective thinking, and similarly limited in their ability to play, to express wonderment, or to use imagination. Whether the result of trauma, conflicts, or constitutional deficits, such children have simply failed to develop a *theory of mind*. One such child is Dante, a severely-disturbed, traumatized seven-year-old boy in residential care who was referred because of a history of violent, destructive aggression and acting out, verbal abusiveness, and phobic behavior. Using such ideas as Winnicott's conception of transitional space, Fonagy and Target's formulation of mentalization, Baron-Cohen's research on children's development of a theory of mind, and the idea of joint attention, Lepisto shows us how the analytic process supports and promotes her young patient's evolving capacity for reflective thought and efforts at meaning-making. In her conclusion, Lepisto acknowledges that such ideas, though representing fields of research generally considered to fall outside the domain of mainstream psychoanalytic thought, can both deepen our understanding of the children we treat and enhance our technical repertoire, thus leading to meaningful augmentation of the analytic play space.

"The Impact of Early Loss on Depression: Dynamic Origins and Empirical Findings," by Irene M. Bravo, assays a range of psychoanalytic theories and research investigations that link early object loss to subsequent depression. This integrative essay is compelling, indeed revitalizing, in an epoch dominated by biological models and treatments for depression, for it approaches depression and grief as the biologically mediated, *psychological* outcome of identifiable, traumatogenic events and experiences. Bravo begins with a methodical description of the rich contributions classical psychoanalysis, Kleinian and middle tradition object relations theories, attachment theory, ego psychology, and self psychology have made to our understanding of the relationship between early experiences of loss or deprivation and both chronic and acute depressive reactions. This discussion is broadened by her summary of important empirical investigations that test various psychoanalytic theoretical premises about the causes of depression. Though the findings reported are mixed, ideas such as the influence of maternal depression on young children, experiences of early childhood bereavement, and the nature of the infant-maternal attachment do appear to predict later problems with depression. In a series of illustrative clinical vignettes, Bravo describes three children and an adult female with depressive conditions rooted in particular developmental experiences in infancy and early childhood. In two cases, the original fixation is hypothesized to have occurred at the pre-ambivalent oral phase of development, while in a third case, the ambivalent oral phase is identified as the locus of the original depressive reaction. These three are in contrast to a fourth case in which oedipal themes predominate, and the depression has more of an introjective quality, reflecting the involvement of superego in the original conflict.

Judith Mishne, in "Transformation of Narcissism and the Intersubjective Therapeutic Exchange: A Depressed Adolescent Patient Shares His Music and Lyrics with His Therapist," explores the topography of adolescent depression in both descriptive and phenomenological terms. She reviews several different bodies of literature, examining such ideas as separation-individuation, affective disorders, bipolarity, and co-morbidity, as well as examining various historical controversies in our psychoanalytic understanding and clinical approach to adolescent depression. Dynamic ideas regarding adolescent substance abuse are also presented and discussed, from the early contributions of Rado and Knight, which emphasized intrapsychic conflictual themes, to more recent views placing greater emphasis on the influence of familial, sociocultural, and self structure variables. In the second portion of her article, Mishne presents a detailed, carefully reconstructed adolescent treatment case involving a very bright seventeen-year-old boy, Mark, who presented with symptoms of depression, multiple substance use, declining academic performance, and explosive anger and defiance. Mishne's clinical understanding of this gifted, yet narcissistically entitled and rebellious, young musician is filtered through the theoretical lenses of psychoanalytic self psychology and intersubjectivity. His extreme aggression and propensity to react with unbridled rage to perceived narcissistic slights thus become more comprehensible as the disintegration products of an enfeebled, structurally compromised self. Ultimately, the principal goal of Mishne's treatment with Mark becomes that of assisting him in modifying primitive narcissistic structures through the clinical equivalent of optimal responsiveness and attunement.

The next two chapters, "Two Systems of Self-Regulation," by Jack and Kerry Kelly Novick, and "A Two-Systems Approach to the Treatment of a Disturbed Adolescent," by Howard D. Lerner, are complementary contributions that explore theoretical and clinical dimensions of a new psychoanalytic developmental model. Rooted in their earlier work on sadomasochism and its organizing omnipotent beliefs, the Novicks present their latest work on what they have termed a dual track, two-systems model for conflict resolution and self-regulation. They identify some of the inherent limitations of a single-track developmental approach to normality and pathology, suggesting an alternative model that encompasses two distinctive developmental trajectories. One is termed an *open system* and is characterized by attunement with reality and such attributes as competence, effectance, and the capacity for pleasure in learning, playing, and socializing. The other is described as a *closed system* and is characterized by misattunement with reality, omnipotent and sadomasochistic fantasies, and a variety of pathological symptoms. In the remainder of their article, the Novicks explore various implications of a two-systems approach relative to the building of a therapeutic alliance and within each phase of treatment, from evaluation to termination. They locate their model within a tradition that has sought, though without notable success, to make psychoanalysis a general psychology–an aim originally linked to Freud and further advanced by such dual track developmentalists as Robert White, Heinz Hartmann, Erik Erikson, and Anna Freud. Although the Novicks' contribution shares certain characteristics with each of these, their framework also achieves a balance between experience-distal theory and experience-near observations of clinical processes and of developmental phenomena that may well bode for greater success in achieving this, heretofore, elusive goal.

Howard D. Lerner's richly detailed case presentation, which describes a nine year course of psychoanalytic treatment with a very disturbed adolescent boy, both illustrates and operationalizes many of the ideas discussed in the Novicks' chapter, particularly those having to do with the formation and development of the therapeutic alliance. Lerner begins by exploring the sociocultural context within which omnipotent beliefs are supported, if not fostered, noting that adolescent problems such as violence, drug use, promiscuous sexuality, eating disorders, body piercing, and other self-destructive activities reveal both core sadomasochistic pathology and efforts, albeit ill-fated, at self regulation. He then applies the two-systems model to his patient, Chris, a very bright 14-year-old high school freshman at the time he was originally referred by his school guidance counselor, parents, and local police. Though the evidence was not incontrovertible, Chris was under strong suspicion of having been involved in the theft of $23,000 from an elderly relative, as well as in a series of neighborhood burglaries. There was additional evidence that he was both dealing and using illegal drugs. In the material that follows, Lerner offers a revealing narrative process summary of his work with this adolescent boy. Important details from Chris's family history, such as his early traumatization by both a paternal uncle and his maternal grandfather, are explored. Lerner also details his efforts to identify therapeutic tasks that are resonant with Chris's interests and level of comprehension, and how these ultimately lead to an effective therapeutic alliance. The technical handling of Chris's defensive use of omnipotence and avoidance of reality is also described, as are therapeutic efforts to support and strengthen his autonomy, healthy assertiveness, and adaptive attempts to extricate himself from family pathology.

"The Therapeutic Process with Children with Learning Disorders," by Joseph Palombo, explores the complexities of treating children with neuropsychological deficits in the context of individual psychotherapy. Palombo, whose theoretical

framework is that of psychoanalytic self psychology but who has also incorporated such narrative concepts as *emplotment* and *conventionalization* into his
clinical approach, believes that children and adolescents with learning disorders have neither been especially well understood nor effectively treated by
psychoanalytic clinicians. In an effort to enable such patients opportunities to
create increasingly coherent self-narratives, he advocates that psychotherapy
with neurocognitively impaired children and adolescents be redefined as a
nonlinear process consisting of discrete "moments" that are *concordant, complementary,* or *disjunctive.* Concordant moments involve the establishment of
a holding environment through the clinician's empathic immersion in the
child's subjective experience, while complementary moments focus on aspects of the transference-countertransference matrix. Disjunctive moments,
which are believed to be both inevitable and necessary for psychological
growth, involve breaches or ruptures in the clinician's capacity to remain in
empathic attunement with a child or adolescent patient. During such moments,
the most essential task of the therapist is to repair the rupture, thereby reestab-
lishing his/her empathic availability and ability as an attuned listener. Using
several clinical vignettes that highlight transference and countertransference
reactions, *inter alia,* Palombo concludes his paper by highlighting some of the
unique therapeutic challenges posed by neuropsychologically impaired children and adolescents.

In the final contribution to this collection, "Attention Deficit Disorder,
Anxiety Disorder, and Learning Disabilities: Preliminary Results of an Ob-
ject-Relational/Psychoeducational Treatment Approach with an Eight-Year-Old
Girl," Vivian Farmery presents an unusual and finely detailed clinical case involving an eight-year-old girl, Emily, who suffered from attentional deficits,
hyperkinesis, associated learning disabilities, and anxiety symptoms. At first impression, the clinical approach used in this girl's treatment appears to contrast
sharply with the primarily individual treatment approach proposed by
Palombo, who incorporates concepts derived from narrative theory into an
overarching framework of psychoanalytic self psychology. Farmery's work
with Emily doesn't involve traditional therapy at all, inasmuch as this had not
proven useful to her. It is characterized as both object-relational and
psychoeducational and includes contributions from a multidisciplinary treatment team of educational specialists, part-time teachers, a social work clinician, an occupational therapist, a consulting senior child analyst, and the
child's mother. In other respects, however, the two approaches may not be so
dissimilar. For example, Farmery, like Palombo, emphasizes the importance
of a supportive "holding environment," though, in her case, it is achieved
through a milieu-like structure created especially for Emily, whereas Palombo
frames a highly similar phenomenon as a *concordant moment.* The

Winnicottian concepts of *true* and *false self,* by which Farmery explores the concatenation of problems culminating in Emily's performance failures, may also have a rough parallel or homologue in Palombo's use of the concept of *emplotment.* Emplotment is described as a mechanism through which subjects "become characters in other persons' narratives . . . (taking on) . . . the themes of the narratives of those they wish to please"; and it appears, like the false self, to possess a defensive cast, obscuring the motives, desires, and ambitions of the subject. The false self is, of course, a façade that the child erects so as to achieve compliance with caregivers' inadequate adaptations; while it permits the child to survive impingements and deprivations, it is always at the cost of "living falsely" (Winnicott, 1960, 1965). Finally, Palombo uses the concept "adjunctive functions" to refer to those particular, non-transference-based functions that neurocognitively deficient children may seek from therapists. Palombo observes that such needs may require the modification of psychotherapeutic technique insofar as they are "brain driven" rather than solely determined by unconscious motives. Somewhat analogously, Farmery speaks of a dual educative-therapeutic role played by Emily's teachers, who often provided coaching and training to assist her in negotiating with various systems, performing cognitive tasks, making transitions, and so forth.

In an important sense, these last two articles illustrate the abiding principle in the field of contemporary child and adolescent psychoanalysis and psychotherapy to which we earlier referred: theoretical heterogeneity. It might be argued that, in one respect, very little has changed in the past 65 years, when a contentious debate was being waged between Melanie Klein and Anna Freud over their respective positions on the process of child treatment, the role of transference, use of interpretation, and so on. We have never really had a unitary model of child or adolescent psychoanalysis and appear to be even further from that elusive goal now than at any point in the past. In fact, represented within this anthology are no less than four distinctive theoretical frameworks for understanding development, psychopathology, and the process of child and adolescent treatment. On the other hand, there appears to be greater acceptance today of the *value* of contrasting theoretical and clinical approaches; in effect, most psychoanalytic clinicians agree that there is always more than one answer to any given clinical conundrum or developmental dilemma. Ego psychologists and Lacanians, self psychologists and Winnicottians, relationalists and drive theorists, have each discovered a *truth*–or to borrow from a contemporary parable, one part of the elephant.

In the pages that follow, the reader will find abundant evidence of consensus and conflict, disparity and complementarity, resonance and dissonance. That one might cogently and convincingly argue each of these positions illustrates both the beauty of the psychoanalytic approach and the complexities of the human condition it seeks to understand. It may also offer us reassurance that our most highly valued traditions in child and adolescent psychoanalysis remain alive and well, even as they continue to evolve.

NOTE

*As William Blake once wrote, "The Child's Toys and the Old Man's Reasons / Are the Fruit of the Two Seasons." (from "Auguries of Innocence" in *The Pickering Manuscript*).

REFERENCES

Abrams, S. (1993). The developmental dimensions of play during treatment: Conceptual overview. In *The Many Meanings of Play*, A. Solnit, D. Cohen, & P. Neubauer (Eds.). New Haven, CT: Yale University Press, pp. 221-228.

Cohen, P. & Solnit, A. (1993). Play and therapeutic action. *Psychoanalytic Study of the Child*, 48:49-63.

Erikson, E. (1959). *Childhood and Society*. New York: W.W. Norton & Co.

Erikson, E. (1977). *Toys and Reasons*. New York: W.W. Norton & Co.

Neubauer, P. (1993). Playing: Technical implications. In *The Many Meanings of Play*, Ed., A. Solnit, D. Cohen, & P. Neubauer. New Haven, CT: Yale University Press, pp. 44-53.

Winnicott, D. (1960). The theory of the parent-infant relationship. In *The Maturational Process and the Facilitating Environment*. New York: International Universities Press, 1965.

The Play Relationship
and the Therapeutic Alliance

Morton Chethik

ABSTRACT. This article examines the function of play in normal development and within the treatment relationship in both child and adult psychotherapy. Noting its developmental function and the natural role that play has as a mode of communication with children, the author emphasizes the centrality of play in the construction of the therapeutic alliance. The therapeutic alliance is characterized here as a libidinal attachment, a new object relationship through which developmental experiences involving play may be revivified and, ultimately, may lead to the forging of more enduring and successful adaptations. Two detailed clinical vignettes furnish illustrations of the ways in which play themes and scenarios develop in therapy, and how their association to the therapeutic alliance and transference relationship may be understood and interpreted. *[Article copies available for a fee from The Haworth Document Delivery Service: 1-800-HAWORTH. E-mail address: <getinfo@haworthpressinc.com> Website: <http://www.HaworthPress.com> © 2001 by The Haworth Press, Inc. All rights reserved.]*

KEYWORDS. Play, therapeutic alliance, child psychoanalysis, dynamic play therapy

INTRODUCTION

The function of play in child development has been given increasing importance in recent years. Various topics involving play have been developed in

Morton Chethik, MSW, is Emeritus Professor, Department of Psychiatry, University of Michigan; Faculty, Michigan Psychoanalytic Institute.

[Haworth co-indexing entry note]: "The Play Relationship and the Therapeutic Alliance." Chethik, Morton. Co-published simultaneously in *Psychoanalytic Social Work* (The Haworth Press, Inc.) Vol. 8, No. 3/4, 2001, pp. 9-20; and: *Psychoanalytic Approaches to the Treatment of Children and Adolescents: Tradition and Transformation* (ed: Jerrold R. Brandell) The Haworth Press, Inc., 2001, pp. 9-20. Single or multiple copies of this article are available for a fee from The Haworth Document Delivery Service [1-800-342-9678, 9:00 a.m. - 5:00 p.m. (EST). E-mail address: getinfo@haworthpressinc.com].

9

whole sections of *The Psychoanalytic Study of the Child* (volumes 42 and 53), and in the recent publication of the book *The Many Meanings of Play* (Solnit, 1993). The role of play in adaptation (Plaut, 1979), in mastery (Peller, 1954), and in creativity (Oremland, 1998) has been explored. The value of play as a direct therapeutic force in work with children has also been amplified in recent years (Scott, 1998; Mays and Cohen, 1973). The importance of the function of playfulness in adulthood as a legacy of childhood play is discussed by a number of recent authors (e.g., Solnit, 1998; Colarusso, 1990). Generally, there is much interest in the changing qualities of play: in its phases of development, in its therapeutic value, in its fate in adulthood, and in its origins in the early parent-child relationship (Winnicott, 1968).

The purpose of this article is to contribute to this literature, particularly the interface of play development and therapy. The thesis is that there are significant connections in the origin of the play relationship in early childhood with parents and in the therapeutic alliance with both children and adults.

CLINICAL MATERIAL

In order to focus on the developmental process of play and its implications for the alliance and the therapeutic process, clinical material from three vantage points will be discussed:

- Early toddlerhood–a written description of a short training film of a mother with her 13-month-old child, where play and learning are evident in their interaction.
- Oedipal phase of development–clinical material of the treatment of a 6 1/2-year-old boy where vigorous play erupts.
- Adulthood–clinical material of an adult patient in intensive treatment where emerging transference reactions become evident and are explored.

Toddler's Interaction with Her Mother

Description: Jenny (13 months old) and her mother are in a nursery school, both sitting on the floor. Jenny sits up, aware of her surroundings. She speaks about ten words, but understands many more.

Mother picks up some toys; she shakes a rattle with bells on it. Jenny takes the toy and imitates her mother. Mother hugs a teddy bear, and Jenny takes the bear and hugs it as well. Mother bounces a large rubber ball, and this too is imitated by Jenny. They talk and smile together throughout this activity. Jenny takes a few faltering steps. Walking is a new activity for her, and, as she reaches her mother, she squeals with delight. Mother is very approving.

Mother hides the rattle behind her back after shaking it. Jenny crawls around mother to retrieve it. Mother exclaims pleasurably, "Oh, you little devil," and then hides the rattle at her side. Jenny toddles after the rattle and mother coos the "devil" remark again.

Mother picks up a blanket and plays peek-a-boo, hiding her face repeatedly. When mother's face appears each time, Jenny smiles broadly and waves her arms. Then Jenny takes the blanket and mother exclaims when Jenny's face appears.

A nursery school teacher comes in and sits on the floor near them. Mother places Jenny in the arms of the teacher, although she remains in the room. Jenny begins that special cry that starts strongly, loses its sound and breath, and finally a strong crying sound emerges. Mother quiets Jenny by taking her back into her arms.

Discussion: A number of important elements highlighted in this vignette describe the early development of play. There is evidence of the sense of joy and an intensity of pleasure in the child. Play is entwined with the object. There is a mutual affective sharing, and the format of the play develops between the mother and child. The "good enough" mother elicits both pleasure and learning and she gratifies through play and teaches through the play. Winnicott (1968) calls this the basis for the development of a "transitional play space" that becomes established between them. In the close unit there is not only an attachment and cathexis to the mother, but also an intense attachment they naturally develop together–the function of play.

The simple parent-child interaction highlights elements of pleasure, empathy, affect-regulation, dependability, and creativity. The intimacy is created in part by the mother's capacity for *empathy*. She knows her child and is attuned to what her child feels and to her child's moods. In fact, in this example we see a generative empathy (Emde, 1980) since the mother provides an environment to pull the child forward to a higher level of development but is sensitive and does not demand too much. Mother, therefore, acts as an *affect-regulator* because she stimulates affect to help learning but can also limit the flooding of affect if the child becomes uncomfortable. This union also develops because the mother has been a stable object who has been *adequately available and dependable* in a consistent way. When a new person appears who has not earned the mother's dependability, the child turns away. In this pleasurable interaction between mother and child we also see the emergence of early *creativity* in this shared time between mother and child. Reality and logic may become suspended in the service of exploration and playfulness.

Treatment of a 6 1/2-Year-Old Boy

Description: Douglas was a handsome, intelligent, vigorous youngster, the older of two brothers in an intact family. Both parents were professionals and effective and thoughtful individuals.

In Douglas's history, the parents described that he had always been active motorically since birth. Since toddlerhood, he had evidenced impulsive, aggressive behavior. He hit, kicked, bit other children, had temper tantrums, and always needed limits. There seemed to be problems modulating all affects. In school, he had a poor attention span, attacked other children, and was easily distracted.

He was diagnosed as a youngster with an attention deficit disorder and, while the use of Ritalin appeared to help some, many problems persisted. In my evaluation, it was clear he was a counterphobic child, who was very frightened internally. He anticipated attackers and punishments, and he handled this by becoming the attacker. The purpose of the treatment was to help Douglas learn of his internal fears and to become comfortable with them. There was no evidence of particular early difficult or traumatic events in his life. I felt his mother could be somewhat intrusive and controlling at times, and a tonsillectomy at age 4 had exacerbated his difficult behavior for a period of time.

I am going to describe two phases of the early treatment of Douglas. First, a period of non-engagement with little or no play. Second, a shift after five months into vigorous play between us.

In the early months of treatment, Douglas was a difficult patient, as many of these youngsters are. He was often angry with me. He said he would "slap my face." He was provocative–he turned on the clock radio, put his shoes on the wall, and he tried to open the window on the 19th floor (my office). He used many curse words to see my reaction–"fucker," "mother-fucker," "bitch." Often this behavior was accompanied with anxiety, expressed in eye-blinking or rocking. He told me that when he became 17, he would be so strong nobody would mess with him. If I commented that he might be frightened of me, he yelled that was a stupid idea coming from a retard.

Any attempt at play was aborted. He might make several ships out of clay but would quickly break and damage them. Or sometimes, bodies emerged out of clay, and he would use a scissors to cut off body parts. But he could tolerate no words or even my attention to what he was doing. Yet, in a general way, over this period of time, he was becoming more comfortable in the office, more comfortable with the toys and routine, and he smiled at me increasingly when our eyes met.

After about a five month period, Douglas told me he was "Jack the Ripper." I asked him who I was, and he said "the worry doctor." I wondered how old Jack-the-Ripper was, and he said "eight." Then he added, "I guess I'm Jack the little Ripper."

Jack and the worry doctor had clay guns. The game he developed was that he knocked on the doctor's door. I asked who was there. He said Jack the Ripper. I was to act very upset and get my gun to shoot at him. He hid behind the chair and shot back. I hid behind a pillow. We'd fight for a long time.

Now Jack wanted to play every hour, and we took a long time to fashion our clay guns. There were triggers and sights, bullet cartridges, and even sequins.

During our play, after several vigorous shooting encounters, I would take a time-out to talk. I'd comment about the play. I noted he worried about the big worry doctor hurting him, and boys his age also worried about big daddies hurting them. He liked to shoot me, and sometimes he had ideas, like all boys, about hurting his daddy.

While Douglas said nothing to me, he began to talk to his mother at home. He worried about his dad–he was too skinny. (His father was having some stomach trouble at the time.) Would his dad become very sick? When his father took a trip during this period, he was very anxious–he said he feared his dad would be killed on the airplane.

In his Jack-the-Ripper play, Douglas now became very interested in my elaborate gun. He wanted to shoot it out of my hand. He shot the gun so it went flying. (In the play, I had to throw it.) He gave it karate chops so it broke into pieces. He extracted the bullets.

I began to talk in our time-outs about feelings boys had about their daddies' guns. How jealous boys felt since they thought their own guns were too small. They want, at times, to break their daddies' gun-penises. Douglas picked up my gun, punched holes in it with a pencil, so all the "piss" could come out from everywhere.

At times during this play, he felt very guilty. In play, he wanted me to kill Jack-the-Ripper and riddle him with bullets. I refrained, telling him that all boys had these jealous, Ripper feelings. At home he told his mother and father, "I do bad things," "You should send me to an orphanage," "I don't think when I'm doing things."

Douglas now wanted to come to treatment, and he talked of me in an affectionate way to his parents. He would say, "I'm going to see my Chethik." Or if he passed my office building, he would comment, "This is my Chethik's building. Is he there now?" He was becoming much less of a behavior problem, somewhat generally but particularly in the office, though he remained vigorous.

Characteristically, after our Jack play for the day, we played sports. We developed a vigorous basketball game, using a nerf ball and hoop attached to my door. We constructed fair rules, so either of us could win with the handicap I had. If he cheated, which was very often, I would comment that we were using the Douglas rules rather than the real rules we made.

In our Jack games he was now shooting off parts of my body. Fingernails and thumbs went, and I would need immediate surgery. I began to comment about his tonsillectomy during this play, and we constructed a tonsillectomy book.

He now decided, after shooting off parts of my body, to play Jack-the-Dick-Ripper. He would shoot off my penis. I would hold myself (according to his direction) in the crotch area and wail. This would produce intense laughter, and I could slowly verbalize again how jealous boys were about worry doctors and their daddies' dicks. Douglas's creative variations continued. After the Dick-Ripper hit his mark, he had my wife enter in play and look aghast at my vital wounds.

In my discussion, I knew he was very jealous because now, in reality, his mother was pregnant again. This made him feel small and left out. He screamed at me that she wasn't pregnant, she was fat. Eye-blinking ensued, and he said he wouldn't let the baby use his toys. He now allowed me to talk for longer periods about his jealous feelings, his baby-killing wishes and so forth, but he kept his eyes closed. When I asked him if he was asleep, he said, no, he was in a coma and wouldn't come out for years.

But with this play and talk, we saw less and less acting out in treatment, at home, and in school, and more vigorous sport games after the Ripper stories adhered to the real rules. He could lose at times in basketball with some grace.

Discussion: How can we understand the play relationship that developed between Douglas and his therapist? Two aspects emerge simultaneously. One component is the transference relationship. Clearly, the "worry doctor" is a displacement of the father. Combat with the feared, castrating father is lived out in his play. Jealously and castration themes are very evident. The phallic-oedipal conflict, with a pre-oedipal aggressive coloring, is verbalized, and some aspects of the conflict are worked through.

A second component of the play relationship is the therapeutic alliance, the play alliance that develops between the two players. Clearly, Douglas comes to love the play, the developing enactment of his internal story. The therapist becomes "my Chethik," "my Chethik lives here." There is a growing, loving tie to the therapist.

Douglas and his therapist appear to recreate the transitional play space that Winnicott describes. The therapist is not only the "bad worry doctor" but also a special person who plays, explores, discovers, and elicits ideas. Douglas becomes creative: Jack-the-Ripper; Jack-the-Little-Ripper; Jack-the-Dick-Ripper. Douglas is an author who unfolds new scenes and chapters.

Why does the alliance unfold? In this play situation, the therapist is especially attuned to the child's internal life. Through the therapist's *empathy* and understanding, he can verbalize and clarify Douglas's inner turmoil. Over the months of regular work with regular appointments, the therapist becomes a *dependable* and enduring object that the child can rely on. The therapist also functions as an affect-regulator. He can allow the emergence of very intense and important affects and erects a safe atmosphere so that these affects are not overwhelming and flooding.

These qualities of the therapy—empathy, dependability, affect-regulation, and creativity—foster the libidinal aspect of the alliance and form the context in which the interpretive work can occur. This attachment has its history in the early "good enough" parent-child relationships, and in their early libidinal play.

What are the curative aspects of this interplay? Douglas's acting out diminishes generally and almost totally within the therapeutic hour. The interpretive work is important. Douglas has those "Ripper" feelings toward his dad. When his primitive aggressive feelings are understood and verbalized, structural change is fostered with Douglas. The harshness of his superego reactions, the intensity of his guilt, diminishes because he has ideas that all boys share.

There is another critical cure component stemming from the play relationship, and this should be understood in object relations terms. The therapist welcomes Douglas' internal life that unfolds through play. His inside ideas, his mind, is valuable. Just as the toddler Jenny felt enhanced when her mother approved of her child's creative productions, Douglas experiences an accepting regard for his material and elaborative productions.

Treatment of a Young Adult

Description: Ms. A is a young adult in intensive psychotherapy who begins to experience the emergence of transference.

There is an interesting quote of Freud's (1914) in his article on "Remembering, Repeating and Working Through." He comments that the

> patient's compulsion to repeat is not only rendered harmless but useful by virtue of its admission into the transference as a *playground* in which it is allowed to expand in almost complete freedom and which it is expected to display to us everything in the way of pathogenic instincts that is hidden in the patient's mind. (Freud, 1914, p. 147)

Therefore, associated with the transference is the emergence of a playground where the pathology is exposed.

Ms. A was a subdued single woman in her mid-thirties. She was a school teacher (art teacher) who conveyed an air of listlessness, hopelessness, and passivity that overshadowed her natural gifts. She came into treatment because she felt she could not adequately develop her artistic talents and because of a pattern of disturbing relationships with men. She "fell into" relationships where she let herself be used and humiliated. Though her artistic work had been promising in her younger years, she had given it up for the routine drudgery of teaching and she felt stifled.

Ms. A came from a wealthy, intact family. Salient in her history was the striking narcissism of both parents, who also seemed rather disturbed. Much of her early care was left to maids. Her mother, who was often gone, was always critical of how her daughter reflected on her–critical of her looks, dress, and bearing. The father, a successful businessman who had little patience with his daughter, was also very critical. But he could alternately be quite seductive with her, throughout both her early years and as an adolescent. As far as we could reconstruct, there was not an open sexual relationship between them, but a lot of physical interaction occurred. The parents had a poor marriage, and they divorced when the patient was in her early twenties.

For Ms. A, her background was experienced as an enormous assault on her sense of self, her self-esteem, and individuality. She had always felt there was something very wrong with her, and, as a child, she was plagued by the quest to find out what she did that incurred the rejection she received (in contrast to an older brother whom, she felt, fared much better).

In our early work together Ms. A fought to keep a loving image of her parents. She, not they, was to blame. She tried to undo evident memories and events that showed their blatant disregard for her and their dismissal of her that continued to the present. They never remembered her birthday. They never initiated contact with her. She, not they, did all the calling.

As she came to understand more of her parents' narcissistic limits, she could see that she was repeating in new relationships what she did with her parents. She chose men who could exploit her and attempted to ingratiate herself with them; she felt she had no rights; she became a helpless victim.

The period of work I will focus on emerged about 1 1/2 years after the beginning of treatment. I began to feel a growing change in Ms. A's demeanor. There was a growing comfort and trust, and a freedom in her associations. Ms. A smiled more often in greeting me, was dressing better, using make-up well, and wearing attractive perfume. There was a definite feeling of a sexual ambiance.

In her sessions, Ms. A related she was beginning a new relationship with a man who had many of the old qualities. His name was "M." He was married, had known her for several years, but now openly wanted her. What could she do? She had no one; she would submit and meet his needs so she could get a little for herself.

After meeting with him for a number of weeks, she described a growing sexual relationship. She was being used–she was only an aside, not central to him. As I listened to this material, I was struck by one odd factor: When she referred to him, she used the initial M. All other men she had called by their full first names. I called this to her attention–"Did she have any idea why this was so?" When she drew a complete blank, I commented that my first name began with an M. She laughed spontaneously and pointed out that her father's first name also began with an M. From that point on, she would only refer to this man by the initial M, and it was clear she enjoyed this. It often left an ambiguity–was she talking only about her lover, or about her therapist or about her father? Did her discussion have double or triple meanings? In my mind, I called this the M game.

One day she described sitting on M's lap. She could feel his erection. She had a sudden association to all the times she sat on her father's lap. Did her father get excited like M did? She then recalled seeing me and my wife on the street. She will never forget my look. I was so cold and severe. (I didn't recall seeing her.) I wondered if my cold and disapproving look doesn't come up now, as she discusses getting men excited. Could there be some internal feeling of disapproval? Her reaction was to tell me that recently she is feeling more and more like a "slut."

Over the next few weeks, as we followed the slut theme, we uncovered how she would often, as a child, get her father to lie down with her. She would only have to complain that she couldn't sleep, and then they would snuggle together for a long time. Ms. A was now more openly seductive in her sessions. One day in this period, she came to the hour wearing an attractive red dress. She reported a dream: She is driving a little red sports care, a Miata. She parks it near an elegant hotel in a no-parking zone. She leaves her car there, and she doesn't care if she is doing something wrong. I commented that as she parks her little red sports car on the couch today, perhaps she likes the "wrong" forbidden feelings she is experiencing. She laughed and told me her relationship with M is changing. She is turning on the charm, and he now finds her adorable. And she added, "Do you know, I really don't want him, I just want to win." I commented, "You mean you want to see if you can beat out his wife." She associated to seeing me and my wife at a concert. She felt terrible, left out. She said sarcastically, "You looked so cozy with all those intelligent professors and intelligent couples."

This material ushered in themes of being shut out as a child and an adult. She gets furious every time M talks about the dinners he attends, the tennis couples he plays with, the parties he goes to with his wife. She can't stand being shut out. She reacts every session when I close the door at the end of the hour.

A lot of memories emerge about the parental bedroom. Her father could snuggle with her, or play with her, but on some occasions he would just put her out and lock the door. It was all right to play with her, but when he wanted the real thing, she was left out. Now, in her relationship with M, this would be avenged; this would be reversed. This time M was never going to want to reenter the bedroom with his wife, because of her.

Throughout this period, as I noted earlier, it was often deliberately unclear to which M Ms. A was referring. While ostensibly talking about her lover, and how M found her irresistible, could she be wondering how M the therapist was feeling? I commented how much she enjoyed this ambiguity. She enjoyed teasing me and wanted me to chase her to find out her meaning. She enjoyed being the tease.

Immediate memories came of play with her father. But also a great deal of her play as a latency-aged girl, which had been repressed. She and her girlfriend played chasing games with boys in her neighborhood for several years. The boys would chase and capture them. The boys would then tie the girls up, and the girls would allow them to touch in all forbidden places. These were very exciting games, which persisted for a long time–and contributed to a compulsive masturbation (which had also been repressed). She also had these boys watching her as she went to the bathroom, where she would disrobe for them. These very exciting, persistent games in her childhood had subsequently created intense guilt, shame, and fear of her impulses.

This was a period of very effective work with Ms. A. We began to see, stemming from the transference development, Ms. A's hidden oedipal sexuality and competitive aggression. Ms. A defended against these affects by her listlessness, depression, and helplessness. She developed punishing and self-defeating relationships because of her intense guilt. In this period, she began to recover a good deal of her vitality. We began to see a real person–sexual, vital, attractive, angry, and, with further work, these gains became lasting. Ms. A closed the M game by breaking off with her lover; she appropriately felt that he wasn't worth it, and there was no future for her.

Discussion: I wish to use this clinical material to highlight certain aspects of the therapeutic alliance with Ms. A. The transference itself is an illusory object relationship. Ms. A developed the M game with her therapist to live out currently the past seductive, frustrating relationship she had with her father, much of which was repressed. The therapist was a sexually desirable father, the rejecting father who shut the door at the end of the hour, and the disapproving father with the icy stare.

While Ms. A attributed these qualities to the therapist, it became clearer and clearer that these were make-believe, as if features in their relationship. The players, therapist and patient, had roles of father and daughter which stood outside of reality. The alliance coexisted with the transference. Ms. A became "allied" with the therapist, in constructing and reconstructing a critical relationship of the past. In a sense, as with Douglas, she became intensely involved in a play process.

An important quality of play in childhood is the capacity of "letting go." Within play, children can (up to a point) abandon themselves. They experience a sense of freedom and are less bound by the demands of reality. This "letting go" has its parallel in the transference regression. Ms. A clearly began to let go both for gratification, but also discovery. Ms. A became a little red sports car, parking in the therapist's forbidden zone. She became the sexual tease, taunting the therapist with ambiguity. The parallel letting go mirrors the healthy regression interplay that children use.

When mother and child play together over a period of time, they develop special code words, signals, and signs–a secret and special communication within a little closed group that no one else can understand. An evolving treatment has many of the same qualities. The M game was a metaphor that only the patient and the therapist could understand. The dream material, the red Miata, assumed symbolic meaning that was understood together. The game (or play) of each session became a reenactment of a past seduction, which was lived out and understood in this new closed group.

As with Douglas, the child patient, specific qualities of the ongoing treatment situation promoted both a transference regression in Ms. A and a sense of trust in the alliance. These qualities included the therapist's capacity for: *empathy,* which he demonstrated by his understanding verbalizations; the sense of *dependability* and availability as a constant object; the therapist's capacity as an *affect-regulator* where the expression of intense affects could emerge safely with the therapeutic hour; and the ability to be *creative,* to understand the metaphors and symbolic dream material that emerged in the unfolding treatment.

CONCLUSION

In this article there has been an attempt to focus on the central aspects of the therapeutic working relationship and with its connection with play. Earlier, authors primarily highlighted the rational interaction between patient and therapist. For example, Greenson (1965) noted that the patient and the therapist shared similar goals of cure and change, and this formed the basis for their union. Stone (1961) added some affective features for developing the alliance. He noted that "tolerance, friendliness and the frank physicianly commitment" were necessary qualities of the therapist to enhance the alliance. Loewald, (1960) in a seminal article titled "On the Nature of Therapeutic Action in Psychoanalysis," moved beyond this emphasis on the rational. He declared that the relationship was central–the analyst was a new object, and, within this relationship, new integrative experiences took place. He suggested that this interaction was comparable in its structure to the early parent-child relationship.

The clinical material in this article supports and explicates Loewald's contention that the alliance is less a rational connection and much more a libidinal attachment. The early object ties that are infused with play help motivate the child to grow and prosper within his family. In effective therapy, this satisfying experience becomes unconsciously reactivated in the therapeutic relationships developed by child and adult patients.

REFERENCES

Colarusso, C.(1990). Play in adulthood. *Psychoanalytic Study of the Child, 45*:225-245.

Emde, R. (1980). The developmental orientation in psychoanalysis. *Psychoanalysis of Contemporary Thought, 3*:123-133.

Freud, S. (1973 [1914]). Remembering, repeating, and working through. *Standard Edition, XII*, 145-156.

Greenson, R. (1965). The working alliance and the transference neurosis. *Psychoanalytic Quarterly, 34*:155-165.

Loewald, H. (1960). On the therapeutic action of psychoanalysis. *International Journal of Psychoanalysis, 41*:16-27.

Mayes, L. and Cohen, D. (1992). Playing and therapeutic action in child analysis. *International Journal of Psychoanalysis, 73*:1235-1244.

Oremland, J. (1998). Play, dreams and creativity. *Psychoanalytic Study of the Child, 53*: 84-93.

Peller, L. (1954). Libidinal phases, ego development and play. *Psychoanalytic Study of the Child, 9*:182-190.

Plaut, E. (1979). Play and adaptation. *Psychoanalytic Study of the Child, 34*:217-232.

Psychoanalytic Study of the Child. (1987). *42*, 3-219.

Psychoanalytic Study of the Child. (1998). *53*, 45-110.

Scott, M. (1998). Play and the therapeutic action: Multiple perspectives. *Psychoanalytic Study of the Child, 53*, 94-101.

Solnit, A. (1998). Beyond play and playfulness. *Psychoanalytic Study of the Child, 53*: 102-110.

Solnit, A. (1993). *The Many Meanings of Play.* New Haven: Yale University Press.

Stone, L. (1961). *The Psychoanalytic Situation.* New York: International Universities Press.

Winnicott, D. (1968). Playing: Its theoretical status in the clinical situation. *International Journal of Psychoanalysis, 49*:591-603.

Discovering the Inner Life of a Child: Exploration, Illumination, and Elaboration of Play Space

Brenda Lovegrove Lepisto

SUMMARY. Using Winnicott's concept of transitional space, joint attention, theory of mind, and a case vignette, the author describes techniques in elucidating and elaborating a child's play space, hence, psychic life. Explicating the child's theory of mind uncovers the dynamics, motives, conflicts, and unconscious material used by the analyst to form interpretations and encourage the child's self-reflective function (Fonagy & Target, 1996). Finally, a case vignette illustrates the enhancement of play space by elucidating the child's theory of mind. *[Article copies available for a fee from The Haworth Document Delivery Service: 1-800-342-9678. E-mail address: <getinfo@haworthpressinc.com> Website: <http://www.HaworthPress.com> © 2001 by The Haworth Press, Inc. All rights reserved.]*

Brenda Lovegrove Lepisto, PsyD, is a psychologist and psychoanalyst in private practice in East Lansing, MI. She is an adjunct professor at Michigan State University in the College of Human Medicine and in the Department of Psychology.

A modified version of this article was presented to The Michigan Psychoanalytic Council, March 19, 2000 in East Lansing, MI. The author would like to thank Lawrence R. Lepisto, PhD, for his support and suggestions for this article, and Sophie L. Lovinger, PhD, for her comments on this manuscript. I also wish to thank Jerrold Brandell, PhD, for his helpful suggestions and editorial review of this manuscript.

Correspondence concerning this article should be addressed to: Brenda Lovegrove Lepisto, PsyD, 4572 S. Hagadorn Road, Suite 2D, East Lansing, MI 48864. (E-mail address: lepisto@msu.edu).

[Haworth co-indexing entry note]: "Discovering the Inner Life of a Child: Exploration, Illumination, and Elaboration of Play Space." Lepisto, Brenda Lovegrove. Co-published simultaneously in *Psychoanalytic Social Work* (The Haworth Press, Inc.) Vol. 8, No. 3/4, 2001, pp. 21-46; and: *Psychoanalytic Approaches to the Treatment of Children and Adolescents: Tradition and Transformation* (ed: Jerrold R. Brandell) The Haworth Press, Inc., 2001, pp. 21-46. Single or multiple copies of this article are available for a fee from The Haworth Document Delivery Service [1-800-342-9678, 9:00 a.m. - 5:00 p.m. (EST). E-mail address: getinfo@haworthpressinc.com].

KEYWORDS. Theory of mind, child psychoanalysis, transitional space, case vignette of a seven-year-old boy, mindblindness, joint attention

Coming to know the psychic life and theory of mind of a child is an inherent endeavor of the child psychoanalyst. The analyst creates a space, usually through play, to observe, explore, and discover the inner workings of the child's mind. Many children who are referred for treatment, however, have not developed mental space necessary for thinking, playing, wondering, puzzling, and imagining, especially in regards to their own philosophy of life, theory of mind, and understanding of others' behavior. They have difficulty playing and making sense of their world and the people that inhabit it. This limited ability to explain their own and others' actions and words that draw on acts of mind–beliefs, feelings, memories, desires–reduces the world to a sensory-perceptual experience in which cause and effect seem related to concrete material, that is, directly perceivable events (Mayes & Cohen, 1996). With a developed theory of mind, one can call upon mental phenomena to interpret and give meaning to the actions of oneself and of others. It is only then that a child's internal world can expand to include mental states such as loving, wanting, and remembering, which cannot be directly perceived. Adaptation and quality of life are enhanced because they can predict and interpret the actions of those around them. Other people, and themselves, are defined "not so singularly by what they do but can include mental states, how they feel, believe, or think. Actions become mirrors of the other's mind or representational world" (Mayes & Cohen, 1996, p. 128). The internal object world is enriched by experiences that build a child's theory of mind. Children who are referred to treatment have suffered most likely a delay or underdevelopment of these abilities, due to conflict, trauma, or constitutional deficits. Analytic technique must include preliminary work on the explication of the child's theory of mind for the analyst to formulate interpretations based upon the child's experience and for the child to develop a more sophisticated self-reflective function.

Because children possess linguistic immaturity, variable cognitive development, unpredictability, intense and raw emotional experiences, and tendency toward action, the analytic technique must include unique measures to enhance their understanding of themselves, others, and life. Despite different ages, stature, ways of thinking, and experiences, the child and the analyst attempt to come together in their voyage toward understanding. Forming the basis of technical considerations in child analysis is a case study, incorporating (a) Winnicott's 1971 conception of transitional space, (b) research in the development of joint attention, (c) Baron-Cohen's 1995 theory of mind research, and (d) Fonagy and Target's 1998 view of mentalization.

TRANSITIONAL SPACE

Creating a safe, exploratory, transitional space of being with another while at the same time being alone promotes symbol formation, especially when nonintrusive, useable comments link together the concept and the symbol, the feeling and the symbol, and the object and the symbol. Alvarez (1992) advocated children's rights to explore what is of interest to them. When adults (i.e., parents, therapists, or analysts) determine what needs to be explored based upon their own fantasies, worries, thoughts, memories, and theories, children are prohibited from learning their own mental contents. The freeing of the mind opens increased possibilities that can be used for age appropriate growth, development of cognitive flexibility, and problem-solving abilities. In essence, it helps children discover who they are, who they might want to become, and who they were. I believe this occurs when two parties have an "agreed state of mind," and "joint attention" that occurs in transitional play space during creative moments.

Winnicott (1971) introduced the concept of "transitional space" as a ". . . designation of the intermediate area of experience . . ." (p. 2). Winnicott wrote, "I put forward for discussion of its value as an idea the thesis that for creative playing and for cultural experience, including its most sophisticated developments, the position is *the potential space* between the baby and the mother" (p. 107). Because caregiver and baby implicitly decide upon the allotment of space, it is only potential space, never actual or guaranteed. In the neonatal follow-up baby clinic where I worked, I could visualize play space between babies and their care givers because it was so mutual, lively, and pleasurable to watch; at other times, I saw little room for play, a lack of spontaneity, and a tension that makes every action literal and serious business: "As one approaches the state where nothing is felt to represent anything but itself, one becomes more and more imprisoned in the realm of the thing in itself " (Ogden, 1985, p. 134). For there to be room to play, each participant has to acquire an agreed upon *state of mind,* very much like children pretending. This *state of mind* is mental activity that is "nonlinear and associational" (Meares & Lichtenberg, 1995, p. 53). At nursery school it is common to see children fall into the role of mother or father. Each knows it is play; each knows the lines; each knows how far to go within the role. These activities represent "an agreed state of mind" and a space used to create metaphors, symbols, and analogies, all of which enhance meaning and richness of life.

Many of the children who are referred for treatment have not been afforded play space for one reason or another; either environmental or constitutional factors interfered with the development of creativity, transforming concrete to symbol to representation. The act of playing always requires "space" to merge, blend, and experiment with reality and fantasy, although for children who are referred for mental health services that space has been collapsed. Meares and Lichtenberg described the inability to play as a result of deficient "interplay" with those who make up the environment. Thus the child, and subsequent adult, becomes "trapped in what might be called a 'hypertrophy of the real' " (Meares & Lichtenberg, p. 47). If play space within the analytic hour can be established, conflicts can be discovered, understood, and resolved, as new, flexible, and expansive structures are constructed. With the possible alternatives played out, new interactions created, and a focus on what might happen, there is a future orientation to play that is built upon present and past experiences.

The analytic frame holds and protects the analyst and child so that trust, exploration, playfulness, and creativity can develop. In other words, there is room for the development and exploration of "that which is known but not yet thought" (Bollas, 1987, p. 4). "The interplay between the dyad has a fluid patterning form, which brings to mind such words as 'dance' and 'music' " (Meares & Lichtenberg, p. 52). The task for the analyst is to make her presence known in a way that is not frightening, and, therefore, does not have to be denied or in other ways defended against by the child; a space needs to be created where dance and play take place.

Describing Winnicott's potential space, Ogden (1985) wrote "That space between symbol and symbolized, mediated by an interpreting self, is the space in which creativity becomes possible and is the space in which we are alive as human beings, as opposed to being simply reflexively reactive beings" (p. 133). Further, he posited that in "the absence of potential space, there is only fantasy; within potential space imagination can develop" (p. 133). Fonagy & Target's 1996 research suggested, for patients whose primary disturbance is thought to be at the level of distortions in mental processes (i.e, method of thinking or not thinking), rather than mental representations (i.e., the actual contents of thought, which may include fantasies, conflicts, etc.), an intensive treatment with a focus on loosening the inhibitions and distortions of mental processes. Particularly crucial is the capacity to think about the mind of the other and one's own mind. These children are not able to verbalize internal states, differentiate affects, break down unmanageable affects into smaller manageable entities, develop a reflective self, and develop the capacity for "as if" thinking/pretending. In order to develop these crucial capacities, the child analyst facilitates the opening of creative play space where self-reflection and observation will be developed and enhanced.

Not only will self-reflection be increased but the opportunity and capacity for empathy will be enhanced. When one can think about another's mind (theory of mind), figure out what might happen, and how the other might react and feel, empathy is more likely to occur, and that leads to more accurately perceived world and more satisfying interpersonal relationships. While it is beyond the scope of this article to discuss the various conceptualizations of empathy (see Lepisto, 1994a, 1994b for a review of the literature), generally it is accepted that feeling understood as a child is related to the ability to understand others, emotionally and cognitively. For this reason, joint attentional behaviors, mentalization, transitional play space, and the child's construction of a theory of mind will likely contribute to the development of empathy and altruistic behavior.

SHEDDING LIGHT ON THE STAGE

Pedder (1992), in his article "Conductor or Director? Transitional Space in Psychotherapy and in the Theater," suggested "therapist and director share a common task of facilitating the right conditions and the right level of tension for creative play to occur" (p. 264). Further, he stated that the "task of therapist or theater director is to be a guardian of *potential space* in which there can be a willing *suspension of disbelief* [italics added]" (p. 265). Despite my lack of experience as a theater director, Pedder's description adequately describes my experience with analysis and therapy with children. For example, as we began the session, a 7-year-old youngster said, "Today I am going to finish the movie I did yesterday." Funny, I was just thinking that yesterday his "play" looked like a movie. We had to recapture the character's and our own mental states from the previous session. A director helps the actor understand, feel, and express another's mental state, emotion, and thoughts. Analysts aid their patients in a similar manner by setting up a condition, a frame that promotes the relaxation of defensiveness, an exploratory state of mind, and a willingness to jointly investigate the patient's mind.

Various techniques can be used to increase the probability that potential play space will be created. Not a psychoanalytic term, the word "illumination," as defined by *The American Heritage Dictionary,* means "spiritual or intellectual enlightenment" and "clarification; elucidation," which closely reflects the process of learning about oneself and others. The definition of illuminate is to "make understandable, clarify" and "to enlighten intellectually or spiritually; enable to understand," which clearly captures the process of psychoanalysis. In working with children, we continually learn how what we do and say as analysts (i.e., adults) influences the material uncovered, shared, worked through, and resolved. We hope the potential play space is increased through illumination of the child's inner experience before interpretations are made.

Still, because children are by definition smaller in stature, immature in cognitive development, and very accustomed to perceiving and adapting to what adults expect and desire of them, they often react with superficial compliance. Contrarily, some children oppose the analysis with the same straightforward, direct manner that they oppose other situations (i.e., refusing sessions, screaming, breaking toys, or passing gas/burping/spitting during sessions). Both of these tendencies, compliance and opposition, can limit openness to discovery. Using various techniques of reflection and interpretation, "thinking possibilities" can be increased. With unwavering adherence to psychic unfolding, the voyage–illumination of psychodynamics, affects, impulses, conflicts, and fantasies–has a rudder, helping us find our way through stormy weather and seas, although it takes some courage to discover and experience those "sea monsters" along the way.

Moreover interpretation can enhance the transitional play space or dampen it. Interpretation can be used to help children clarify thinking, reveal conflicts, and add to understanding, but different theorists use interpretation differently. Melanie Klein (1975) believed that ". . . not only a timely interpretation but a deep-going one is essential" (p. 25). Anything short of an interpretation that not only explicates "the representational content but also the anxiety and sense of guilt associated with it right down to that layer of the mind which is being activated . . ." (p. 25) was considered superficial. Further, she stated:

> An interpretation which does not descend to those depths which are being activated by the material and the anxiety concerned, which does not, that is, touch the place where the strongest latent resistance is and endeavor in the first place to reduce anxiety where it is most violent and most in evidence, will have no effect whatever on the child, or will only serve to arouse stronger resistances in it without being able to resolve them again. (p. 25)

She explained the "right interpretation" as one that penetrated to the level of the mind that is being activated by anxiety. However, the child's ability to take the analyst's interpretation, relate it to the appropriate circumstances, and then be able to apply the newly gained knowledge is dependent on a sophisticated level of abstraction. The level of the most primitive anxiety lies in an abstract area of intrapsychic functioning, which is the furthest from the child's level of mental maturity, so an interpretation is by definition an abstraction and of questionable use without preparatory analytic work. If it is delivered before the child has reached this level of mental operation, there is the danger of creating pseudo understanding or the closing of analytic space.

In contrast to Klein, A. Freud (1965) advocated a slower progression to interpretation that, most likely, allowed the child time to elucidate the material enough to experience it. "Verbalization and clarification of the preconscious play a definite role, especially with children, in preparing the way for interpretation proper and in lessening the impact of anxiety which goes hand in hand with it" (p. 227). Clearly, this expressed a respect for potential analytic play space that was geared to the child's ability to handle anxiety. Another reason A. Freud (1945) did not interpret deeply and quickly was her feeling that the interpretations that resulted were "rigid, impersonal, and stereotyped" and without corroboration from the child. Following A. Freud's (1971) technique, Bornstein's (e.g., 1935, 1945, 1948, 1951) technique of collaboration with the child in the analytic work demonstrated her willingness to provide play space for the children with whom she worked.

Bornstein (1945) did not insist on interpreting play material directly, as Klein did, because the ". . . multiplicity of meaning in a child's play is likely to lead to misinterpretations" (p. 156). Further, she likened it to dream interpretations that only rely on generic symbolism rather than associations, history, and symbols. Since play is the first important step in developing sublimation, she hypothesized that interpreting play themes may interrupt the development of sublimation. With constant interpretation of its symbolic meaning, play might be disabled as a precursor to sublimation. For the same reason, she felt that children's drawings, stories, and other creations should not be interpreted but rather used as information about the child's internal psychic development and functioning (Bornstein, 1951). Hence, what is known is not always what is shared. Not only might constant, deep, complex interpretations interfere with sublimation, it seems quite likely that it may encourage intellectualization and superficial, pseudo-understanding that remains far from emotional experience. Further, it may undermine the child's creativity by blocking potential fantasies and thoughts from taking place. Despite adults' vast experience and more mature cognitive skills, a hierarchical attitude interferes with the process of unfolding intrapsychic functioning that only occurs in adequate play space. Only by extricating themselves from engaging in hierarchical interactions and forming collaborative relationships with children will children begin to explore conflict and the internal working of their minds. When we link the pretense to a past event or reality, we form the possibility of reflective thinking. We are saying, "Look, this can be used to try out new ideas, think about new things in a safe place–your mind–just as you have been doing without realizing it." This implies a collaborative relationship within a therapeutic frame rather than a relationship based upon authoritarianism.

The danger with sophisticated interpretations is that "children get caught between the words and their experience" (Saxe, personal communication, November 11, 1996). She explained, "Words don't articulate the experience at the moment. If you are talking to their cognition, which undermines their experience, it doesn't help them move their experience to one that is better articulated." Furthermore, if children are spoken to in intellectualized language, they build up defenses to illuminating their experiences, affects, and fantasies, which prematurely closes potential play space. "Interpretation is effective when it utilizes the feelings of the child that he recognizes to be *real*. Those are discovered in the 'real' experiences in his life and in the analytic situation" (Feigeson, 1974, p. 25). The communication of understanding illuminates further exploration into the child's experience.

Chused (1990) described her technique of "illumination":

> By articulating, putting into words, that which is expressed nonverbally, I demonstrate the value of my understanding, and by choosing preconscious, relatively unconflictual material to address, I *avoid linking observation to discomfort* [italics added]. I do this initially in a way unlikely to stir up much resistance or stress. (p. 47)

Further, she wrote, "Speaking to behavior that was almost conscious but had not yet been articulated even in thought," increases the play space and the willingness to jointly attend to an exploration of the meaning of behavior as long as it does not result in self-consciousness or discomfort (p. 47). If material discussed is too far away from the child's perceptions and experience, it may sound like "superego condemnation or omniscient declaration" (p. 50), neither of which are valued by the child and may close off possible opportunities for exploration. Potential play space occurs when a child's experience expands in understanding and awareness. A. Freud (1965) stated that the "aim of analysis remains the widening of consciousness without which ego control cannot be increased" (p. 31). She is speaking of widening of the transitional play space that increases cognitive flexibility and opportunities for new thoughts, fantasies, and representations. Fonagy and Target (1996) add that "Therapeutic work must therefore initially focus on assisting the child to lift the inhibitions on his mental functioning which in turn may make access to his mental world easier and, in extreme cases, possible for the first time" (p. 62). What is shared experience has the potential of becoming, under optimal analytic circumstances, part of one's autonomous ego functioning. When transitional play space, developmentally appropriate interpretations, and joint attention can occur during the analytic experience, children can begin to learn about their theory of mind and use it to understand themselves and others.

JOINT ATTENTION AND THEORY OF THE MIND

Recently there has been a rapidly growing body of theory and research concerned with the developmental origins of early joint-attentional behaviors (Moore & Dunham, 1995). "Joint attention" can be inferred by gaze-following behaviors that begin when a baby is about six months old. For instance, in the baby clinic where babies are developmentally assessed, Anna, 9 months old, sits on the psychologist's lap as her mother talks about her developmental history. Then Anna's mother's eyes wander from the psychologist and settle on Anna's 3-year-old sister, Sarah, who is contemplating opening the dresser drawer. As the mother continues talking to the psychologist, she is watching Sarah; soon Anna references her mother and is now looking at Sarah. Anna's mother needs only to look in a certain direction and soon Anna will be looking in that direction, too. They both attend to Sarah. Then Anna looks back at her mother, seeming to check on her mother's continued attentional focus. Anna's mother warns Sarah from opening the drawers to the nightstand, because they are not hers. Anna attends, listens, and learns about her mother's tone of voice when she is talking to Sarah, and the feelings that emanate from the interaction. Anna will hear her mother apologize to the psychologist for interrupting the conversation, comment on Sarah's inquisitiveness, and then return to telling the developmental history. There was a wealth of social information communicated in this very short interaction all of which was initiated when Anna noticed the direction in which her mother was looking.

To explain the development and sophistication of the above described mother-child interaction, Baron-Cohen's (1995) theory on the development of a theory of mind may be helpful. In his book *Mindblindness,* Baron-Cohen described the mechanisms by which infants, including primate infants, develop a theory of mind, the ability to understand that others have knowledge, thoughts, and feelings that, may be different from one's own. Based upon research in comparative psychology, developmental psychology, and neuropsychology, he proposed that, as part of evolutionary endowment, infants possess the potential to actualize three mental mechanisms used in the development of a "Theory of Mind," that is, a system for inferring the full range of mental states from behavior. The three mechanisms are an "Intentionality Detector," "Eye-Direction Detector," and a "Shared-Attention Mechanism."

Utilizing the results of a number of interesting studies designed to establish evidence of the first mechanism, the "Intentionality Detector," which is "a perceptual device that interprets motion stimuli in terms of the primitive volitional mental states of goals and desire" (p. 32), Baron-Cohen (1995) supported the notion that infants, as well as people of all ages, perceive agents in motion as having desires and goals. This is the rudimentary beginning of self and other representation. As evidence, Baron-Cohen described several studies, including one classic and very interesting study performed by Heider and Simmel in 1944. According to Baron-Cohen, Heider and Simmel showed participants a film in which there were only geometric shapes as actors. Then they had the subjects describe the film. All but one subject anthropomorphized their account of what transpired during the film. In other words, most subjects used a rich vocabulary of volitional mental state terms. For example, a typical subject described the scene like this, "A man has planned to meet a girl, and the girl comes along with another man. The first man tells the second to go; the second tells the first, and he shakes his head." Interestingly, one participant described the geometric shapes with a lack of intentionality and agency, in a sterile manner using only concrete terms. For example, "A large solid triangle is shown entering a rectangle. It enters and comes out of this rectangle, and each time the corner and the one-half of one of the sides of the rectangle form an opening." Not only is this passage boring, it lacks intentionality and agency and is described in the most concrete of terms; "a hypertrophy of the real" has occurred. This subject was trapped in the concrete without the play space that we all use when describing what we see and experience. In all likelihood if this person were given a Rorschach test, she would not be able to see beyond inkblots. We have all worked with people who have had significant difficulty extricating themselves from the actual, concrete description of experience to move toward the development of a rich and meaningful understanding of observations, experiences, and thoughts that are based upon imagination and "as if" characteristics. The subject in Heider and Simmel's experiment who only used a concrete description of the picture may have been, as Baron-Cohen termed the phenomena, "mindblind," as this participant did not attribute agency and intentionality to the figures in the film. This may be some of the difficulty that our patients experience when they are not able to use transitional space to understand their mental states, thoughts, and feelings and the mental states, thoughts and feeling of others.

A related fundamental mechanism that adds to understanding others' intentions and behavior is the Eye-Direction Detector (EDD) (Baron-Cohen, 1995). The Eye-Direction Detector (EDD) has three basic functions: detecting the presence of eyes or eye-like stimuli, computing of whether eyes are directed toward it or toward something else, and inferring from its own case that if another organism's eyes are directed at something, then that organism sees that thing. Anna's behavior suggested that she performed these functions and then she looked in the direction in which her mother looked. So far, the mechanisms described are based primarily on a dyadic relationship. Once two people are attending to a third object, then a triadic relationship has been formed.

Another mechanism contributing to the development of the theory of mind is what Baron-Cohen (1995) termed "The Shared-Attention Mechanism" (SAM), which is based on triadic relationships. The self and the other are attending to the same object. Others have termed this mechanism as joint attention (Moore & Dunham, 1995). Following along with Baron-Cohen's proposal, Shared Attention Mechanism "builds triadic representations by using any available information about the perceptual state of another person (or animal)" (p. 46). The idea is that the Shared-Attention Mechanism needs dyadic representations to build triadic ones and relies on Eye-Direction Detectors because this is the easiest way to identify objects of joint attention.

Furthermore, joint attentional behavior initiates a rudimentary social understanding of mental life, which is the beginning of the development of a theory of mind. If the baby is developing adequately, joint attentional behavior will continue to become more sophisticated. Mobile babies seek toys and then they hand them to their mothers to look at, they look where their fathers are looking, and they follow siblings around the house to do, see, and hear what they are doing, seeing, and hearing. In response, their parents are helping to shape their understanding of others, situations, and experiences.

> Wood and his colleagues (Wood, 1988; Wood, Bruner, & Ross, 1976), for example have demonstrated in detail how the adult caretaker provides scaffolding for the young child's intentions, keeps her attention focused, protects her from distractions, reduces the degrees of freedom she must manage. Mother and child are not simply sharing common foci of attention, but are also constructing them, extending them over time by embedding them in task structures, and conventionalizing them in the terms of canonical forms in the culture. (Brunner, 1995)

As toddlers, they like to listen to stories and look at books with caregivers, another way to attend to a phenomenon jointly. Early social insights can be observed by the child's verbalizations or facial expressions while listening to stories. Often toddlers and young children want to talk to their mothers and fathers about the pictures they see and the stories they listen to. These are all joint attentional behaviors that build the theory of mind. Baron-Cohen (1995) employed Leslie's (1994) description of the development and necessity of a theory of mind. Theory of Mind Mechanism (ToMM) "is a system for inferring the full range of mental states from behavior–that is, for employing a "theory of mind." A way of representing the set of epistemic mental states (which include pretending, thinking, knowing, believing, imagining, dreaming, guessing, and deceiving) is needed along with a way to tie all of these mental-states concepts (volitional, the perceptual, and the epistemic) into a coherent understanding of how mental states and actions are relayed. Once this connection is developed, the child has a theory of mind.

In slightly different language, Stern (1985) agreed with this observation as he identified this stage of infant development between 7 months and 15 months as one in which the *subjective self* begins to develop. Infants discover that they have minds and that other people have minds, too. Stern (1985) stated:

> This discovery amounts to the acquisition of a "theory" of separate minds. Only when infants can sense that others distinct from themselves can hold or entertain a mental state that is similar to one they sense themselves to be holding is the sharing of subjective experience or intersubjectitivy possible. (p. 124)

Parents treat the young child's gestural or preverbal signs as intended, treat the child as an agent, and even construe these attributed intentions in quite conventional ways (Meltzoff & Gopnick, 1993). Parents begin to treat the baby as more of a separate person. Incidently, Greenspan's (1992) research found that impairment in intentional two-way communication at age 9 months is one of the first predictors of delayed development requiring active intervention. At 9 months one would expect the "Shared-Attention Mechanism" to be used as a scaffold for developing a theory of mind. Both Baron-Cohen (1995) and Greenspan (1992) studied children with problems in the pervasive developmental disorder spectrum, such as autism, Asperger's, or other problems in communicating and relating, to formulate their ideas about what went awry and what natural mechanisms children use. Although Greenspan (1992) uses different terminology, many of his interventions are related to Baron-Cohen's (1995) proposed model of theory of mind and mindblindness. One may wonder what this has to do with child psychoanalysis, discovering the inner life of a child, and play space.

Creative play space may develop and be enhanced when two people collaboratively participate in focusing their attention on the same idea, pretend sequence, theme, or story. How this occurs and is enhanced may be a function of the ability of both participants to jointly attend to the same phenomena. "Sharing attention" may provide the scaffold for creating a theory of mind. It is the space where one can jointly attend to a play sequence, one's mind, music, objects, or any other experience with another. Mayes and Cohen (1996) described how the development of a theory of mind is intricately involved with internalization, the creation of an inner psychic relation, and a basis of object relations.

One of the crucial elements of psychoanalysis with children and adults is helping the child or adult attend with the analyst on their mental contents, emotions, fantasies, thoughts, sensations, and perceptions. We jointly attend to these. We create an analytic space where we can observe mental functioning in all of its various dimensions. With adults we create an analytic third by attending to the patient's thoughts, behavior, associations, and emotions, as though they are a subject in and of themselves. Ogden (1997) stated, "In sum, the analytic third is not a single event experienced identically by two people; rather it is a jointly, but asymmetrically constructed and experienced set of conscious and unconscious intersubjective experiences in which analyst and analysand participate" (p. 110). With children we create play space where we experience joint attention in play, experiences, and conversation. By jointly attending to a phenomenon such as the free association of ideas, the development of a play theme, or actual toy scenarios within the treatment setting, opportunities to learn about life, oneself, and others are established.

Fonagy and Target (1996, 1998) proposed that, "mentalization" or a reflective function permits children to respond not only to another person's behavior, but also to the child's conception of others' attitudes, intentions, or plans. Therefore, children who possess a reflective function can step back, respond flexibly, and adapt to the symbolic, meaningful qualities of others' behavior (Fonagy & Target, 1998). Likewise, "Exploring the meaning of others' actions, in turn, is crucially linked with the child's ability to label and find meaningful his own psychic experiences, an ability that we suggest underlies affect regulation, impulse control, self-monitoring, and the experience of self-agency" (1998, p. 92). In an article titled "Predictors of Outcome in Child Psychoanalysis: A Retrospective Study of 763 Cases at the Anna Freud Centre," Fonagy and Target (1996) identified the ability to recognize one's own and others' states of mind, a reflective ability, as a crucial variable in predicting outcome of treatment. It follows that focusing on a child's understanding of the world, philosophy of life, and mental states would open the transitional space to allow for a reflective function to develop. Once the space is opened, interpretation and a more classical psychoanalytic approach may be necessary to bring the analysis to a successful conclusion. The knowledge gained from research in joint attentional behavior and the development of the theory of mind can guide technique away from premature abstract interpretation until a solid basis of reflective function or mentalization has taken place. Therefore, child analysts can reflect on mental states, principally in relation to the child, both conscious and preconscious, rather than interpreting repudiated feelings about past and present relationships and experiences.

All of the above-mentioned material is not meant to suggest abandoning the classic and traditional approaches to child psychoanalysis, or psychoanalysis in general. What I am proposing is that analysts pay attention to a person's ability to attend jointly and develop a theory of mind before any interpretive work is undertaken. If these capacities are lacking, a preparatory step of focusing technique on mentalizing may be beneficial. The following vignette will illustrate the technique of focusing on the child's theory of mind during an analytic treatment. Rather than selecting a child who had no ability to use theory of mind (autistic), I have selected a child who represents the more typical child treated in outpatient or residential programs. There are subtle but important changes that take place during the analysis.

CASE VIGNETTE OF A SEVEN-YEAR-OLD CHILD

When I met Dante, a 7-year-old boy, he lived in a residential treatment facility because his mother, a drug addict, and his father, unknown whereabouts, were unable to care for him. The first Protective Services report occurred when Dante was one month old when his mother, addicted to cocaine, left him alone for long periods of time. The next few Protective Service reports came in response to Dante's injuries and reported physical abuse, and finally as a result of his mother's drug addiction. For a short period of time he lived with his grandmother and then in a foster home, but neither place could contain his violent outbursts, aggressive behavior, property destruction, verbal abusiveness, and phobic behavior. Behaviors included wiping mucus on the walls, vomiting, verbal disrespect, enuresis, biting, threats, kicking, and disrespect for rules.

Dante was moved into residential treatment when he was just under 7 years old. An attractive, slightly built child with long black eyelashes and dark brown eyes, Dante quickly acquainted himself with the adults and children with whom he resided at the residential treatment facility. At first, adults were flattered that he knew their names, and they liked him, but his verbal outbursts, opposition, running away, threats, and aggressive behavior strained their patience. Quickly, sadomasochistic relationships (Novick & Novick, 1996) were reproduced with staff and peers, and that resulted in management problems. Dante presented a picture of multiple fears, intense anxiety that led to temper tantrums, and clinging dependence. Dante participated in thrice weekly sessions, on-grounds school, and milieu treatment.

During our work together, Dante investigated, explored, and played out many themes having to do with aggression, sexuality, cannibalism, and some tenderness that spanned over several sessions. The toy babies would snuggle with one another, then become "hooked" together, then one of them would eat the other one (with all of the concomitant slobbering, chewing, eating noises), and then some sadistic fighting would occur between them, again with all of the sound effects. Over the course of the analysis, the toys became real to both of us. He knew exactly which 50 or so toys were in the box and treated them as companions, and I was dreaming about them coming alive. There were few words to couch the anxiety of being raped, devoured, and tortured; he played it; I watched. Conflict and anxiety around bodily functions, dominance/submission, gender differences, maternal longing, questions about race, fears of intimacy, phallic aggression, questions about reproduction (connection of sexual relations with cannibalism), distrust of what people say and do, seeing and not seeing, secrets, sibling rivalry, and body boundaries were presented. Dante was ambivalent about the treatment; sometimes he raced to the room, other times he refused to attend, and at first he demonstrated difficulty forming the necessary therapeutic alliance.

Using the first process note that was written after our first session, I hope to illustrate the beginning of a slow, painstaking analytic process that allowed for expansion of his thoughts, fantasy, and imagination based upon elaboration and exploration of his theory of mind. Anxiety became manageable and drive impulses could be contained in thought. During the first session, in hopes of setting the stage for further exploration and understanding of his mind, his relationships, and his behavior, I explored his preconceived notions of therapy, how adults treat him, his fears emanating from within but felt as a threat from the environment, and the ways he copes with his feelings, conflicts, and anxiety.

The second process note is from the 99th session when we are working through my leaving the facility. We had been talking about the termination, who might be his therapist, and why I was leaving. He begins to speculate and question what I am thinking and how it matches up to his idea. Again, we explore the questions, fantasies, feelings and thoughts he has as a way to understand the conflicts that reside inside him.

The third process note is the 105th and last session. It is in this last session that Dante uses his theory of mind to predict what others might think and how he might express his feelings in a way not likely to cause a negative reaction in the other person. He can speak clearly about his feelings and plan for the future.

Before each session I walked to the school, which was in a building next door to my office building, to accompany Dante to our sessions, because early in his stay he demonstrated a propensity for running away from his living quarters. Dante's approach to analysis began with trepidation and fear that evolved into ambivalent feelings of contempt and excitement, and finally has become an eagerness to explore and play. Over time, Dante has developed the practice of running ahead of me and waiting in a chair near my office. Or he "arrives" at my office after I unlock the door and sit down. It feels as though he has just dropped in for a visit.

Session 1

On the day of our first session when I arrived at his classroom to accompany Dante to my office, he was ready and promptly came to the door. After introducing myself, I told him it was time for therapy. He said, "I know that I have to have therapy." I said, "Oh, you have heard about therapy?" He said, "Yes, I have to have it." I asked him what he knew about therapy. He said, "That I have to have it." I said, "We will talk about what therapy is when we get to my office." He asked where my office was. I told him that he was probably in the building when he first came here and that I would show him where the office is so he will know his way. He ran his hand along the brick wall of the school hallway. Once we reached the door of the school building, he grabbed his arms with his hands, hugging himself tightly, and asked, "Are there bees in your office?" I said, "No, I did not see any." Then once we were outside the school building, he asked if the noise he heard were bees. I said that they were probably cicadas, not bees, and that they make a noise like bees. He said they sounded like bees. When we reached the building where my office is, still clinging to himself, he said, "I'm afraid." I said, "You are feeling afraid?" He looked tiny, scared, and worried. At this point I was very cognizant of feelings of wanting to try to soothe his fears, yet his experience was far from being understood, and, furthermore, it was quite unlikely that anything I would say or do would calm him. He was preparing himself to be stung. He did not trust that anyone, including himself, could offer him protection.

After climbing the stairs to my office, I opened the door and told him that I was putting out the sign that says that we are having therapy. He immediately went to the toy box and started getting out male action figures and the house, which was sitting in the toy box. He said, "I like big men, men that move." After I reflected that he likes big men, men that move, he nodded. I said that he must have heard about therapy. He said, "I have to go to therapy." I asked what he thought happened in therapy. He said, "I don't know," and then he thought he heard a bee–again he is preparing himself to be stung. His "big men" in play are in stark contrast to his smallness as he readies himself for a sting. This sequence is a window to his defense of portraying strength (physical and verbal outbursts) when he feels impending "stinging" and helplessness. In his psychic world one dominates, one submits; one is the stinger, one is the stung.

I introduced Dante to the process of therapy by telling him that therapy is a place where we talk about our ideas, thoughts, and feelings, anything he likes. It is a special place because he is in charge of what will be talked about. Again, cognizant of his smallness and theory of mind, he asserted, "I'm not in charge of anything." I said, "That is what makes therapy special. You are in charge of what we talk about, and we can talk about anything and everything." Again, he revealed that using his theory of mind, we have one who is in charge and one who will take orders. As we talked, he collected several toy action figures, four men and two women. When I spoke to him about our possible meeting times, he preferred to arrange our meeting times from a distance, looking at the calendar from several feet away.

After we settled on our meeting times, Dante spotted a Dinosaur head that when opened revealed a little scene where little creatures nestled into its mouth. He examined the teeth and opened and closed the mouth a few times. He said, "He can eat anything." After a bit of reflection, he said, "I like dinosaurs. I know a kid who has a dinosaur that eats men." Again, he is revealing his understanding of relationships: big people can overcome little people just as little people can overcome big people with the aid of a dinosaur. According to his theory of mind, this is how people relate to one another. This is the basis of his object relations.

In a little house there was a dog, boy, and car. He looked this toy over and said, "He's a little boy looking out a window." After I repeated his observation, he expanded the idea with, "He sees her," referring to the woman. Referring to the boy or dog in the window, he repeatedly asked, "Can you see him?", inviting me to jointly attend to the toy much like a younger child who wants a mother to see and validate what he sees. He engaged me in conversation about the toys by asking me who the men were. I did not answer at first. Then he asked me again. I said that I did not know and that they could be whomever he wanted them to be. He said, "They are climb and smoke men." I thought but did not say that maybe he was referring to firemen as he now had them posed on top of the house. Dante said that the man sees the woman. I asked, "What does he see?" He said, "I don't know." It felt as though he was teaching me not to ask questions.

Dante continued playing with the characters fighting or changing from good guys to bad guys and back again, making sure that I saw every movement. If he was unsure if I saw a movement or interaction, he drew my attention to it with a question. Whenever I moved my foot or made any noise, he asked me if there was a bee in the room.

Later during the session he decided that the men turned into bad guys, robots that the woman created. He found a little rubber net and asked me what it was. I did not answer. He said, "You would rather not say? I think it is a net. Doesn't it look like a net?" I said, "Yes." He used it to catch the woman and the bad guys. He said, "He didn't see the net because he was looking at the ground because he was scared." Dante wrapped up the man in the net so he could no longer move. Then Dante took another man and said, "This guy was looking up but he doesn't know there is a net there. He has a knife that he cuts through it. Sometimes when you are looking down you get caught." To avoid being caught off guard, Dante has developed the defenses of being very wary, sensitive to others' slights, and explosive.

Then Dante set traps for the action figure men by laying the net over the chimney and letting them walk on it and fall, again taken by surprise. He asked me if I would be scared to be on a house. When I did not answer right away, he expanded his question, adding that I would be by myself on the top of the house. Referring to the man on the roof, I asked, "Umm, what does he think?" He said, "I would be scared." He made traps for the men a little bit longer, and then I told him that our session was over for today and that I would come for him tomorrow. He said, "OK" and picked up the toys. After picking up, he came close to me, looked out the window, and said, "I'm scared." Knowing that we were talking about much more than was apparent but wanting to let him tell me what he knew about being scared, I commented on his direct experience, "You are scared when you look out the window?" He said, "Yes," and then after the session ended, I walked him back to his classroom.

This was my preview to Melanie Klein's oral sadistic, greedy, and devouring baby. "I like dinosaurs. I know a kid who has a dinosaur that eats men." In subsequent sessions many oral incorporation themes followed: we discussed the size of creatures' teeth; we discussed babies sucking on their mothers; animals licking one another; daddies eating babies; dinosaurs eating people and animals; and the dinosaur head roaming the office looking for food, chewing, spitting, and swallowing. Unlike Klein's technique, these themes were not interpreted in terms of their unconscious, symbolic themes, but rather they were "illuminated" and allowed to develop to their fullest. The ambivalence of taking in and expelling was played out until it developed further into overtly sexual themes.

This first session illustrates the fear, ambivalence, and confusion with which children approach treatment. Often, just as Dante did, they approach with compliance but with feelings of being overpowered, dominated, and persecuted. Sensing his worries about being attacked, I explained therapy to him but this did nothing to calm his fears. He defended himself by fantasizing about a small kid, like himself, who owns a powerful enough creature that could eat me up if necessary. In his daily life he demonstrated this fear by becoming powerful by using cuss words, making "big man" threats toward staff, and throwing objects around. However, his strengths show themselves in this session, as well. He tolerates attending the session, uses displacement in the play, and engages me in conversation about the characters. To use the reflective function as a guide, Dante can reflect a little on the characters' minds, but needs my confirmation of his perceptions. I tried to set up an environment where we would be able to jointly attend to Dante's play, thoughts, fantasies, feelings, and behavior. I showed interest in Dante's mental states, his emotions, and the emotions and mental states of the characters in play. With little understanding of his own fear, he talked about his mental state by ascribing it to his characters; it is he, the man alone on the roof, who feels scared, and ready to be taken by surprise or caught off guard. He feels impingement as though it comes from the outside, always worrying about a bee stinging him.

Session 99

The second process note is from the 99th session after I had told Dante that I would be leaving the facility. For about two months we had been discussing termination, and it was going to become a reality in another two weeks. The session before this one we missed because Dante had an all-day field trip.

Dante had a pouting, angry look on his face when he returned from lunch. He glared at me. Reluctantly, he walked behind me all the way to the office, which is contrasted with his running ahead of me and waiting at the door. Once inside the office he looked at me accusingly and asked why I did not see him yesterday. I said, "Because when I went to get you, you were on a field trip." Dante said, "No, I was in the readiness room (a time-out room)." I said, "Ah, I checked there too." Then he said, "I went somewhere else." I said, "It sounds like maybe you wondered if I looked for you." He asked, "When are you leaving?" I said, "The end of June. Do you want to see the calendar?" He said, "Yes." We counted off the days. Then he accused me of leaving on a Tuesday instead of a Friday. I said, "You are having some trouble keeping straight when I leave." He said, "I will be glad when you leave. You ask too many questions." I asked, "What questions do I ask that you do not like?" He said, "You just talk too much." I said, "I am wondering what we would do if we didn't talk." He said, "You talk too much. Do not say anything else." I said, "Maybe you are practicing for when I am not here." He said, "I do not want you to talk."

From the toy box, Dante got out the little animals. He asked me to get the Topple game down. Holding the dinosaur head, he said, "Now feed me."

I said, "Oh you are hungry again today, Dinosaur?" He said, "Yes, feed me." I said, "Today do you want certain food?" He said, "No, just those one at a time." I said, "OK" and began throwing them into his mouth. If I missed, he said, "You are hurting me." I said, "It hurts if I don't get them in just right." Every now and then he emptied his mouth, meaning that it went into his stomach. He never got filled up, though. Once I was out of food, Dinosaur went roaming the office looking for more. He found the animals and ate some of them. He wanted to eat the snake. Dante wondered if I watched the Discovery Channel on television, and did I know what eats snakes. I asked, "Is it an animal?" He said, "Yes." I asked, "Does it have fur?" He said, "Yes." I said, "OK, um a raccoon?" He said, "Not a raccoon. A snake would eat a raccoon." I said, "Oh, do you know anything more about it?" He said, "It is by the water." I said, "A badger?" He asked what a badger is. I told him, and he said that it was not a badger. He said that it was black. I said, "A mink?" He said, "Yes, a mink." Then Dinosaur ate the snake and began to move around like something was making him feel jumpy. I said, "Oh, that is like when we have a feeling and nobody knows what it is but they can see that something is making us move." He said, "The snake is biting him but nobody can see it." I said, "That is how it is sometimes. We feel things but other people don't know what it is because they can't see it." He played out this theme several times, and each time I talked about how we don't know what is hurting Dinosaur because we can't see it, but Dinosaur still hurts on the inside.

Then he said, "The men are going to hunt him." I asked why, and he said, "Because they are hungry." I said, "Oh, so Dinosaur eats the animals, and then the men eat Dinosaur." But unexpectedly the men got eaten. Some men tried to help the other men out of Dinosaur's mouth with varying success.

Dante opened the Topple game and put the little animals on the summit. He said, "This animal is you." I said, "OK." He said, "This animal and this one and this one are me." I said, "It seems like there is more of you than me. I am just one animal." Then he said, "You talk for the animal." Then he made one of his animals say, "Now get out of here–just leave." Speaking for the animal, I asked, "Are you my boss?" He said, "Yes, now get out of here." I asked, "Why do you want me to leave?" He said, "Because I hate you." I said, "Oh, you hate me and just want me to leave. Did I do something to make you hate me?" He said, "Just leave or I am going to push you over the edge." I said, "Are you my boss?" He said, "Yes. Now leave." Then he decided to leave and all of his friends left with him. They all jumped off the Topple game stand. He said, "Now let's fight" as he put one animal back up there. They fought a little. Then they fell down, and Dante continued to fight and asked me if I saw all of the other guys fighting too. I said, "I do, but sometimes I think that they don't know what else to do but to fight, maybe they are afraid to be friends." He said, "They are not afraid to fight." I said, "I see that. I do not think fighting feelings are as scary as friendly feelings are sometimes." He had them fight some more. He tried to coax my guy back with, "You want to be my friend?" But then he fought me. I said, "Maybe that is a little like you feel . . . that I said let's be friends now I am going away. Sort of like a trick." He did not answer, but just tried to coax me more. Then he said, "You are calling for your mama." I said, "Mama, Mama." Then he asked, "What does your mama look like?" I asked, "Um, how does she look?" He found another rhino and said that this was my mom. He started to fight my mama. I said, "Now wait a minute. You are fighting my mama?" He then looked into the box and found the big bull to be the dad. I said, "Oh so it is dad against mom?" He lined them up and said that it was a fight between mom and dad. I asked, "Why are the mom and dad fighting? Are they from the same family or different ones?" He pointed out that it was a dad of one and a mom of another. Then he decided that the lion would fight a rhino. I said, "The lion is so big. How does the rhino have a chance?" He said, "You don't think it is a fair fight?" I said, "Well, what do you think?" He decided to have the lion and the giraffe fight, and then he wondered if that was a fair fight. I said, "How would we figure that out?" Dante did not say anything. I said, "Well, I wonder if the giraffe can run faster than the lion." Dante said, "He can." I said, "OK, um, I wonder if his teeth are as sharp?" Dante had the lion run after the giraffe, but he then decided to get out the little lion. I said, "Now that doesn't look fair to me. That lion is so much smaller that it looks like an adult against a child." He said, "OK then," and got out one more kid. Then he asked, "Do you think that is fair?" I said, "Interesting question. It is two against one." Dante put the little lion on top of the other lion. Then I said, "Well, now they look more like the same size, but I am still not sure that it is fair. Doesn't the adult have more experience than the child?" He said, "OK then" and got out a guy he called the "teenager." I said, "Oh, so a teenager comes to help." He corrected me, "That is a grown-up." But he was still not satisfied with the size discrepancy. He spied another rhino the same size as the other one and decided that they could fight each other. That will be a fair fight. They just started fighting when it was time to end the session for the day. Dante had Dinosaur pick up some of the Topple game. Then he tossed some of the pieces into the box and left, saying, "I'll see you tomorrow." I said, "You will see me Tuesday, just like always." He said, "OK, I will see you then."

During this session Dante began to deal a little more directly with his feelings about the upcoming termination. He responds to my thinking that maybe he was wondering if I looked for him with an expansion of the underlying issue, which is my leaving the facility. While he argues with me about what day I am leaving, and he accuses me of leaving early, he is able to begin facing the impending separation. He shows his dissatisfaction with my reflection that he is having trouble keeping these dates straight by telling me that I ask too many questions and talk too much anyway. However, contrarily, he wants to be fed but if I do not feed him just right it hurts and he wants to fight. We jointly work on what kind of animal would eat a snake, and, since he is going to be transferred to a new therapist, he has snake eaters on his mind. He also plays out the beginning realization that he can have feelings inside that bother him but that others cannot see. Previously, he was not concerned with whether a fight was fair or not but he is stronger now and can afford a bigger challenge. He also struggles with size discrepancy and fairness. At the end of the hour he wants to see me tomorrow instead of waiting until Tuesday; however, he leaves the session and is able to walk himself back to school.

Session 105: Last Session Summary

During the last session, session 105, it is clear that Dante has begun to consider others' minds and use this newly found knowledge to plan his behavior. He is concerned about being able to express himself, especially when he has all sorts of intense feelings that betray themselves in profanity. He is not comfortable with what he had on his mind and was unsure if his new therapist would allow him to express his true feelings.

> During the last session Dante prepared himself for my departure, reflected on our past together, and planned for the future. Intermittently during the session, Dante wondered why I could not remain his therapist; yet, in the service of letting go of our relationship, he talked about how he had "remembered" the day I came to the treatment center (actually I had been there before he arrived). Often throughout the treatment, when important, arousing, confusing, or otherwise overwhelming issues were being discussed, Dante needed to go the bathroom or get a drink. During this last session, I had a cup of water on my desk, so I offered him one. He proceeded to drink it and talk with me as though we were having tea. After these emotionally close moments of conversation, Dante decided that he would make "pee" and wondered if I wanted to drink it, possibly to keep him with me after I left.

> Dante discussed his worry that my replacement would not be able to listen to his thoughts and feelings as raw as they were. He demonstrated this worry by questioning me about cuss words, took copious notes on the cuss words, and wanted me to look them up in the dictionary. He wanted to know if he could have his box down. I said, "Yes, today, as we talked about, you can take what is in your box home with you. I will give Debbie.

(the replacement therapist) the box." He said, "I'm scared." I asked, "What are you scared about?" He said, "Debbie." I asked, "What about her scares you?" He said, "She won't let me say f– and b–." I asked, "You don't think so?" He said, "She won't." I said, "So one of your worries is that you won't be able to say what is on your mind?" He said, "She is not going to let me say b– and f–." I asked, "How do you know?" He said, "Just look at her. No one who looks like that is going to let you use those words." I asked, "What is it about her looks?" He said, "Just look at her." After he had said f– and b– a few times, I asked if maybe he was thinking that he wanted to say that to me. He said, "No, but I am an expert on those kinds of cuss words." I said, "Oh, so you are an expert on cuss words?" He said, "Yes, let's look them up. What are some? F–. How do you spell that?" Then he started looking up the word in the dictionary. I said, "You have an interest in words and are pretty good looking them up, too." He found the word he was searching for. Then he saw the notebook paper, was very excited, and decided to take notes on cuss words. He asked about another cuss word, "sh–." He said, "Like in 'sh– on Debbie's face?' " I said, "So you are pretty unsure about seeing her." He asked, "How do you spell it?" I told him. Then he asked about another word. I said, "H–." Then he asked how to spell it. I told him. I said, "Since it is important to be able to say what is on your mind, how will you be able to tell if those words are OK with Debbie?" Dante decided that he would say, "uck, with a f in the front of it," "it with an h in the front of it," "sit with a sh in the front of it." I said, "So you will be able to tell by how she acts when you say these words?" He kept writing all these notes. I told him that it was almost time to go. I asked which sack he wanted to put his papers in. He said, "Both." I said, "Dante I have enjoyed working with you." He interrupted me and said, "I am going to miss you." I said, "I am going to miss you too." He asked, "Why can't you just stay?" I said, "I know this is confusing about my leaving." He asked, "Can I show you where Debbie's room is?" I said, "Yes." He said, "It is near the drinking fountain." He read her name tag. He went down the stairs and decided that he wanted just to wait for childcare to pick him up.

DISCUSSION

During the last session it is clear that Dante was beginning to plan his behavior on the basis of newly found knowledge of predicting how someone will react to him. He reflected on his own feelings with some understanding about the origins of them. He was afraid of not being able to say what is on his mind when he interacts with the new therapist, and he worried that because she presented herself as someone who is not used to cuss words that she will not be able to tolerate his feelings and thoughts. Words had become interesting as well as exciting and powerful for him. Dante internalized our work of identifying feelings and thoughts and used it in thinking about meeting the new therapist, something he had not been able to do previously. Instead of externalizing his fears onto the general environment (bees, aggressive behavior and verbalizations, running away, etc.), Dante could now identify the specific source of his fear and devise a strategy to help him feel safer. By loosening the inhibition on his mental functioning, he developed more access to his mental world, thereby demonstrating a genuine ability to comprehend his own and others' mental functioning. Clearly, he was able to use cognition to manage some of his anxiety and confusion. To use Anna Freud's (Sandler, Kennedy, & Tyson, 1980) notion of "transference of habitual modes of relating," Dante assumed that authority figures could not be counted on to understand or accept or approve of his thoughts, feelings, or fantasies. Our work, which included determining others' and his own intentionality and jointly attending to mental contents, allowed Dante to begin to question his characteristic ways of functioning and try out new behaviors. I might add that even before the last session described, Dante's behavior at the treatment center was greatly improved. He was not verbally abusing or threatening others, or generally causing trouble. Reportedly, he was talking with staff more about what made him uncomfortable, angry, or sad. As Fonagy and Target (1996) noted, "being able to make meaning of one's own psychic experiences underlies affect regulation, impulse control, self-monitoring and the experience of self-agency" (p. 92). This was the case for Dante.

Unfortunately, I left the facility before Dante's treatment was completed. We had more work to do before he could resolve some important conflicts and heal the many traumas he endured, nor did we fully explore the abandonment by his parents. By engaging in helpful exploration, illumination, and elaboration of his experience, Dante was better able to understand himself, his experience, and the experience of others, and how to make his way in the world in a more effective manner. He was able to internalize my pondering about his mental life, and now he was able to do the same for himself. In the safe, nurturing, finely attuned analytic space, Dante was able to share his thoughts, question them, and explore his feelings through play and then conversation. My analytic attitude of listening and commenting on his philosophy of life as presented through behavior, play, or conversation facilitated the widening of the mental space where Dante could begin to play with his thoughts and fantasies.

SUMMARY

Transitional play space is important for children and adults. It is where new fantasies, thoughts and ideas can be discovered, and it is also where fantasies, thoughts, and ideas can be rethought, reworked, and understood differently. As child analysts, we need to provide a safe, nurturing, inviting environment conducive to exploration, much like the ideal early environment in which mother and child find an agreed upon state of mind and explore one another and themselves. "Over time, the unconscious past loses some of its grip on life and future alternatives to old maladaptive patterns are *imagined and become possible*" [italics added] (Emde, Kubicek, & Oppenheim, 1997, p. 127). Widening the scope of psychoanalytic techniques to include theory of mind and developmental, evolutionary, cognitive, and neuropsychological research does not take away from the cherished principles and techniques we hold as psychoanalysts. Instead, it offers analysts new techniques, which, when consciously applied, help pave the way for our patients to open analytic play space in a way that expands thinking possibilities and more flexible solutions to problems.

REFERENCES

Alvarez, A. (1992). *Live Company* London: Routledge.

Baron-Cohen, S. (1995). *Mindblindness: An Essay on Autism and Theory of Mind.* Cambridge, MA: The MIT Press.

Bollas, C. (1987). *The Shadow of the Object: Psychoanalysis of the Unthought Known.* London: Free Association Books.

Bornstein, B. (1935). Phobia in a two-and-a-half-year-old child. *Psychoanalytic Quarterly, 4,* 93-119.

Bornstein, B. (1945). Clinical notes on child analysis. *The Psychoanalytic Study of the Child, 1,* 151-166.

Bornstein, B. (1948). Emotional barriers in the understanding and treatment of young children. *American Journal of Orthopsychiatry, 18,* 691-697.

Bornstein, B. (1951). On latency. *The Psychoanalytic Study of the Child, 6,* 279-285.

Brunner, J. (1995). From joint attention to the meeting of minds: An introduction. In C. Moore & P. J. Dunham (Eds.), *Joint Attention: Its Origins and Role in Development* (pp. 1-14). Hillsdale, NJ: Lawrence Erlbaum Associates.

Chused, J. F. (1990). How clinical work with children can inform the therapist of adults. In S. Dowling (Ed.), *Child and Adolescent Analysis: Its Significance for Clinical Work with Adults* (pp. 37-54). Madison, CT: International Universities Press.

Emde, R., Kubicek, L., & Oppenheim, D. (1997). Imaginative reality observed during early language development. *International Journal of Psychoanalysis, 78,* 115-133.

Feigeson, C. I. (1974). Play in child analysis. *The Psychoanalytic Study of the Child, 29,* 21-26.

Fonagy, P. & Target, M. (1996). Predictors of outcome in child psychoanalysis: A retrospective study of 763 cases at the Anna Freud Center. *Journal of American Psychoanalytic Association, 44*(1), 27-77.

Fonagy, P. & Target, M. (1998). Mentalization and the changing aims of child psychoanalysis. *Psychoanalytic Dialogues, 8*(1), 87-114.

Freud, A. (1945). Indications for child analysis. *The Psychoanalytic Study of the Child, I, 127-149.*

Freud, A. (1965). *Normality and Pathology in Childhood.* New York: International Universities Press, Inc.

Freud, A. (1971). *The Writings of Anna Freud: Vol. VII. Problems of Psychoanalytic Training, Diagnosis, and the Technique of Therapy* (pp. 48-58). New York: International Universities Press.

Greenspan, S. I. (1992). *Infancy and Early Childhood: The Practice of Clinical Assessment and Intervention with Emotional and Developmental Challenges.* Madison, CT: International Universities Press.

Klein, M. (1975). *The Psychoanalysis of Children.* England: The Hogarth Press and The Institute of Psycho-Analysis.

Lepisto, B. L. (1994a). Empathy and Psychotherapy. *Voices, 30,* 78-87.

Lepisto, B. L. (1994b). Children's understanding of maternal empathy. (Doctoral dissertation, Central Michigan University, 1994).

Mayes, L. C. & Cohen, D. J. (1996). Children's Developing Theory of Mind. *Journal of the American Psychoanalytic Association, 44,* 117-142.

Meares, R. & Lichtenberg, J. (1995). The form of play in the shape and unity of self. *Contemporary Psychoanalysis, 31,* 47-64.

Meltzoff, A. & Gopnick, A. (1993). The role of imitation in understanding persons and developing a theory of mind. In S. Baron-Cohen, H. Tager-Flushberg, & D. J. Cohen (Eds.), *Understanding Other Minds* (pp. 335-366). Oxford, England: Oxford University Press.

Moore, C. & Dunham, P. J. (Eds.). (1995). *Joint Attention: Its Origins and Role in Development.* Hillsdale, NJ: Lawrence Erlbaum.

Novick, J. & Novick, K, K. (1996). *Fearful Symmetry: The Development and Treatment of Sadomaosschism.* Northvale, NJ: Jason Aronson.

Ogden, T. (1985). On potential space. *International Journal of Psycho-analysis, 66,* 129-141.

Ogden, T. (1997). *Reverie and Interpretation.* Northvale, NJ: Jason Aronson.

Pedder, J. R. (1992). Conductor or director? Transitional space in psychotherapy and in the theater. *Psychoanalytic Review, 79,* 261-270.

Sandler, J., Kennedy, H., & Tyson, R. L. (1980). *The Technique of Child Psychoanalysis: Discussions with Anna Freud.* Cambridge, MA: Harvard University Press.

Stern, D. (1985). *The Interpersonal World of the Infant.* New York: Basic Books.

The American Heritage Talking Dictionary, Third Edition. [CD-ROM] Houghton Mifflin Company, Softkey International.

Winnicott, D. W. (1971). *Playing and Reality.* London: Routledge.

The Impact of Early Loss on Depression: Dynamic Origins and Empirical Findings

Irene M. Bravo

SUMMARY. This article reviews psychodynamic theoretical claims linking childhood losses to depression later in life and explores contemporary empirical studies that are congruent with those claims. Biologically mediated responses to grief, empirically supported pathways that link loss to depression, and factors that distinguish normal from pathological grief are identified. Trajectories that may lead to the development of psychotic-like, instead of neurotic-like, symptoms of depression are also explored, and empirically supported internal and external vulnerability factors that may lead to depression are reported. Several clinical vignettes are included to exemplify theoretical claims. Implications for assessment and treatment are discussed in light of these findings. *[Article copies available for a fee from The Haworth Document Delivery Service: 1-800-342-9678. E-mail address: <getinfo@haworthpressinc.com> Website: <http://www.HaworthPress.com> © 2001 by The Haworth Press, Inc. All rights reserved.]*

KEYWORDS. Childhood loss and depression, dynamic origins, childhood loss and empirical findings

---

Irene M. Bravo, PhD, is Assistant Professor, Doctoral Program, Carlos Albizu University, Miami Campus, Miami, FL.

The author thanks Sheri L. Johnson, PhD, University of Miami, for her comments on an earlier version of this article.

Address correspondence to: Irene M. Bravo, PhD, Carlos Albizu University, Doctoral Program in Psychology, 2173 N.W. 99th Avenue, Miami, FL 33172.

[Haworth co-indexing entry note]: "The Impact of Early Loss on Depression: Dynamic Origins and Empirical Findings." Bravo, Irene M. Co-published simultaneously in *Psychoanalytic Social Work* (The Haworth Press, Inc.) Vol. 8, No. 3/4, 2001, pp. 47-69; and: *Psychoanalytic Approaches to the Treatment of Children and Adolescents: Tradition and Transformation* (ed: Jerrold R. Brandell) The Haworth Press, Inc., 2001, pp. 47-69. Single or multiple copies of this article are available for a fee from The Haworth Document Delivery Service [1-800-342-9678, 9:00 a.m. - 5:00 p.m. (EST). E-mail address: getinfo@haworthpressinc.com].

Loss of loved objects may create feelings of despair and emptiness that are not easily overcome. When the devastation persists, the grieving process may develop into a full-blown depression. Experiencing losses is a common human experience, but it is not clear why some individuals suffer endlessly whereas others traverse grief episodes adaptively. Although a multiplicity of answers related to genetic endowment, temperament, contextual issues, and so forth may explain these differences, one answer lies in how developmental pathways, obstructed at childhood due to severe distress or major losses, result in impaired coping ability to deal with later losses. The nexus between early loss and depression has stimulated a good deal of theorizing and subsequent research, first on the part of psychodynamic clinicians and later on the part of a wide range of researchers. The focus of this article is to trace some of the most salient psychodynamic and empirical findings on loss and depression and to gain understanding–on the grieving process in general and, in particular, on models that link early loss to later depression.

EARLY THEORETICAL BACKGROUND

Karl Abraham (1911/1968), a physician, published the first paper written by a psychoanalyst on depression in 1911. In 1917, Sigmund Freud (1917/1968) wrote an essay, "Mourning and Melancholia," comparing melancholia to normal mourning. In melancholia, there is "a profoundly painful dejection, cessation of interest in the outside world, loss of the capacity to love, inhibition of all activity, and a lowering of the self-regarding feelings to a degree that finds utterance in self-reproaches and self-reviling, and culminates in a delusional expectation of punishment" (Freud, 1917, p. 244). With the exception of the disturbance in self-regard, Freud added, all melancholia's features are present in mourning. Freud observed that in mourning, yearning for the lost object is part of the normal response to loss; it is gradually overcome as the mental representation of the lost object is dissipated or decathected. Conversely, in melancholia, the pathological response is more pervasive; it originates from an ambivalent, narcissistic object relationship between the mourner and the lost person.

Interestingly, although Freud's theories emphasized the importance of early experiences on later development, it was Abraham, in a subsequent paper, (1924/1968) who made this distinction. Abraham defined melancholia as an ambivalent feeling of love and hate toward the self that arises from an early infantile disappointment in love. He suggested that a repetition of this disappointment later in life reactivated the primary depressive condition in vulnerable individuals. According to Abraham, the reactivation of the primary depressive condition in vulnerable individuals required: (a) an inherited predisposition toward extreme oral erotism, (b) an oral fixation of the libido, (c) a severe injury to infantile narcissism arising from disappointments in love (frequently from both parents), (d) the first important disappointment in love before the resolution of oedipal wishes, and (e) the repetition of the primary disappointment later in life, resulting in self-reproaches that are unconsciously directed to the primary love object. Abraham suggested that in unaffected individuals, ambivalent tendencies of love/hatred toward the self (oral stage) and toward others (anal stage) are dispelled after the libido becomes fully formed (genital stage). In melancholics, on the other hand, the libido becomes fixated at the oral, narcissistic level, creating extreme feelings of self-importance and self-debasement that prevent them from focusing on the external world and on processing subsequent losses adaptively. According to Abraham (1924/1968), melancholics introject primary love objects as pathological consciences, whose self-reproaches become unconscious merciless criticisms toward their introjects. In addition to Abraham, several object relation theorists also connected loss at the oral stage to maladaptive coping during subsequent losses later in life.

One of these theorists, W. R. D. Fairbairn (1940, 1941), described the oral stage as a crucial time in the formation of affective relations. Fairbairn divided the oral stage into a pre-ambivalent phase and an ambivalent phase. At the pre-ambivalent phase, infants do not yet bite and remain unaware of the emotional state of hate. Infants attribute great importance to states of fullness and emptiness and may believe that the mother is emptied after suckling. When they feel deprived, infants become anxious over having emptied and thus destroyed the breast or libidinal object and conclude that their love is destructive and bad. If fixation occurs at the pre-ambivalent phase, feelings of anxiety remain repressed in the unconscious, ready to be reactivated by subsequent experiences of deprivation. Fixation at this phase becomes the schizoid position, a stage that is more pernicious and alienating than fixation at the ambivalent oral phase.

Infants fixated at the ambivalent oral phase know how to bite and conclude that their hate, not their love, has the capacity to destroy the mother's affection. Because their badness is isolated in their hate, their love remains good in their eyes. Fairbairn argued that fixation at this stage becomes the depressive position which underlies manic depressive psychoses. During subsequent losses, individuals fixated at the pre-ambivalent oral phase revert to states of deep melancholia or depressive psychosis, whereas individuals fixated at the ambivalent oral phase revert to neurotic depressive states. As a consequence of Fairbairn's and other object relation theorists' emphasis on the quality of the mother-child relationship, interest stirred on child welfare issues, and important questions were posed, such as: Do children have the capacity to mourn?

Controversy ensued at this time as a result of divergent developmental theories of infant mourning elaborated in Vienna and in London (Bowlby, 1982). The main proponents of these opposing theories were Deutsch (1937) and Klein (1940). Deutsch argued that, due to inadequate psychic development, children are unable to mourn. Klein, on the other hand, held that children certainly can and do mourn.

Klein theorized that all infants adopt a primary depressive position when they have to give up the breast, which represents to them love, goodness, and security. In agreement with Fairbairn, Klein argued that feelings of loss are caused by the infant's ambivalence (love/hate) toward the breast's fluctuating availability. However, she believed that the primary depressive position becomes reactivated at the oedipal stage, when children become distressed about the possibility of losing both parents. According to Klein, the depressive position is overcome by a manic position, or the internalization of parents as good objects. This substitution is necessary because a sense of omnipotence, denial, and idealization, coupled with ambivalence (split images as both good and bad), is essential for ego development. Klein argued that as a result of dealing with reality children forgo manic omnipotence and develop the capacity to trust and thus enhance their capacity for love.

During mourning, Klein added, feelings of loss and dejection are related, not only to the lost loved object, but also to the original internal good objects. This implies a regression to a predominant internal bad objects stage that triggers the original infantile depressive position, "and with it, (arise) anxieties, guilt, and feelings of loss and grief derived from the breast situation, the Oedipus situation and from all other sources" (p. 353). Klein's early views were elaborated on and supported by other theorists, such as Erikson (1950/1963), Mahler (1966), Blatt (1974), and Kohut (Tolpin & Kohut, 1980).

Although Erikson (1950/1963) adhered more to Freudian psychoanalysis than to the object relations perspective, he also investigated the etiology of depressive states, linking them to the mother-infant relationship. In support of Klein, Erikson stressed the importance of breast-feeding in the development of a strong bond between the mother and her infant. However, Erikson argued against weaning infants abruptly, as he believed this may provoke in them a depressive reaction. He considered sudden weaning to be appropriate only if it was culturally accepted, and solely in situations in which women similar to the mother were available. Otherwise, Erikson considered it advisable to wean infants in a very slow and gradual manner. Erikson expressed that "a drastic loss of the mother's love without appropriate substitution can lead to infantile depression or to a mild but chronic state of mourning which may give a depressive undertone to the whole remainder of life" (p. 80).

Mahler (1966) also acknowledged that the mother-child relationship is crucial in the development of basic moods, including depression. However, in contrast to Klein, Mahler believed that the depressive position does not occur at the oral stage, but later in toddlerhood, during the separation-individuation period. Mahler claimed that toddlers require the mother's love and acceptance for appropriate ego development. If toddlers perceive that they are not wholly accepted, their self-esteem becomes compromised, and disturbances in the development of object constancy may arise. Mahler argued that toddlers become especially vulnerable at the phallic phase of psychosexual development as a consequence of the double trauma of toilet-training and concomitant castration anxiety. Emphasizing gender differences, Mahler concluded that the higher vulnerability for depression observed in females may derive from the double trauma of toilet-training plus the discovery of anatomical sexual differences during toddlerhood.

Other object relations theorists, such as Blatt (1974), subsequently conceptualized depression in accordance with the child's level of object representation. Blatt made important distinctions between anaclitic (see Spitz, 1946) and introjective depression. Anaclitic depression is oral, mainly concerned about the basic relationship with the mother, where there is relatively low evidence of guilt. In this type of depression, fears of abandonment and of being unloved predominate. In introjective depression, on the other hand, children are more developmentally advanced, often have oedipal wishes, and may suffer intense feelings of guilt (Blatt). Blatt added that introjective depression is characterized by feelings of being unworthy, unlovable, and guilty of not reaching exceedingly high ideals. The superego is overly harsh, and there is constant self-scrutiny and evaluation that may revolve around themes of morality and commitment (Blatt). In addition to object relations theorists, self-psychologists, such as Kohut, examined depression as a disorder of the self.

Kohut (Tolpin & Kohut, 1980) explained that children often present with chronic states of and defenses against depletion. Tolpin and Kohut describe depletion depression as a chronic response that children have to their inability to interact with their parents as selfobjects, or objects that satisfy their needs for mirroring, idealizing, or partnering. Although such children may appear to possess psychological stability, they may become easily fragmented should anything interfere with their selfobject relationships. At such time, children typically become helplessly enraged and "clinging, excessively demanding, coercive, and manipulative" (Tolpin & Kohut, 1980; p. 245). Self-assertion in developmental tasks, such as toilet mastery, peer relations, and so forth, often suffers lasting impairment.

GRIEF AS A NORMATIVE, ADAPTIVE RESPONSE

In contrast with theoretical conceptualizations of grief as a regressive mechanism, other early object relations theorists, such as Fenichel (1945) characterized grief as an adaptive response. Fenichel postulated that grief provides an avenue for the mourner to first introject and then release the lost object. Specifically, he stated that an ambivalent introjection of the lost object is adaptive and that guilt is present to some extent in all grief. Fenichel theorized that infants have the ability to recall states of hunger and satiation. Because hungry infants remember having been satisfied before, they develop a feeling of omnipotence, often manifested in protests and cries. Their omnipotent feelings are lost once they realize their dependence on the care of others, and thus project their feelings of omnipotence onto their parents. As their development progresses, their needs also change. Infants now are no longer content with being fed, but also need to feel loved. If they do not feel loved, their self-esteem becomes compromised, resulting in feelings of self-depreciation. As children develop the capacity to anticipate the future, they learn to use adaptive ego defenses in situations that result in minor feelings of loss of self-esteem. As a result of this strength, they learn to defend against real and definite losses. Once the superego emerges, it becomes the regulator of the child's self-esteem. Feelings of having done the right thing predominate, and guilt arises in situations of failure, thus becoming part of all depressive states.

According to Fenichel, bereaved individuals want to keep the illusion that the lost object is still alive and create a substitute object within the self by switching from object relation to identification. Fenichel argued that "many individuals who have lost one of their parents early in childhood show signs of an oral fixation and tend to establish, along with their object relationships, proper, extensive identifications, that is, to incorporate their objects" (p. 394). Fenichel considered this process adaptive because it eventually relinquishes the introjected object–apparently an easier task than the release of the real object. Mourning becomes complicated when the relationship to the lost object is extremely ambivalent. The incorporation becomes sadistic, as it represents, not only an attempt to preserve a loved object but also an attempt to destroy a hated object. In such cases, the introjection creates renewed feelings of guilt.

Fenichel proposed that guilt is pervasively present in death as seen in the frequent symptoms of remorse observed in normal death rituals. He specifically argued that symptoms of remorse are present when: (a) the object had been previously wished dead, and its death may be perceived as the fulfillment of this wish, (b) feelings of joy arise at the realization that someone else died instead of the self, and (c) narcissistically inclined individuals unconsciously blame the dead person for having abandoned them.

Harry Stack Sullivan (1956) also regarded grief as a valuable protective device. Because grief is dependent on attachment to the deceased, it also provides an avenue to free oneself from the attachment bond. In short, Sullivan believed that grief is valuable because it dissolves attachments that may maintain the illusions of love forever. Similarly, Pollock (1961) thought of grief as inevitable due to the dual role of the mourner. On the one hand, there is a struggle to reestablish internal balance, and, on the other hand, there is a need to readjust to a threatening external environment.

While theorists continued to speculate on the specific timing of an emergent vulnerability to subsequent states of depression, researchers such as Bowlby (1951) became motivated to observe systematically the effects of separation (or threats of separation) from principal caretakers during childhood and the appearance of sensitivity to separation later in life. Specifically, Bowlby and colleagues examined the detrimental effect that institutional care had on children.

During the 1930s and 1940s, several influential investigators, such as Levy (1937), Bowlby (1940, 1944), Goldfarb (1943), Burlingham and Freud (1944), Spitz (1945), and Bender (1947) commented on the detrimental effects of prolonged institutional care or frequent change of caretakers during infancy on later development (Bowlby, 1982). This renewed interest on the effects of deprivation and inconsistent care during childhood was instrumental in the production of two films during the 1950s: Spitz's *Grief: A Peril in Infancy* (1947), and Robertson's *A Two-Year-Old Goes to Hospital* (1952) that promoted radical improvements in institutional-care practices (Bowlby, 1982).

In examining the effects of emotional deprivation in institutionalized infants, Spitz (1946) noted two specific infantile syndromes reminiscent of adult depression: anaclitic (partial emotional deprivation) depression and hospitalism (total emotional deprivation) depression. In partial emotional deprivation or anaclitic depression, institutionalized infants developed normally (for six to eight months of life) as long as they had continued interaction with their mothers. However, when their mothers became unavailable to them (for approximately three consecutive months), these infants deteriorated rapidly. Spitz reported that anaclitic infants wept and clung to observers, they were increasingly distressed, they went from weeping to wailing, and they began to lose weight. On the third month, they refused contact, continued to lose weight, had persistent insomnia, frequent illnesses, motor retardation, and facial rigidity. However, anaclitic infants recuperated quickly upon their mothers' return, usually within a period of three to five months (Spitz, 1965).

In his description of total emotional deprivation or hospitalism, Spitz (1945) reported that infants developed normally (for the first three months of life) as long as they were breast-fed by their mothers or a mother substitute.

However, infants were separated from their mothers in the third month, and a nurse began to take care of their bodily needs, but not their emotional needs. Symptoms of anaclitic depression appeared in rapid order, and in a period of three months these infants became completely passive. They lay supine in their cots and never developed the strength to reach the prone position. "The face became vacuous, eye coordination defective, the expression often imbecile" (Spitz, 1965, p. 278). By the age of four years, most of these children could not sit, stand, walk, or talk, and some of them even died (Spitz, 1946). In addition to Spitz' dramatic findings, other researchers, such as Bowlby, also conducted direct observations of children's reactions to separation from their mothers (Bowlby, 1982).

Bowlby's observations of separation responses were partly motivated by his disagreement with Deutsch's (1937) and Klein's (1940) explanations on childhood loss and depression. Bowlby claimed that Deutsch's and Klein's theories were not based on observations of mourning children, but based on the retrospective clinical analyses of older, emotionally disturbed children who had suffered earlier losses.

During the early 1950s, Robertson and Bowlby observed how young children responded to temporal separations from their mothers. Their response involved a sequence of protest, despair, and detachment (Robertson & Bowlby, 1952) that represented a break in the mother-child attachment bond. According to Robertson and Bowlby, the attachment bond is an innate, human proclivity to "seek proximity to and contact with (an) individual and to do so especially in certain specified conditions" (p. 669). This bond develops very early in life, as most three-month-old infants differentiate their mothers with more smiles, vocalizations, and eye-movements than they demonstrate to others. However, the attachment bond becomes more evident after infants ambulate and their proximity-maintaining behaviors can be clearly observed (Robertson & Bowlby).

Bowlby, his colleagues, and other theorists (Ainsworth, 1982; Bowlby, 1973; Hinde & Spencer-Booth, 1971) closely examined the mother-infant behaviors that lead to attachment. Bowlby, in particular, became immersed in studying attachment from an ethological perspective.

ETHOLOGICAL PERSPECTIVE OF THE GRIEF RESPONSE

Based on direct observations of animal behavior, Bowlby (1969) began to conceptualize grief as a pervasive and universal response to loss that is evolutionarily adaptive because it enhances safety by maintaining proximity to the attachment figure. Bowlby claimed that humans respond to separation with fear like other species, not because the situation engenders a high risk of pain or danger, but because it signals an increase of such risk.

In analyzing the sequence of children's responses to separation from the mother, Bowlby (1969) found that children protest, despair, and finally detach. Bowlby argued that separation threats create not only fear but often intense anger. During the protest phase, children's protestations are charged with anger and fear. If the attachment figure does not return, protest changes into despair, because protest is no longer perceived as useful. Bowlby argued that after an unspecified period of despair, children detach from or no longer seem to care about the attachment figure. After extensive observations of the separation response in children, Bowlby questioned whether this response also would be observed in adulthood.

Bowlby (1982) was surprised to find the same sequential reaction of protest, despair, and detachment in widows who had recently lost their husbands (Marris, 1958). Marris's study encouraged Bowlby to observe mourning in healthy adults. He discovered that the sequence of responses that followed loss lasted longer than the customary six months often suggested by clinicians in those days. Bowlby also discovered that some of the natural reactions to loss observed in healthy adults had common features with reactions widely regarded as pathological. These features included "anger directed at third parties, the self, and sometimes at the person lost; disbelief that the loss has occurred (misleadingly termed denial); and a tendency, often though not always unconscious, to search for the lost person in the hope of reunion" (Bowlby, 1982; p. 672). Bowlby's observations of healthy adults held a striking similarity to the separation response observed in children and, although Bowlby was criticized at first for making such comparison, his views were subsequently supported (Furman, 1974; Kliman, 1965; Parkes, 1972; Raphael, 1982), although other early investigators failed to identify Bowlby's separation response as a separate, unified sequence.

In particular, Lindemann (1944) found it difficult to isolate the sequence of separation protests identified by Bowlby as a separate syndrome. Instead, Lindemann identified a variety of pathological symptoms associated with intense grief reactions, including hostility, hyperactive behavior, acquisition of symptoms of the deceased, "psychosomatic illnesses" (ulcerative colitis, rheumatoid arthritis), disturbances of social interaction, and frank depression. Evolving from diverse theories on mourning, and specifically from theories that conceptualized grief as a natural, adaptive response, biological mediators of the grief response were also explored.

BIOLOGICAL MEDIATORS OF GRIEF

Engel (1961) proposed that the central nervous system (CNS) is organized to mediate both the fight-flight response and also the conservation-withdrawal system. These two opposite systems become engaged at different stages of grief resolution. Engel proposed that shock, disbelief, and awareness are followed by restitution, idealization, and outcome. Obviously, the first stages of grief resolution (shock, disbelief, and awareness) correspond to a time of despair and anger similar to the fight-flight response, whereas the later stages require intense internal work to resolve the loss, akin to a system of conservation and withdrawal. Years later, Sanders (1989) added to Engel's biological theory by proposing an integrative account of grief resolution reflective of the fight-flight and conservation-withdrawal response. Sanders described a sequential account of grief resolution that included phases of initial shock, awareness of the loss, conservation-withdrawal, healing, and renewal.

Similarly, other investigators compared grief to a physiological response. Parkes (1972) argued that grief resembles a physical injury more than any other type of illness. Specifically, it seems akin to receiving a physical "blow." Parkes likened complicated grief to the complications that occasionally arise after potentially fatal injuries, postulating a four-stage theory of grief resolution. This process starts with a feeling of numbness (after the "blow"), is followed by searching and pining (similar to pain after the injury), becomes a depression (need for rest), and ends in recovery.

Additionally, a striking similarity has been observed in the grief response of both infant animals and human infants (Hofer, 1984). Hofer's observations of the normal grief response in infant animals suggest a two-phase model: agitation and yearning (similar to a complicated grief response), and social disinterest (analogous to a detachment response). Interestingly, a range of research now supports a unique profile of short-term and long-term changes associated with early maternal loss (Hofer, 1996), including hypothalamic-pituitary-adrenal responses (Francis et al., 1996).

A word of caution is necessary. Although biological accounts of the grief response and theoretical models may suggest an orderly and universal response to loss, this is not necessarily so. It may be misleading to conceptualize grief in terms of a broadly defined three-stage process that should not exceed one year, as grief theorists and investigators have suggested, such as (a) an initial period of shock, disbelief, and denial, (b) an intermediate period of acute discomfort and social withdrawal, and (c) a period of resolution (Zisook, Schuster, & Lyons, 1987). Indeed, results from empirical research clarify that the time and sequence of grief resolution are subject to individual differences (Morgan, 1994). Thus, research has increasingly focused on discovering the antecedents of both adaptive and pathological grief responses.

EMPIRICAL INVESTIGATIONS ON THE IMPACT OF EARLY LOSS ON DEPRESSION

Brown, Harris, and Copeland (1977) postulated that childhood losses not only provoke a detrimental reaction to later losses, but they increase the likelihood of depression later in life. Although this notion is congruent with early psychodynamic theorists and with Bowlby's observations, Granville-Grossman (1968) found little evidence to support the notion that parental loss during childhood was related to depression in later life. Brown and his colleagues agreed that previous empirical findings had not been consistent in supporting their hypothesis, but they renewed their interest based on epidemiological studies that found a small but statistically significant correlation between loss by death of either parent before the age of 10 and later depression (Birtchnell, 1972).

Brown et al. clarified that both early and recent losses play an important role in the etiology of all forms of depression. They argued that previous inconsistent research results might be due to methodological flaws, such as limiting case recognition to individuals seeking treatment, and theoretical oversights, such as failure to attend to heterogeneity in the etiology of depression. To clarify this view, Brown et al. identified three separate loss pathways that may eventually lead to depression. The first of these pathways conceptualizes loss as a *provoking* factor. The second pathway describes loss as a possible *vulnerability* factor that increases the probability of developing depression, and the third pathway conceives loss as a possible *symptom formation factor* that defines the type and severity of depression, although it is not its precipitating factor.

Each of these three pathways of loss and depression formation have received empirical support. In a group of 114 female patients and 458 women from the general population, Brown and colleagues found that the most common provoking factor linked to the onset of depressive symptoms was a major life event occurring within the last nine months. Of these major life events, a high proportion involved loss. These findings have now been replicated in over 12 cross-cultural studies, using the careful interview-based methodology originally developed by Brown and Harris for assessing life events (1989).

Within Brown and Harris' original studies (1986), the most significant vulnerability finding was the loss of the participants' mother before the age of 11, and all types of past loss by death, which contributed to the symptom formation factor associated with psychotic-like instead of neurotic-like depressive symptoms. Additionally, a series of studies now have suggested that life events can be viewed within a framework of internal and external vulnerability factors (Brown, Harris, & Hepworth, 1994; Brown & Moran, 1994). These studies have important implications for identifying which individuals are most likely to become depressed in the face of severe losses. Internal factors such as low self-esteem and chronic subclinical symptoms and external factors such as low social support seem to be important vulnerability factors in the development of depression (Brown et al., 1994; Brown & Moran, 1994).

Finally, the type of loss appears to have important implications in shaping the nature of later symptoms of depression. Early loss appears tied to the emergence of psychotic versus neurotic symptom patterns (Brown & Harris, 1986), and chronicity of depression appears tied to early childhood adversity (Brown & Moran, 1994; Brown, Harris, Hepworth, & Robinson,1994). In contrast, when loss is an immediate precipitant to depressive episodes, it appears to predict a more rapid response to psychotherapy (Johnson, Monroe, Simmons, & Thase, 1994).

In addition to Brown and his colleagues' research, other investigators have examined such diverse issues as grief severity, distinctions from normal and pathological grief, and problems in attachment or the mother-child relationship. Hays, Kasl, and Jacobs (1994) investigated the severity of the grief response. For over two years, they followed multiple dimensions of distress among the spouses of 440 patients hospitalized for serious illness or elective surgery, according to whether and when the spouses were bereaved. Distress was related to the severity of the patient's illness, the actuality and timing of the bereavement, and the gender and age of the respondent. Surprisingly, middle-aged widows and widowers showed more acute and long-term depressive symptomatology or need for medical attention or both than did older bereaved subjects.

Wolfelt (1988) examined differential factors in the formation of symptoms that lead to normal and pathological grief. Wolfelt observed that individuals who experienced normal grief were more likely to respond to comfort and support from others, to express anger openly, and to link their depressed feelings to their loss than individuals who experienced pathological grief. Although the former had somatic complaints, decreased self-esteem, expressions of guilt, and feelings of sadness and emptiness, their symptoms were transient in nature. Alternatively, bereaved individuals who experienced pathological grief had problems accepting support from others, complained frequently, expressed irritability, and did not express anger directly. They were less likely to attribute their negative feelings to a particular life event (such as a loss) and often projected a sense of hopelessness and doom. Generalized feelings of guilt were common in these individuals, and their physical complaints and loss of self-esteem were typically of longer duration.

In spite of these distinctions, Viederman (1995) proposes that normal and pathological grief can no longer be dichotomized. Rather, the vegetative and psychomotor symptoms of a depressive disorder may accompany severe grief responses, and grief may persist over extended periods of time (Parkes & Weiss, 1983; Wortman & Silver, 1989).

Leik and Davidsen-Nielsen (1991) found that patients who had difficult attachments in childhood seemed more vulnerable to develop protracted grief reactions. More recently, Fraley and Shaver (1999) examined the quality of infant-mother attachment in childhood as a mediator to the loss response in adulthood. To briefly illustrate Ainsworth's (Ainsworth & Wittig, 1969; Ainsworth, Blehar, Waters, & Wall, 1978) classification, the quality of the infant-mother attachment is established by the degree of security or insecurity (avoidant or ambivalent) that infants feel when they are in proximity to their mother. Securely attached children explore the environment freely and greet their mother positively after brief separations. Insecurely attached children, on the other hand, show distress on such occasions. Specifically, avoidantly attached children accept their mother's touch, but do not spontaneously initiate contact with them. Ambivalently attached children seek and avoid contact with their mother at different times (Ainsworth et al., 1978). Using quality of attachment as a mediator to the grief response, Fraley and Shaver (1999) found that individuals classified as avoidantly attached may manage to suppress and mask their feelings of grief to a large extent, without necessarily incurring harmful emotional consequences. Indeed, these individuals may not show the separation response of protest, despair, and detachment that Bowlby believed was necessary for satisfactory grief resolution. For this reason, Fraley and Shaver recommend that clinicians treating bereaved individuals may benefit from assessing their client's individual attachment style. This knowledge may help clinicians avoid forcing avoidantly attached individuals through stages of grief resolution that may not be meaningful to them.

According to Goodman and Gotlib (1999), extensive research supports the notion that maternal depression creates a risk for psychopathology in children. Goodman and Gotlib postulated an integrative model in the transmission of psychopathological risk that includes: heritability of depression; innate dysfunctional neuroregulatory mechanisms; exposure to mother's negative and maladaptive cognitions, behaviors and affect; and exposure to stressful environments. Although all these components have received empirical support, of special interest to this article is the exposure to the mother's negative interactions. Exposure to the mother's negative and maladaptive cognitions, behaviors, and affect implies a loss of nurturing, challenging, and joyful interactions with their mothers. According to Goodman and Gotlib's (1999) review of the literature, in comparison with controls, depressed mothers perceive their parenting more negatively, have a decreased sense of personal control, and feel unable to influence their children in a positive manner. In addition, depressed mothers become more self-focused, engage in more negative conversations, and demonstrate more negative behaviors than controls in interactions with others. In turn, their negative behaviors elicit feelings of depression, anxiety, and hostility in those with whom they interact (Goodman & Gotlib). Because of these reasons, children of depressed mothers may experience a sense of loss that places them at an elevated risk for psychopathology. In exemplifying the role of loss in subsequent episodes of depression, the following four case studies are examined.[1]

CASE STUDIES

The case of Ruth G. Ruth is a Swedish-born, healthy and attractive 9-year-old girl who was referred to her school psychologist for an evaluation. Ruth was extremely suspicious and intolerant of her peers, frequently got involved in fist-fights, and often lied to justify her behavior. Her grades had been dropping consistently, and it was doubtful that she would be promoted to 5th grade. After each violent incident, Ruth was remorseful and cried inconsolably for long periods of time, until she became exhausted and withdrawn. During her initial interview, Ruth exhibited paranoid symptoms and complained to the school psychologist that her parents were physically and verbally abusive toward her. Upon close scrutiny of her family, it was learned that Ruth had been adopted by a stable, loving, childless couple when she was 3 years old. Her adoptive parents eagerly looked to the day when they could bring Ruth home. Upon arrival, Ruth was irritable, had frequent temper tantrums, and was unruly and difficult to calm down. Her history revealed that her biological mother was a single woman, living at poverty level, who had been verbally and physically abusive toward Ruth since birth. Because of her mother's abusiveness, protective services intervened, and Ruth was separated from her several times. Eventually, the mother decided to give Ruth up for adoption and return to her country of origin. Ruth was in foster care for approximately six months until she was adopted. Her adoptive mother was overprotective of her, and Ruth struggled in her efforts to separate and individuate.

Given that Ruth's inconsistent care and abuse started at birth and that her behavior did not improve after adoption into a stable family, it seems plausible that she was fixated at Fairbairn's pre-ambivalent oral phase of development. When infants become fixated at the pre-ambivalent oral phase due to loss or inconsistent care, feelings of deprivation and guilt persist over time. These children may conclude that their love is destructive and bad, and feelings of anxiety may remain repressed in the unconscious, ready to be reactivated by subsequent experiences of deprivation. Ruth's adoptive mother was strict and overprotective, and her attitude did not provide Ruth with the nurturing that she needed to help her resolve her feelings of anxiety and deprivation. According to Fairbairn (1940), fixation at the pre-ambivalent oral phase develops into the schizoid position in which psychotic-like symptoms predominate. Additionally, it is recalled that in Brown and Harris's (1986) studies, early loss appears tied to the emergence of psychotic versus neurotic symptom patterns. Ruth's symptoms included extreme suspiciousness and intolerance of her peers, and delusional ideas relative to the manner in which her adoptive parents treated her. These psychotic-like symptoms seem related to her primary relationship or to the treatment she received from her biological mother, who maltreated her and ultimately abandoned her.

The case of Gina F. Another case example that seems to indicate fixation at the pre-ambivalent phase of development is the case of Gina F. Gina F. is a 40-year-old Hispanic female who has a 14-year-old son from her second marriage. Gina was brought to the local hospital's emergency room by a rescue team after passing out in the street. Numerous scans and laboratory tests revealed no significant medical problems, and Gina was referred to Dr. B. for psychological treatment. During the initial interview, Gina exhibited *flight of ideas* and paranoid ideation about her husband and son who "do not care about or love me, and who have a liaison against me." She was agitated and restless, left her seat several times, cried incessantly, was concerned about "going crazy," and wanted to leave both husband and son. Gina reported wanting to know what could have happened to her during "extensive memory lapses." She had been a bookkeeper at a real-estate office for over 20 years, but quit her job after she became extremely angry at her demanding boss, who "abused me and never appreciated me." Gina's history revealed that her mother had been depressed after Gina's birth and that "she never wanted me or cared for me." During her illness, Gina's mother intermittently delegated Gina's care to her paternal grandmother, until she ultimately left the marital home when Gina was 3 years old. At that time, Gina's stern and rigid paternal grandmother and aunt took care of her. When Gina was approximately 8 years old, her father died, and her paternal grandmother was awarded sole custody of her.

Like Ruth's symptoms, Gina's symptoms seem tied to a pre-ambivalent oral phase of development. After Gina's birth, her mother became depressed and felt incapable of dealing with her. Gina's paternal grandmother tried to help by telling Gina's mother about infant care, but Gina's mother perceived this help as a threat, became even more depressed and hopeless, and eventually abandoned the marital home. It is very likely that Gina felt deprived and very anxious in response to her mother's erratic behavior. Indeed, infant Gina may have felt that she had destroyed her mother's breast, due to her mother's inconsistency in providing for her needs. A possible sequela of her mother's neglect and abandonment, Gina may have felt guilty and responsible for her mother's behavior, concluding that her love was destructive and bad. Her psychotic-like symptoms seem to support this hypothesis, as evidenced by her ideas of paranoid persecution by her boss, husband, and son.

The case of Luke P. While Gina seemed to have been developmentally fixated at the pre-ambivalent oral phase, Luke's case seems related to fixation at the ambivalent oral phase of development. Luke is a slim, disheveled, 8-year-old boy of Arabic and Hispanic descent, who was brought to his neighborhood mental health clinic at the request of his school counselor. Luke had been implicated in several incidents of petty stealing at school shortly after his parents' divorce. Luke's mother expressed that Luke's twin-brother, Roger, was slightly taller, heavier, and smarter than Luke, as evidenced by his grades in school. Roger was close to his mother, while Luke was close to his father. Upon further examination, it was found that Luke's mother functioned at borderline intelligence, was hearing impaired, and had difficulty communicating with her twins. After the stealing incidents, Luke's father stated that he was going to leave for good if Luke continued engaging in such behaviors. Luke's history revealed that he was born prematurely, weighed 1.5 lbs. at birth, and he was placed in an incubator for three months. His mother could not carry him until he weighed 2 lbs., at one month of age. At the time of the initial interview, Luke's mother reported that Luke was crying "too much, like a baby." He did not fight much with his brother, but was easily distracted, often forgot his home work, and did not seem to listen. Luke read at kindergarten level, and he was in treatment for speech problems that began at age 3.

Although Luke's problems were severe, they did not reach psychotic proportions. Luke was deprived of his mother's care until his first month. However, given modern advances in neonatal care, it is likely that he received appropriate care at the hospital's intensive-care unit until his third month, when he was sent home. Because she had twins who were born prematurely, it is also very likely that Luke's mother received special help from her own mother, after the twins' arrival at home. In fact, Luke's maternal grandmother was instrumental in bringing Luke to psychological treatment. Luke's mother was partly, not totally, unavailable (given her hearing problems and her preference for Luke's brother). Once settled down at home with her twins, it is likely that Luke's mother became progressively inaccessible to Luke during the second half of his first year and the first half of the second year, when toddlers actively ambulate and have an increased need for attention. Thus, it is plausible that Luke became fixated at the ambivalent oral phase of development (depressive position). Infants fixated at the ambivalent oral phase know how to bite and conclude that it is their hate, not their love, which has the capacity to destroy their mother's affection. Although fixation at this stage is more developmentally advanced than fixation at the pre-ambivalent oral stage, it results in the depressive position which underlies deep melancholia or manic depressive psychoses (Fairbairn, 1940). During subsequent losses, individuals fixated at the ambivalent oral phase revert to neurotic depressive states. Luke's symptoms included frequent crying, distractibility, not following instructions, and a submissive stance towards his brother that are indicative of a depressive neurosis.

The case of Pablo G. Pablo G. is a child who exemplifies a case of introjective depression (Bemporad & Gabel, 1992; Blatt, 1974) or fixation at a higher level of object representation. Pablo G. is a tall, overweight, 10-year-old boy of Italian descent, who was referred to a mental health clinic due to problems of encopresis, low self-esteem, distractibility, and poor grades. His mother indicated that Pablo was only able to control his encopresis by "pinching his arms and hands until he literally makes holes in them." His peer relations also were problematic, as his peers picked on and made fun of him. Pablo is the third child of a family of four siblings. Pablo's mother stated that all her pregnancies were unplanned. Pablo's prenatal history revealed that his mother had diabetes and pneumonia during pregnancy. He weighed 9 lbs. 12 oz. at birth, and his mother suffered from some type of seizures after delivery. Pablo's mother returned to work when Pablo was six months old. He slept with his mother until he was two years old, at which time his youngest brother was born. The newborn had a strong resemblance to Pablo's father, and, instantly, he became his mother's favorite. Pablo resented being moved away from his mother's bed, and he protested, waking up and crying in the middle of the night, but adapted after two or three nights because, according to his mother, "Pablo is very conforming." Because of frequent ear infections, Pablo had surgery at age three, at the same time his parents were divorcing. During the initial interview, Pablo revealed that he often fought with his brother, who teased him frequently. Pablo expressed, "I want to kill myself after (the fight)," thus revealing both his sadness and his strong feelings of guilt.

Pablo seems to be suffering from an introjective depression (Blatt, 1974), as evidenced by his jealousy of his younger brother, who dethroned him from his favored position with his mother. It is likely that Pablo's encopresis is, at an unconscious level, the only way in which he can elicit his mother's attention. According to Blatt (1974), children who suffer an introjective depression often have oedipal wishes and may suffer intense feelings of guilt. The superego of these children is overly harsh, and there is constant self-scrutiny and evaluation that may revolve around themes of morality and commitment (Blatt). Pablo's suicidal despair after the fights with his brother suggests that a severe and uncompromising sense of morality does not provide room for this type of rivalry. Bemporad and Gabel (1992) describe the despair and self-loathing of these youngsters that "often lead to suicide as a means of removing themselves from what appears to be an irresolvable conflict" (p. 123).

CONCLUSIONS

This review has focused on the nexus between loss and depression, tracing early psychoanalytic claims and examining empirically supported pathways of loss that lead to depression. Several theoretical propositions have received empirical support. First, an early disappointment in love may lead to depression later in life. Second, childhood losses may be linked to the quality and severity of symptoms observed later in life. Third, internal vulnerability factors such as low self-esteem may be associated with severe responses to loss. Last, the quality of childhood attachments may have important implications for subsequent grief reactions.

Specifically, Abraham (1924) postulated that individuals with a melancholic temperament are especially vulnerable to having strong reactions to loss. A melancholic temperament arises from genetic factors, fixation at the oral stage, and early disappointments in love. Likewise, Klein claimed that childhood losses trigger the original infantile depressive position and with it all the anxiety and negative feelings derived from crises at all stages of psychosexual development. Mahler added that toddlerhood is a especially vulnerable period in which children need to be treated with warmth and attention to prevent the development of a depressive reaction. In line with these theoretical claims, Brown et al.'s (1977) findings–replicated in over 12 cross-cultural studies–showed that the most significant vulnerability factor of loss leading to a full-blown depression was the loss of the mother before the age of 11, and all types of past loss by death.

The second claim was related to the severity of symptoms of depression observed later in life. Fairbairn (1940) theorized that oral fixation at the pre-ambivalent and at the ambivalent phases become precursors of the schizoid position (psychotic-like symptoms), and of the depressive position (neurotic-like symptoms), respectively. Although empirical findings do not specify loss in infancy (oral stage) in creating a vulnerability to depression later in life, loss of the mother before the age of 11 includes the stages of infancy, toddlerhood, and early-to-middle childhood (0-11 years). Thus, loss of the mother before age 11 contributes to the symptom formation factor that may lead to psychotic-like instead of neurotic-like symptoms of depression.

Further, research on the impact of life events on depression has supported other early theoretical claims (Freud, 1917). For example, empirical findings on the impact of life events on depression suggest they be viewed within the framework of internal and external vulnerability factors (Brown et al., 1994; Brown & Moran, 1994). These studies seem to suggest that individuals who are vulnerable to depression may have low self-esteem, chronic subclinical symptoms of depression, or low social support. It is recalled that Freud (1917) believed that the crucial distinction between mourning (or normal grief) and melancholia was the substantial loss in self-esteem he observed in melancholics.

Last, research on attachment has shown that patients who had difficult attachments during childhood may develop a vulnerability to protracted grief reactions later in life (Leik & Davidsen-Nielsen, 1991). It is also relevant to examine the quality of attachment in conjunction with reactions to loss and bereavement (Fralcy & Shaver, 1999), as not all individuals traverse grief episodes showing behaviors that resemble the separation response of protest, despair, and detachment that Bowlby believed was necessary for satisfactory grief resolution.

Implications for treatment. Altogether, these findings may be useful in alerting clinicians to become more thorough in their assessment of depressed individuals. It is frequently observed that clinicians focus on clients' presenting problems without closely examining the history and timing of previous losses. It is plausible that old losses become reactivated with each new loss. This is particularly relevant in older adults who have experienced multiple losses (Parkes, 1992). It is plausible that the history of patients suffering from a lingering depression, such as dysthymia, chronic depression, melancholic depression, or double depression may be associated with early loss or with having had interactions with a depressed mother (Goodman & Gotlib, 1999). Moreover, patients who had lost one parent at or before the age of 11 may regress to experience symptoms associated with all the psychosexual crises (oral, anal, and oedipal) when experiencing subsequent losses. Feelings of hopelessness, desolation, and despair–resembling the helpless state of infancy–may appear in response to later losses, and previous psychosocial gains (Erikson, 1963) may disappear, returning patients to a state of mistrust, shame and doubt, guilt, and inferiority.

Psychotherapy that examines the developmental level of depressed patients at the time of their initial losses may be helpful in clarifying why these patients become despondent, often voicing catastrophic cognitions and expressing feelings of hopelessness and doom. Working through unresolved feelings of loss arising from initial losses and disentangling them from feelings related to present losses may be invaluable in the resolution of complicated grief.

NOTE

1. Names and situational details have been altered to protect clients' confidentiality.

REFERENCES

Abraham, K. (1911/1968). Notes on the psycho-analytical investigation and treatment of manic-depressive insanity and allied conditions. In *Selected papers of Karl Abraham*. New York: Basic Books, Inc.

Abraham, K. (1924/1968). A short study of the development of the libido, viewed in the light of mental disorders. In *Selected papers of Karl Abraham*. New York: Basic Books, Inc.

Ainsworth, M. D. S. (1982). Attachment: Retrospect and prospect. In C. Parkes and J. Stevenson-Hinde (Eds.), *The place of attachment in human behavior*. New York: Basic Books.

Ainsworth, M. D. S., Blehar, M., Waters, E., & Wall, S. (1978). *Patterns of attachment*. Hillsdale, NJ: Erlbaum.

Ainsworth, M. D. S., & Wittig, B. A. (1969). Attachment and exploratory behavior of one-year-olds in a strange situation. In B. M. Foss (Ed.), *Determinants of infant behavior* (Vol. 4, pp. 113-136). London: Methuen.

Bemporad, J. R., & Gabel, S. (1992). Depressed and suicidal children and adolescents. In J. R. Brandell (Ed.), *Countertransference in psychotherapy with children & adolescents*. Northvale, NJ: Jason Aronson, Inc.

Bender, L. (1947). Psychopathic behavior disorders in children. In R. Lindner & R. Seliger (Eds.), *Handbook of correctional psychology*. New York: Philosophical Library.

Birtchnell, J. (1972). Early parental death and psychiatric diagnosis, *Social Psychiatry*, 7, 202-210.

Blatt, S. J. (1974). Levels of object representation in anaclitic and introjective depression. *The Psychoanalytic Study of the Child*, 29, 107-157.

Bowlby, J. (1940). The influence of early environment in the development of neurosis and neurotic character. *International Journal of Psychoanalysis, 21,* 154-178.

Bowlby, J. (1944). Forty-four juvenile thieves: Their characters and home life. *International Journal of Psychoanalysis, 25,* 19-52, 107-127.

Bowlby, J. (1951). *Maternal care and mental health. W.H.O. Monograph No. 2.* London: HMSO.

Bowlby, J. (1969). *Attachment and loss, Vol. 1: Attachment*. New York: Basic Books.

Bowlby, J. (1973). *Attachment and loss, Vol. 2: Separation-anxiety and anger*. New York: Basic Books

Bowlby, J. (1982). Attachment and loss: retrospect and prospect. *American Journal of Orthopsychiatry, 52,* 664-678.

Brown, G. W., & Harris, T. O. (1986). Establishing causal links: The Bedford College studies of depression. In H. Katsching (Ed.), *Life events and psychiatric disorders*. Cambridge: Cambridge University Press.

Brown, G. W., & Harris, T. O. (1989). Depression. In G. W. Brown & T. O. Harris (Eds.), *Life events and illness*. New York: The Guilford Press.

Brown, G. W., Harris, T., & Copeland, J. R. (1977). Depression and loss. *British Journal of Psychiatry, 130,* 1-18.

Brown, G. W., Harris, T., & Hepworth, C. (1994). Life events and endogenous depression. *Archives of General Psychiatry, 51,* 525-534.

Brown, G. W., Harris, T., Hepworth, C., & Robinson, R. (1994). Clinical and psychosocial origins of chronic depressive episodes II: A patient enquiry. *British Journal of Psychiatry, 165*, 457-465.

Brown, G. W., & Moran, P. (1994). Clinical and psychosocial origins of chronic depressive episodes I: A community survey. *British Journal of Psychiatry, 165*, 447-456.

Burlingham, D., & Freud, A. (1944). *Infants without family.* London: Allen and Unwin.

Deutsch, H. (1937). Absence of grief. *Psychoanalysis Quarterly, 6*, 12-22.

Engel, G. L. (1961). Is grief a disease? A challenge for medical research. *Psychosomatic Medicine, 23*, 18-23.

Erikson, E. H. (1950/1963). *Childhood and society.* New York: W. W. Norton & Co.

Fairbairn, W. R. D. (1940). Schizoid factors in the personality. *Psycho-analytic studies of the personality.* London: Tavistock.

Fairbairn, W. R. D. (1941). A revised psychopathology of the psychoses and psychoneuroses. *Psycho-analytic studies of the personality.* London: Tavistock.

Fenichel, O. (1945). *The psychoanalytic theory of neurosis.* New York: Norton.

Fraley, R. C., & Shaver, P. R. (1999). Loss and bereavement: Attachment theory and recent controversies concerning "grief work" and the nature of detachment. In J. Cassidy & P. R. Shaver (Eds.), *Handbook of attachment: Theory, research, and clinical applications.* New York: The Guilford Press.

Freud, S. (1917/1966). Mourning and melancholia. In J. Strachey & A. Freud (Eds.), *The standard edition of the complete psychological works of Sigmund Freud.* London: The Hogarth Press.

Francis, D., Diorio, J., LaPlante, P., Weaver, S., Seckl, J. R., & Meaney, M. J. (1996). The role of early environmental events in regulating neuroendocrine development: Moms, pups, stress, and glucocorticoid receptors. In C. F. Ferris and T. Grisso (Eds.), *Annals of the New York Academy of Sciences, 794, (pp. 136-152). New York: New York Academy of Sciences.*

Furman, E. (1974). *A child's parent dies.* New Haven: Yale University Press.

Goldfarb, W. (1943). Infant rearing and problem behavior. *American Journal of Orthopsychiatry, 13*, 213-223.

Goodman S. H., & Gotlib, I. H. (1999). Risk for psychopathology in the children of depressed mothers: A developmental model for understanding mechanisms of transmission. *Psychological Review, 106*, 458-490.

Granville-Grossman, K. L. (1968). The early environment of affective disorder. In A. Coppen & A. Walks (Eds.), *Recent developments in affective disorders.* London: Headley Brothers.

Hays, J. C., Kasl, S. V., & Jacobs, S. C. (1994). The course of psychological distress following threatened and actual conjugal bereavement. *Psychological Medicine, 24*, 917-927.

Hinde, R., & Spencer-Booth, Y. (1971). Effects of brief separation from mother on rhesus monkeys. *Science, 173*, 111-118.

Hofer, M. (1984). Relationships and regulators: A psychobiologic perspective on bereavement. *Psychosomatic Medicine, 46*, 183-198.

Hofer, M. M. (1996). On the nature and consequences of early loss. *Psychosomatic Medicine, 58(6),* 570-581.

Johnson, S., Monroe, S., Simmons, A., & Thase, M. (1994). Clinical characteristics associated with interpersonal depression: Symptoms, course, and treatment response. *Journal of Affective Disorders, 31,* 97-109.

Klein, M. (1940). Mourning and its relation to manic-depressive states. In *Love, guilt and reparation and other papers* (pp. 1921-1946). Boston, MA: Seymour Lawrence/Delacorte.

Kliman, G. (1965). *Psychological emergencies of childhood.* New York: Grune & Stratton.

Leik, N., & Davidsen-Nielsen, M. (1991). *Healing pain: Attachment, loss, and grief therapy.* London and New York: Tavistock/Routledge.

Levy, D. (1937). Primary affect hunger. *American Journal of Psychiatry, 94,* 643-652.

Lindemann, E. (1944). Symptomatology and management of acute grief. *American Journal of Psychiatry, 101,* 141-148.

Mahler, M. S. (1966). Some preliminary notes on the development of basic moods, including depression. *Canadian Psychiatric Association Journal, 11(Suppl.),* 250-258.

Marris, P. (1958). *Widows and their families.* London: Routledge & Kegan Paul.

Morgan, J. P. (1994). Bereavement in older adults. *Journal of Mental Health Counseling, 16,* 318-326.

Parkes, C. (1972). *Bereavement: Studies of grief in adult life.* New York: International Universities Press.

Parkes, C. (1992). Bereavement and mental health in the elderly. *Reviews in Clinical Gerontology, 2,* 45-51.

Parkes, C. M., & Weiss, R. S. (1983). *Recovery from bereavement.* New York: Basic Books, Inc.

Pollock, G. N. (1961). Mourning and adaptation. *International Journal of Psychoanalysis, 43,* 341-361.

Raphael, B. (1982). The young child and the death of a parent. In C. Parkes & J. Stevenson-Hinde (Eds.), *The place of attachment in human behavior.* New York: Basic Books.

Robertson, J. (1952). *A two-year-old goes to hospital.* [Film]. New York: New York University Film Library.

Robertson, J., & Bowlby, J. (1952). Responses of young children to separation from their mothers. *Courrier Center Internationale Enfance, 2,* 131-142.

Sanders, C. M. (1989). *Grief: The mourning after.* New York: John Wiley & Sons.

Spitz, R. (1945). Hospitalism: An inquiry into the genesis of psychiatric conditions in early childhood. *Psychoanalytical Study of the Child, 1,* 53.

Spitz, R. (1946). Anaclitic depression: An inquiry into the genesis of psychiatric conditions in early childhood II. *Psychoanalytical Study of the Child, 2,* 53.

Spitz, R. (1947). *Grief: A peril in infancy.* [Film]. New York: New York University Film Library.

Spitz, R. (1965). *The first year of life: A psychoanalytic study of normal and deviant development of object relations.* New York: International Universities Press, Inc.

Sullivan, H. L. (1956). The dynamics of emotion. In H. L. Sullivan (Ed.), *Clinical studies in psychiatry (Chapter 5)*. New York: W. W. Norton & Co.

Tolpin, M., & Kohut, H. (1980/1989). The disorders of the self: The psychopathology of the first years of life. In S.I. Greenspan & G.H. Pollock (Eds.), *The course of life: Psychoanalytic contribution toward understanding personality development* (pp. 229-253). Washington, DC: U.S. Government Printing Office.

Viederman, M. (1995). Grief: Normal and pathological variants. *American Journal of Psychiatry, 152*, 1-4.

Wolfelt, A. D. (1988). *Death and grief: A guide for clergy*. Muncie, IN: Accelerated Development. (Available from publisher, 3400 Kilgore Avenue, Muncie, IN 47304).

Wortman, C. B., & Silver, R. C. (1989). The myths of coping with loss. *Journal of Consulting and Clinical Psychology, 57*, 349-357.

Zisook, S., Schuster, S. R., & Lyons, L. E. (1987). Adjustment to widowhood. In S. Zisook (Ed.), *Biopsychosocial aspects of bereavement* (pp. 51-74). Washington, DC: American Psychiatric Press.

Transformation of Narcissism and the Intersubjective Therapeutic Exchange: A Depressed Adolescent Patient Shares His Music and Lyrics with His Therapist

Judith Mishne

SUMMARY. Clinicians and researchers have redefined adolescence and depression in adolescence and no longer consider depression as typical of "normal" adolescence. Depression during the teenage period is differentiated from a depressed mood, replete with misery and anguish, and depression proper, i.e., a real illness with specific symptoms which are depressive equivalents. These symptoms often include aggressivity, substance abuse, school refusal, and delinquency. A detailed case presentation is offered of a 17-year-old depressed, substance abusing adolescent who shares his lyrics and heavy metal rock music in sessions, thereby transforming his aggression and narcissism. Use of self psychology and intersubjectivity theory stimulated the formation of a therapeutic alliance and a corrective selfobject relationship, with this young patient's subsequent gains in self-regulation, decreased temper eruptions, and school involvement. *[Article copies available for a fee from The Haworth Document Delivery Service: 1-800-342-9678. E-mail address: <getinfo@haworthpressinc.com> Website: <http://www.HaworthPress.com> © 2001 by The Haworth Press, Inc. All rights reserved.]*

Judith Mishne, DSW, is Full Professor and Chair of the Social Work Practice Curriculum Area at the Shirley M. Ehrenkranz School of Social Work, New York University.

[Haworth co-indexing entry note]: "Transformation of Narcissism and the Intersubjective Therapeutic Exchange: A Depressed Adolescent Patient Shares His Music and Lyrics with His Therapist." Mishne, Judith. Co-published simultaneously in *Psychoanalytic Social Work* (The Haworth Press, Inc.) Vol. 8, No. 3/4, 2001, pp. 71-94; and: *Psychoanalytic Approaches to the Treatment of Children and Adolescents: Tradition and Transformation* (ed: Jerrold R. Brandell) The Haworth Press, Inc., 2001, pp. 71-94. Single or multiple copies of this article are available for a fee from The Haworth Document Delivery Service [1-800-342-9678, 9:00 a.m. - 5:00 p.m. (EST). E-mail address: getinfo@haworthpressinc.com].

KEYWORDS. Adolescence, depression, substance abuse, transformation of narcissism, intersubjectivity, self psychology

ADOLESCENT DEPRESSION

Most research about treatment of depressed children is recent because only in the more recent decades has the concept of childhood depression come to be recognized and accepted by theorists and researchers. Previously, there were prevailing assumptions that depressive disorders rarely occurred in children and adolescents (despite descriptions of melancholia in children which can be traced back to the mid-eighteenth century). This view of depression stems from classic psychoanalytically oriented theorists and researchers who argued that children were too developmentally immature to have developed the superego necessary for the onset of depression. Other writers maintained that depressive symptoms were transient phenomena or experiences associated with the onset of depression. For example, Essau and Peterman (1999) said:

> In considering the possibility of depressive disorders in children and adolescents, the concept of "masked depression" was proposed during the late 1960's and 1970's. According to this concept, depressive disorders do and can occur in children, but depressive symptoms are manifest primarily as somatic symptoms, conduct disturbances, enuresis and encopresis. It is now widely accepted that depressive disorder in childhood and adulthood is phenomenologically equivalent, but with some age-appropriate symptoms. (p. ix)

There is now an accepted general consensus that to understand depression in children and adolescents, a developmental perspective is needed to consider the emergence, evolution, and organization of affective and cognitive behavior and biological processes (Kazdin, 1989). In adolescents, ages 12 to 18, depressive symptoms include volatile mood, rage, intense self-consciousness, low self-esteem, poor school performance, delinquent behaviors, substance abuse, sexual acting-out, social withdrawal, problems with overeating, oversleeping, and suicidal ideation (modified from Kronenberger & Meyer, 1996). The developmental perspective suggests that the clinical depression of adolescence usually evolves out of developmental phases of earlier childhood rather than those of adolescence itself. Differentiating between normative depression and clinical depression is difficult, but, generally, the presence or absence of significant mood disturbances in earlier childhood is of diagnostic and prognostic importance.

Initially, depression in adolescence was considered as part and parcel of normal adolescence, characterized by normal developmental turmoil and age-appropriate ego regression. Anna Freud's classic paper on adolescence (1958) emphasized that adolescent upset is inevitable, desired, and "no more than the external indication that inner adjustments are in progress" (p. 264). She believed that normal adolescence is a disruption of peaceful growth and that basic disharmony is the norm. By contrast, longitudinal studies by Masterson (1967), Masterson and Washburne (1966), Rutter, Graham, Chadwick, and Yule (1976), Offer (1967), and Offer, Sabshin, and Marcus (1965) challenge this classic perspective and question the prevailing view that persists in its expectations that adolescence can be marked by anything except stability. They discredit the turmoil view of adolescence and propose that severely symptomatic youths are not simply traversing a stressful developmental stage and will not grow out of it.

There is no suggested compromise or reconciliation between the classic definition and descriptions of adolescence and the newer views formulated by Offer and others (Offer & Offer, 1975a, 1975b, 1977; Offer & Sabshin, 1963; Rutter et al., 1976; Oldham 1978). "Defining and describing the contemporary adolescent requires some references to current societal changes which have affected familial style and roles, parental employment patterns and adolescent peer behavioral norms" (Mishne, 1986, p. 11). The above social realities, including the breakdown of the extended family and easy availability and use of drugs, have made it difficult for many adolescents to develop and sustain meaningful emotional involvements with others or to tolerate ambivalence, ambiguity, grief, and mourning.

Although there is some controversy over the notion of masked depression, we do find it as the underlying feeling, even if not initially reported by the adolescent patient who presents varied forms of delinquency and acting-out. Berkowitz (1981) cited late adolescence as a critical period for dealing with depression and feelings of powerlessness and hopelessness. These feelings, if overpowering, can lead to actions, "violent or controlled, intentional or accidental, random, or a mixture of these" (Berkowitz, 1981, p. 477).

If earlier emancipation, separation, and individuation have not resulted in competent autonomy, the young person is overwhelmed with a sense of failure and of "time running out." Longstanding inability to adequately express aggression interferes with the development of autonomous identity and frequently results in eruptions of anger or extreme impulses of homicide and suicide. Drugs may be used as self-medication to blur these highly charged feelings, but drug use will lessen control and impulse due to diminished ego function. Berkowitz's only optimistic observation of these dire proceedings is that violent actions or accidents "seemed to function almost as traumatic events around which external as well as internal changes become organized, especially the formation of a new, more responsible, less narcissistically oriented superego and a new relationship to family and society" (1981, p. 479).

It is necessary to attempt to clarify whether one is talking about a depressive mood, which occurs as a response to a variety of stressors and disappointments, or about depression as a serious and lasting effect and, therefore, an illness. Carlson (1981) puts it this way: "In depressive illness one has the depression syndrome which is out of proportion to environmental stressors and is not relieved with environmental manipulation. Furthermore, there is ample evidence from the adult psychiatry literature that the entity of depressive illness has psychological, biochemical, pharmacological and genetic cohesion" (p. 412). Thus, we always attempt to distinguish between misery and anguish and depression proper.

In sum, the development of operationalized criteria to ascertain depression in adults was accompanied by a similar effort for children. Pearce (1977) defined depressive disorder in children and teenagers by the presence of depressed mood, plus at least two of the following symptoms: suicidal and morbid thoughts, irritability, hypochondriasis, school refusal and altered perceptions such as delusions, and overvalued ideas of guilt and worthlessness. The most commonly used classifications are from the *Diagnostic and Statistical Manual of Mental Disorders* (DSM) which notes *Mood Disorders*, i.e., mood episodes, namely major depressive episode, manic episode, mixed episode, and hypomanic episode. *Depressive disorders* include major depressive disorders, single episode; major depressive disorders, recurrent; dysthmic disorders; and depressive disorders not otherwise specified. *Bipolar Disorders* include Bipolar I disorder, or a single manic episode; Bipolar II disorder (recurrent major depressive episodes with hypomanic episodes); and *Cyclothymic Disorder*. Other mood disorders include *Substance Induced Mood Disorder*.

Co-Morbidity

Depression tends to predominate in co-morbidity profiles in adolescents as well as in adults and in children (Anderson & McGee, 1994; Angold & Costello, 1992; Angold, 1993; Nottelmann & Jensen, 1995). Despite advances in childhood and adolescent depression research over the last ten years (Birmaher et al., 1996a, 1996b), co-morbid forms of the disorder and evaluation of their impact on the course and outcome of depression continue to present major challenges.

A breakdown by co-morbid condition is possible only with consideration of the most prevalent disorders in children and adolescents, which are: anxiety disorders, attention deficit hyperactivity disorder (ADHD); oppositional defiant disorder (ODD), and conduct disorder (CD) (Nottelmann & Jensen, 1995). Co-morbidity in depressive disorder also includes consideration of major depressive disorder (MDD) and dysthmic disorder (DD). This co-occurrence is often referred to as "double depression" (Nottelmann & Jensen, 1999, p. 139).

Understanding co-morbidity and its implications demands clarity in the definition of remission, relapse, and reoccurrence, as well as in our definition of the clinical course that a child with depression may experience. Such terms as "stable and unremitting," "episodic and recurring," or "progressive, pernicious and persistent" are employed (ibid, p. 184). Obviously significant are the severity of symptoms and levels of impairment. Additionally important is the assessment of the young patient's functioning, family and environmental factors, and service outcomes. Co-morbidity must be taken into consideration to plan appropriate treatment interventions.

Affective Disorders

Primary affective disorder refers to depressed patients without a preexisting condition. Those with previous emotional disorders are diagnosed as having a secondary affective disorder (Woodruff, Goodwin, & Guze, 1974). One of the legitimate dilemmas in recognizing the bipolar affect disorder or manic-depressive illness in teenagers is that one is often seeing the first episode, or only one side of a process which will in the future become bipolar. Feinstein (1982) noted the presence of most or all of the following characteristics in children and adolescents diagnosed as manic-depressive:

1. Early evidence of affective instability;
2. Separations usually lead to exaggerated reactions to loss frequently manifested as temper tantrums or periodic hyperactivity;
3. Dilation of the ego with persistence of grandiose and idealizing self-structures owing to failure of normal transformation of narcissism. This may manifest itself as an outgoing dramatic quality with a theatrical flair. Many histories reveal early interest in (performances and competitions) and an early willingness to (be on stage).
4. Bizarre eating and sleep patterns and impulsivity may continue in spite of all efforts to enforce normal daily rhythms.
5. There is very frequently a family history of affective disorder. In addition to the presence of bipolar and unipolar patterns, equivalent states such as alcoholism or compulsive gambling may be elicited. (pp. 258-259)

Diagnosis is most confusing in adolescents when one sees adolescent-specific symptoms that are depressive equivalents–truancy, disobedience, excessive drug use, delinquent behaviors, hyperactivity, and aggressiveness. These can signify short-lived and transient adjustment reactions or they can occur in adolescents with primary and secondary depression. Bipolar illness and schizophrenia are frequently confused and misdiagnosed in adolescents because of their puzzling and atypical presentation, and the all too common psychosis that is due to extensive drug abuse by a depressed teenager. There is considerable conflict and uncertainty about the contributions of genetic predisposition and the role of family stress, as well as possible underlying neurophysiological mechanisms. These uncertainties pose major questions about medications, psychotherapy, or some combination of both, with family therapy also part of the therapeutic plan. Some researchers note the similarity of depressed adolescents to those assessed as borderline. Such symptoms as impulsivity, untempered and unwarranted anger, mood shifts, and fear of being alone are due to feelings of boredom, estrangement, loneliness, and emptiness.

Overall, there is general agreement that it is critical to monitor and carefully assess depression in adolescents to distinguish most neurotic (milder) depressions from the more severe bipolar affect disorders superimposed on a personality riddled with significant ego deficits–as we see in the borderline adolescent. Kestenbaum (1982) has a positive view of adolescents presenting with even severe depression and recurrent affect disorder:

> On a positive note, I would like to add that young patients with an affective disorder are often among the brightest, most sensitive and creative individuals we encounter. They are often endowed with special gifts and should be encouraged to develop them, whether in the sphere of music, art, literature, or human relationships. They are most capable of tenderness and empathy when they do not feel threatened themselves. By helping such children negotiate the difficult adolescent years (because they do need protection from the intensity of their drives as well as from the events of the external world) we are protecting them from future psychotic breakdown or at least ameliorating such breakdowns as well as enhancing the quality of every day life. Thus the rewards of "at-risk" research (and clinical treatment) speak for themselves. (p. 253)

Adolescent Substance Abuse

Richard Gardner (1999) notes that, without exception, youngsters who abuse drugs have little in their lives that they can point to with pride. He suggests that prior to adolescence most children gain a sense of esteem from one or more areas, be it academic success, social success, or admirable performance in sports, theater, art, or music. "If, however, a youngster reaches the teen period and doesn't have a sense of high self-worth in at least one of these areas, then that individual is a prime candidate for abusing drugs" (p. 48). A drop in competence or a lack of competence in adolescence is not automatically equated with addictive behaviors, but such adolescents suffering shame, humiliation, and lowered self-esteem are at higher risk. Other factors and variables are operative, but the failure to acquire competence in a peer valued activity has extremely important consequences. Director (2000) observes that the problem of drug use and abuse is "unique because it sits astride several domains of human experience, and is a crossroads, involving the law, government, popular culture, ethics, physiology, family life and individual psychology . . . the problem-solving skills and perspectives of each of these disciplines is needed to affectively address the problem" (pp. 97-98).

Therapists concerned with adolescent patients who use drugs can find relatively few extensive, dynamic studies of substance abusers. Rado's seminal early work (1933) dealt with adult drug addicts, and he stressed not the toxic agent, but the impulse to use it which makes an addict of a given individual. Others (Hartman, 1969; Wieder & Kaplan, 1969) likewise emphasized basic depressive character and wounded narcissism, intolerance for pain and frustration, poor object relationships, and attempts to self-medicate to blot out reality, or to maintain self-regard. Ego deficits, permissive or inconsistent parental restrictions, peer presence, and aggressivity were also stressed to explain drug abuse. Zinburg (1975) differed with the above noted explanations and criticized any concept of a one-to-one relationship between personality maladjustment and drug use and addiction. He noted what he called "retrospective falsification," that is, "looking at drug users and especially addicts, after they have become preoccupied with their drug experiments, authorities assume these attitudes and this personality state are similar to those the user had before the drug experience and thus led to it" (p. 568). Zinburg claims he does not completely disregard internal personality factors and family history, but he discounts any accurate consistent profile or pattern of ego deficits or phase-specific patterns that can be considered the determining factors in the history of drug abuse and addiction. In contrast, he and many others emphasize the power of the social setting which sustains drug and alcohol use. Studies of drug-using college youths and Vietnam veterans support the Zinburg thesis, given the enormity of these substance-abusing populations, which cannot be reduced to a few discrete profiles of the typical addict. Miller (1973) concurred with the emphasis on social and cultural determinants rather than personality conflicts as the cause of drug dependency. He also noted that drug use differs from country to country and within communities, social class, and groups and also varies with fashion and culture. He cited adolescent age-appropriate, specific tasks that can stimulate drug use. Problems of identity formation and emancipation from parents can slow down maturation. Such problems originate not from the adolescent's deficits but are due to isolation from extra-parental adults.

Stanton and Todd (1982) coined the term "pseudo-individuation" to describe how drug use and abuse can serve as a parent-free playing ground for an adolescent's independent strivings, all the while causing sufficient dysfunction to insure that the youth never leaves home. Similarly, teen pregnancies and teen runaway behaviors are regarded as steps of independence, but, in fact, only serve to more closely bind parent(s) and child in anxiety and worry. Wurmser (1978) focuses on the role aggression plays in drug addiction, often appearing in masochistic or sadistic forms. Director (2000) notes that chronic drug use is by definition self-abuse, but most serious drug use also entails a dynamic of self and family sabotage. The user knows that hurting the self is the surest way to hurt the parents. Core feelings of shame, a sense of failure, and a failure to achieve ambitions cause the feelings of emptiness and worthlessness (Morrison, 1996) that commonly stimulate substance abuse.

Sexual conflicts, including anxiety about heterosexual strivings, normal masturbatory activity, and normal preconscious homosexual impulses can stimulate relief-seeking drug experimentation and drug use. Struggles with intrapsychic pain, feelings of deprivation, inferiority, or the loss of a love object can stimulate drug use. Drug abuse to deal with an adolescent's depression, loss of the dependency of childhood, shame, and anxiety is commonly accompanied by "playing loud music and by listening to lyrics that express both conflict and solution. The more disturbed the youngster is, the more that violence in lyrics and their delivery will appeal" (Miller, 1986, p. 204).

Many adolescents also abuse alcohol. Distinction must be made between alcohol abuse, alcohol dependency, alcoholism, alcoholic psychosis, and alcoholic intoxication. There is considerable controversy about the causes of alcoholism. As with drug abuse, earlier explanations were based in symbolic and other psychological theories. Rado's (1933) conception created the formal psychological equation that bottle equals or signifies breast and that drinking, like drug abuse, is a symbolic, infantile incorporation of the symbiotic mother.

Ego psychologists explain alcoholism in terms of ego deficits (Knight, 1937; Mack, 1981) or flaws (Balint, 1969) in the infant/mother relationship. Kernberg (1975) believed that a borderline character structure is basic to alcohol addiction, with alcohol used to separate and individuate, and then reunite with the mother. For self psychologists, alcohol is viewed as an attempt at self-repair (self-soothing) of the structural selfobject flaws (Pattison, 1984, p. 364). Again, Zinburg (1982) and others (Bean, 1981; Vaillant, 1981) contended that pre-morbid and morbid personality studies of alcoholics do not consistently demonstrate the presence of pre-oedipal borderline or narcissistic character disorder. The seeming borderline and narcissistic behaviors are, rather, the *outcome* as a result of regression due to the effects of alcohol or drugs or both on ego operations.

Miller (1986) observes that society is "almost terrifyingly tolerant of alcohol abuse from middle adolescence onward" (p. 230). Injunctions from parents may be to caution not to drink and drive, but Miller notes parents are too unconcerned about drinking itself, buying kegs of beer for their teenagers' parties, and serving them beer routinely. Clinical studies reflect a rise in the incidence of adolescent alcohol abuse, used equally by both boys and girls. Alcohol and marijuana use are not mutually exclusive. An adolescent's interpersonal relationships will change with chronic use of either or both. All of a teenager's friends will tend to be alcohol or marijuana abusers or both. Alcoholism is at least partly determined by genetic sensitivity and vulnerability. Some large-scale studies link excessive alcohol use with an affective disorder. Many studies view alcoholism as familial. Commonly, alcohol consumption replaces, with increasing social penalties, other interests and activities. There will be familial and work difficulty–blackouts, temper eruptions, and family violence–followed by episodes of remorse and depression, thoughts of suicide, and futile attempts at self-cure. Then something shocking happens: school expulsion, injury in a drunken fight, an auto accident, legal problems.

Regular alcohol use by adolescents who are not primary alcoholics is symptomatic of emotional problems. Miller (1986) notes that some teenagers are not capable of involving themselves with peers and so need alcohol to lubricate sexual and social relationships. With some teens, their drinking may represent an identification with the parents' alcohol abuse or is used to cope with stress, loss, and mood disorders. Teen drinking is generally associated with delinquent behaviors. Alcoholic youngsters in therapy do not usually agree to stop drinking because of emotional attachments to their families and therapeutic personnel. "If they do agree to stop, it is because of anxieties about the consequence of their drinking and this is rare until late adolescence and young adulthood. Young alcoholics have difficulty realizing that they have a problem, and alcohol only reenforces their feelings of omnipotence, their poor time sense and concrete thinking. Thus they cannot emotionally understand the necessity of stopping" (Miller, 1986, p. 236). Antabuse has been used with teenagers, but the drug can have rare side effects; it may cause a temporary psychosis. Moreover, when they leave the hospital, some teens in their omnipotence, disregard instructions and use alcohol while they are taking Antabuse.

Case Example: Mark, Age 17

Mark's parents were at their wits' ends, when they initially contacted this therapist. To date, over a six-month period, I have been working with Mark and his parents, seen at times together and, more frequently, in separate sessions. We are engaged in an extended evaluation and trial course of individual treatment and family therapy.

Mr. and Mrs. W are a very attractive and engaging couple: articulate, highly intelligent, and most committed to their children, and to Mark in particular, given the enormity of his problems, which are in total contrast to his successful, very high functioning siblings. Because none of their other children posed any problems in early or middle adolescence, the parents are bewildered, hurt, anxious, and very angry at and overwhelmed by Mark. Father and mother both are university professors. They have six children, and Mark is the fifth. His older sisters are 28 and 26 and both were superior students, attended Ivy League colleges on scholarship; both are now completing PhDs. One sister is married and recently had a baby, and the next sister is just formally engaged. The youngest sister, 13, is described as a superior student and a well-adjusted child. Mark has two brothers, ages 23 and 21. They did well academically, but never were as scholarly or intellectually motivated as the sisters. One brother out of college is working in real estate and the other is completing his senior college year. All children attended demanding, academically prestigious Catholic schools on scholarships. Mark, age 17, is viewed as the estranged "middle" child in the family. He is excluded from the very warm relationship that exists between his oldest sisters and, likewise, from the relationship between his brothers, who are such good friends with one another. Mark is described as adoring his younger sister, but the age and gender differences preclude any social peer activities together. Despite being excluded from the special intimacy that exists between his older siblings, he feels positively connected to them.

The parents describe Mark historically as an adorable and engaging youngster, articulate, very intelligent, mischievous, and given to testing the limits of others. Sometimes his funky humor is amusing, but now and for some time, he has been depressed, angry, defiant, and explosive. He had extensive problems with alcohol and drugs (pot, cocaine, and mushrooms), which are believed to be the cause of his original academic decline, which has been accompanied by a volatile temper, his bizarre and excessive sleeping patterns, and his propensity to lie and steal. He socializes with boys the parents feel are the worst influence possible. Mark is said to have stolen beer from a grocery store in the 7th grade; he started to smoke cigarettes in the 8th grade, and began to use beer, pot, and cocaine. His temper mounted and explosions were constant. He lost his scholarship in the 8th grade and, because he was so demoralized, his parents took him out of his prestigious school, giving him the benefit of the doubt and hoping to give him a fresh start. He was expelled from the second parochial high school after making menacing, rageful remarks about a teacher. His words were heard during the week of the Columbine horror; schools were on high alert and did on occasion overreact, which seemed to be the case in this situation.

Professional help was sought, and psychological testing completed. Overall testing reveals "a young man with superior intellectual potential (full scale IQ of 127, a verbal rating of 131 and performance at 117), but with very uneven functioning." The following notations are from the psychological report: "Long-standing attentional gaps are suggested along with subtle problems with retrieval, especially with respect to rote information and labels. While Mark can approach simple tasks in a relatively organized fashion, he can become overwhelmed when he is required to organize more complex tasks. Time management appears problematic." (How much of this is due to adolescence proper, ADHD, or substance abuse is not clear.) However, the psychologist states that he is a highly intelligent young man who can experience a successful academic career once he has developed study skills that work for him. He tends to "space" out, and has an uneven attention span and low frustration tolerance. Projective testing revealed he has great difficulty integrating his feelings, concentrating, and handling anger. He can scream and yell, slam doors, and put a fist through the wall when most distraught. Aware of his volatility, he is rageful and argumentative; he projects blame, however, onto his parents, at first mostly his mother for "harassing" him. He feels parental pressure to achieve academically and professes total disinterest in school. His explosive episodes seem linked to periods when he's using drugs or alcohol.

He is obsessed with heavy metal rock music and the lyrics he's continually writing; he hopes to gain membership in a rock band some of his friends have formed. He hopes to be the singer and writer of lyrics for a group, but to date has had no music lessons. He indicates some interest in voice, piano, and guitar instruction, but has not pursued setting this up despite his parents' willingness to provide lessons. He is remarkably dependent on his mother to handle all for him . . . concurrent with his vile and rageful outbursts at her. She has been the primary parental force in the family but upon recommendation is backing off as his father becomes more active in handling Mark. His mother is anxious and can nag and obsess about things Mark should be attending to. She and Mark also have some close and warm exchanges, though negativity is the current norm.

Once we began a lengthy assessment process and trial course of treatment, effort was directed to securing a number of resources; namely, an appropriate school setting, a music instructional site, a psychiatrist to evaluate Mark's affective disorder and to supervise his medication, and a sleep disorder evaluation. Mark had previously seen a psychiatrist, who placed him on Prozac for depression, and, according to the parents, dismissed the family history of depression (I heard the same in a phone contact with this prior therapist). Mark's maternal grandfather was diagnosed with major depression and committed suicide, and a maternal uncle (whom the mother says Mark reminds her of) was bipolar. Prior to my contact with the family, Mark had seen the psychiatrist and had undergone about ten months of supervision and group treatment in a well-known day-treatment drug program. He claimed, at first, to have completely given up pot and cocaine. His recent admissions of "occasional" pot usage are less than clear.

He had opted out of school attendance and has been enrolled in several courses in a home-schooling arrangement, which has involved endless parental nagging to get him to handle the written assignments, which he could easily complete. Mark sleeps excessively and even falls asleep in the shower. He has regressed greatly since being home full time with only the minimal structure his parents are able to provide or enforce. Parents, usually his mother, awaken him. Left to himself, he'd sleep and read in bed all day. He wants to be out and about with his rock-band friends nightly. They all are drinking excessively, using pot, and, on occasion, when using alcohol they have had physical confrontations and arguments. Mark seems to have had several black-out experiences while drinking, with resultant lack of memory about what exactly occurred to explain his having been beaten up on two occasions. He is just beginning to acknowledge the possibility that he might be a vicious and wild drunk who suffers from complete blackouts when inebriated.

Prior to this current substance abuse in adolescence, the parents report a very uneventful history, with achievement of normal developmental milestones, and a total absence of traumata, separations, illnesses, etc. There is a question about co-morbidity (attention deficit disorder). Mark's sleeping patterns are thought to be related to depression, that is, a bipolar condition. He generally is up very late at night, reading or writing poetry and lyrics.

Mark presents himself as being at complete odds with his parents: "the only ones I supposedly explode at." Most recently, he's surrendered some of his denial and faced the reality of his drunken outbursts at others, at friends, and at one of his brothers. Despite a slowly evolving, more realistic account, Mark holds fast to his denigration of his parents, his mother especially, their academic expectations about school, and any notion of college for him in the future. He presents unrealistic scenarios about how he wants to move out and rent a place with friends, to avoid any or all parental oversight. He splits off major portions of reality, like how he can or will support himself or find employment and an affordable place to live. He has not been successful in finding, or rather, holding down a job on his own. He was fired from several places because of missing money, and mismanagement of a cash register. Currently through the parents' contacts, he's gotten and is holding down a part-time job, which has involved using a library, getting materials copied, painting an office, cleaning out a storage area, and so forth. Here he's been praised for doing a good job, and has not suffered from organizational problems which appeared to interfere in his two prior jobs.

As noted by Director (2000), drug abuse summons up consideration of several different resources, and, in this case, this involves planning and referral: (a) to a medical analyst regarding medication and further assessment for affective disorder, (b) referral and planning for some alternative school work and study setting to provide structure and to help Mark surrender his routine of sleeping all day, and (c) referral for a sleep disorder evaluation. All of these referrals have been accepted and real progress has become evident since the beginning of contact; Mark and his parents have been very responsive to my various recommendations, moving quickly into a warm alliance with excellent rapport.

After some initial, very stormy family sessions, Mark has opted for individual sessions where he is indeed less combative and defensive. We can examine various family exchanges in a calmer fashion; Mark feels less attacked and thinks he is treated fairly, as we attempt to look at the interplay and at various exchanges between him and his parents. Mark clearly feels less defensive or enraged when separate from his parents, as we attempt to analyze the patterns of his outbursts.

Mark is clearly relieved that I have been able to relate to him and his parents and that I reframe events that show him that his parents are worried, anxious, or bewildered, not simply enraged or disapproving. Thus he is beginning to see his rage responses are due to his super-sensitivity to "criticism," whereas he's missed seeing the depth of his parents' concerns for his welfare. Our treatment process relies on specific techniques of understanding, explanation, and interpretation, and my efforts to immerse myself empathetically to gain a depth of emotional understanding of Mark's and his parents' demands, hopes, ambitions, struggles, and symptomatic behavior (Mishne 1993). "To put it another way, the theory of self psychology removes the focus from the patient's faulty functioning in favor of learning to understand the underlying structured responses for the faulty functioning" (Basch, 1986, p. 409). This treatment approach alters the classic use of confrontation in regard to Mark's evasions, lies, demands, and raging outbursts. As he responds with more cohesion, he now has fewer explosions at home.

As the treatment relationship has deepened, Mark tells his parents and me how much he is enjoying his sessions. He has taken to bringing in all of his poetry and lyrics, and to sharing them with me, reading, or singing them in the heavy metal rock style he so admires and aspires to perform. Rosenblum, Daniolos, Kass, and Martin (1999) reflect on the unique challenge adolescents often present to their therapists due to defensiveness, resistance, and hesitancy to reveal their vulnerability. "The role of music in the popular culture may be used by adolescents in therapy towards potential therapeutic alliance formation, dynamic understanding and working through developmental conflicts in displacement" (pp. 319-320). These authors also remind us that children in treatment, similarly, express themselves in play, art work, and enactments, and of Bettelheim's account of fairy tales aiding children in the mastery of the psychological tasks of growing up. These tasks include: (a) overcoming narcissistic disappointments and the oedipal dilemma; (b) relinquishing childhood dependency and escaping separation anxiety; (c) organizing the chaotic pressures of the unconscious; and (d) gaining a feeling of self-hood and self-worth (Bettelheim, 1976). In like fashion, teenagers may use music and the popular culture to help them express preconscious and unconscious material and better handle age-appropriate developmental tasks.

Mark is very deliberate in differentiating himself from the rest of his family. He sees himself with distinctly different tastes, interests, hopes, and aspirations. While he does not mock his parents professionally, or his siblings, and, in fact, sees them as all highly accomplished, he professes little use, in fact, disdain for traditional American education, either parochial or at the college level. Like the rest of his family, he is and acknowledges being a "wordsmith" and a voracious reader, but, unlike them, he has no interest in going to college. He is obsessed with becoming a heavy metal rock musician and lyricist. His garb and self-presentation is that of a wholesome and attractive, well-groomed adolescent, who often nervously pulls at his hair. He no longer adorns himself with the trappings of a heavy metal rocker, whereas last year he had nails in his boots.

Mark's musical aspirations alarm his parents for a number of reasons, especially their perception of their son as possessing no musical talents and having no interest in beginning music lessons. Thus, in their view, he is living in a total fantasy, in futile search of an identity. Rock and roll music has been an expression of

> the outsider, the lonely, the alienated. It purports to supply a voice for the rebel who chooses to stand apart from the mainstream or adult culture. Musical affiliation also plays a role in adolescent peer relations. Musical preferences as a means of communication becomes a nexus for group identity, extending to clothing style and expressed beliefs as well as on occasion, drug use, other risk-taking behavior. With music, teenagers form their own distinct subcultures–hip-hop, dead-heads, Goth, heavy metal, as a challenge to their parents' culture, in part as a resistance to growing up, but also, paradoxically, as a way of staking out their own territory upon which to grow. (Rosenblum et al., pp. 321-322)

This has been compared to Winnicott's (1958) concept of a new holding environment. For Mark, heavy metal is his chosen environment, which reflects narcissistic rage and injury, profound aggression, the devil, and questions of good and evil. Mark and his parents do refer to his interests in religion, moral and aesthetic theology, and the writings of C.S. Lewis, particularly *The Screwtape Letters.* With similar examinations of evil, the titles of his songs and poems are striking–for example, "Doomsday," "Predator of Society," "Corpse on Display," "Paralyzed," and so on. He attempts in his lyrics to courageously defy and call to task the adult world. The chorus of his song "Predator of Society" is as follows:

> And if you believe that there's no way to win
> You should take another look at what the world calls
> sin.
> And if you stand for justice and truth
> You should take another look at what the world calls
> youth.
> And if you think conforming is your only use
> Challenge their authorities, don't take their abuse.

In other lyrics Mark renders harsh judgments. In addition, lack of separation/individualization appear to be continual themes.

"REFLECTIONS"

> Whenever you've done wrong i'm always there
> Singing a rage song in my glass lair
> My eye's always on you grim icy stare
> My judgement is always nowhere near fair
> You know its been so long since i had a friend
> Who wouldn't begrudge me or make morals bend
>
> And even when i was wrong i tried to mend
> The misconception that the mirror's your friend
> I'M THE MAN IN THE MIRROR LOOKING AT YOU
> REFLECTING ALL YOUR FAULTS
> WITH MAGNIFIED VIEW
> I WANT YOU TO WEAKEN SO THAT I CAN BEGIN
> TO MAKE YOU SEE
> THAT I'M PART OF YOU AND YOU'RE PART OF ME

Like so many rock musicians, reading music and a formal musical education is atypical, even, in the eyes of some, a disadvantage. Thus, Mark seems quite unconcerned about his lack of actual skill on a musical instrument. With friends he's becoming adept at the new form of music making, namely, digital technology (digital editing, use of software and other computerized tools to stitch together prerecorded sounds). The new alternative high school he's just enrolled in has this technology and related courses, as well as internships in record companies of various sorts. Thus, school attendance is no longer a battle and, on the basis of my various referrals and manner in sessions, Mark has come to feel that I accept him and his passionate aspirations. Of late, he shares his lyrics and songs with me, stating his growing belief that I am not aligned with his parents against him, but rather, am very "fair," with great respect and regard for him and his parents, despite their very "different agendas." He observes that I don't dismiss his lyrics and musical goals but, in fact, am attentive, admiring, and respectful of his ambitions.

As we attempt to sort out why, unlike his siblings, he feels so very different and alienated from his parents and enraged with them, he states it's because he's been depressed for so long and his parents didn't see how miserable he was most of his childhood. Before his adolescent experimentation with pot and alcohol, he, like his siblings, was a solid and successful scholarship student at a prestigious and demanding parochial school. Once pot use began, academics suddenly were no longer a source of easy achievement and pride. He had never had much ability, interest, or involvement in sports, and socially, he states, he always felt like a misfit, a dork, a short kid, blind without glasses; he read too much, was picked on, and couldn't hold his own. He offered a number of bemused vignettes of himself, totally isolated from peers, all but hiding out in the cloak room–reading away while sitting atop a pile of coats and jackets. Now he feels less shy and disconnected from peers; but to his parents' despair, his friendships are with youths who are only marginal in school, given to substance abuse, and all from highly problematic homes. In his parents' eyes, Mark is even more dysfunctional than his substance abusing peers, because of his being out of school so long and his excessive sleeping and regression.

Mark feels his parents should have been more aware of the depth of his unhappiness sooner, possibly seeking some sort of help for him when he was much younger. He now is able to acknowledge more openly his ambivalent as well as affectionate feelings for his entire family, a family he recognizes as so much better than the fractured and dysfunctional ones of so many of his friends. Mark is also facing the strong possibility that he might suffer from a genetic bipolar disorder, since he slowly is recognizing that his rage and depression are out of proportion to the reality of his family life. Under supervision with a new psychiatrist, he's recently begun a trial course of Depocate, in addition to his Prozac, prescribed by the doctor he saw prior to our contact.

Mark doesn't want any parental supervision or curfew and resents *any* restriction or parental expectation about what he does and when he does it. He feels entitled, endlessly and excessively, to sleep in and to require his parents to rouse him. He believes since he does dinner dishes and walks the dog, he should not have more oversight; yet, he sets things up to embroil them, by not being autonomous, not independently doing his home schooling assignments, and not finding a job. Guidance for the parents successfully decreased parental nagging, and, instead, some sort of structure was created, so that the English course was finally completed, and the final exam was taken.

Mark is becoming more aware of his hostile dependency, feelings of love that alternate with hatred toward his parents, his rebelliousness versus his acceptance of them. He recently raged that if not allowed out to sleep over at a friend's, he'll "vanish for the next five years." He stormed out and was gone from home at a friend's for two days. We could ultimately laugh together over his acknowledged excessiveness and theatrics. I shared with him the old joke about the five-year-old, threatening to run away, while requesting that his parents take him across the street "since I'm not allowed to cross streets alone."

Since we've worked together, things are more stabilized; temper explosions are much less frequent, and normal exchanges are more common. He seemingly is not using drugs, by his own account, and by urine tests his parents conduct (through the recommendations in the prior drug prevention program he attended). Most important, the parents, mother especially, are also calmer and not overwhelmed with thoughts and fantasies about a non-voluntary hospitalization for Mark or about placing him in a punishing and remotely based Outward Bound program. There is considerable relief that he's finally willing to try medications and surrender all alcohol use and that he cooperated and enrolled in a creative, alternative high school program. To everyone's surprise, the total accumulated credits reveal that Mark is quite close to qualifying for high school graduation, with a very decent overall grade point average. His priority is to use his school program and courses to help him produce and distribute a CD of his work on the Internet and secure a music-related internship which might possibly develop into a paying job. College in the immediate future is of little interest, but not completely dismissed, as was the case when we began our work together. He is actually beginning to speak about possible programs and schools. Mark most recently asked a wholesome girl out for a date, his first in over one and a half years, also representing a notable shift from his previous pattern of socializing solely with substance abusing male buddies.

Therapeutic Optimal Responsiveness and Intersubjectivity

Optimal responsiveness, as explicated by Bacal (1998), describes both the analyst's therapeutic function and the patient's therapeutic experience as a result of an increasing awareness of the interactional/relational nature of the psychoanalytic process. Bacal's conception deals with the "responsibility of the analyst that is therapeutically most relevant at any particular moment in the context of a particular patient and his illness and as the therapist's acts of communicating to his patient in ways that that particular patient experiences as usable for the cohesion, strengthening and growth of his self" (Bacal, 1998, p. 142). Bacal also notes the clinician's response which facilitates therapeutic relatedness; that is, it is understood as a corrective selfobject relationship and experienced within an interactive reciprocal system. The therapist cannot expect, or aim for perfection, but rather, must be "himself or herself in the best way that he or she can, in order to enable the patient to use him or her therapeutically" (ibid, p. 167).

Optimal responsiveness entails the utilization of affect attunement to apprehend and understand the patient's subjective experiences, and this takes place in a relational or interactional system. Kohut (1984) spoke of self-selfobject relationships, and Model (1984) referred to a two-person psychology. Mitchell (1988) described the relational matrix, and Beebe and Lachman (1988) label the treatment a dyadic system with a mutual influence structure. Atwood and Stolorow (1994) utilized the term intersubjective context to describe the treatment process, shaped by the "continually shifting psychological field cast by the interplay between the differently organized subjective worlds of patient and (therapist)" (Stolorow, Atwood, & Brandchaft, 1994, p. 28).

It should be noted that the theory of intersubjectivity is not considered an outgrowth of self psychology, nor is the intent that of superseding self psychology. According to Stolorow (1994), it developed in parallel with it and "became greatly enriched by the framework of self psychology" (p. 38). In sum, Stolorow perceives the concept of the intersubjective field as a theoretical construct "precisely matched to the methodology of empathic introspection." Further comparisons are provided by Trop (1984). He points out that both theories are relational and "both reject the concept of drive as a primary motivational source." Both theories use the stance of empathy and introspection as a central guiding principle. Self psychology is centered on the concept of selfobject and selfobject transferences and in contrast the "motivational principles of intersubjectivity theory is not centered in the concept of selfobject, but is more broad-based, striving to organize and order experience" (p. 78). Trop (1994) emphasizes the unconscious organization of experience and posits that the theory of intersubjectivity is "uniquely suited to facilitate a clinical understanding of the patterning and thematizing of experience when selfobject functions are missing" (p. 89). This is in contrast to a self-psychology perspective which aims to promote a "gradual internalization of the analyst's selfobject functions." The goal of the "curative process is the patient's enhanced capacity to choose more mature selfobjects in future relationships" (ibid).

CONCLUSIONS

Mark, the primary patient, has increasingly become able to share his inner life, his feelings of self-consciousness, and his low self-esteem. With piercing intensity, he has recounted embarrassment and shame in his previous peer group that caused him to take flight and to identify with a group of angry and marginal male friends who shared a common interest in expressing themselves in heavy metal rageful lyrics and pulsating angry music. Mark has begun to recognize that his feelings of inferiority cause him to overreact to the smallest perceived slight or insult. Mirroring and the provision of terrain regulation were offered in a context of accepting the patient's subjective experiences (Stolorow, Brandchaft, & Atwood, 1987, p. 115).

On the few early occasions when extreme aggression surfaced in a treatment hour towards the clinician and the parents, the therapist suggested to Mark her possible failure of attunement. This was based on the self-psychology perspective that aggression "is not etiological, but rather a secondary reaction to the therapist's inability to comprehend the developmental meaning of the patient's archaic state" (Kohut, 1972; Stolorow, 1984). The therapeutic task was not to avoid any and all expressions of selfobject failure but to attempt to understand them "within the unique aspect of the patient's subjective world" (Stolorow, Brandchaft, & Atwood, 1987, p. 131).

Mark feels his mother doesn't see him for himself, but rather links him with her brother and father. His mother sees no similarity between her son and her father who killed himself, but does acknowledge some striking similarities between Mark and her brother, though her brother was never non-functional or as regressed as Mark has been the last 10-11 months, sleeping endlessly, and being out of regular school. By contrast, her brother was a super-achiever, both academically and athletically, who attended and excelled at one of the nation's finest universities, despite suffering from an apparent bipolar condition and resultant excessive drinking and volatility.

The goal of all of the treatment interventions has been to stimulate the development of a cohesive self or self-system in the family. This is accomplished through a process Kohut (1971) called transmuting internalizations, that is, the internal changes that occur as individuals and the family as a whole develop a capacity "to accept the hurts that are caused by failure of optimal responses to important others" (Solomon, 1991, p. 132). With increased tolerance of feelings that previously caused shame and anxiety, family members have less need to feel helpless, hopeless, and overwhelmed. Ideally, family members are now learning to relate to one another in a more benign, nontraumatic environment in which imperfections and small failures are experienced as manageable with no damage to the newly cohesive nuclear self and more cohesive nuclear family.

It is apparent "how certain facets of popular culture intersect with adolescent developmental needs" (Rosenblum, 1999, p. 337). My real interest in Mark's poetic and musical longings has strengthened the therapeutic alliance and helped the parents see that music and style are in relation to transitional and developmental phenomena. Thus, their fears and anxieties could abate and all could be seen in the context of internal developmental issues, needs, and longings (ibid, 1999). The therapeutic alliance in this essay is not framed in terms of traditional ego psychology and is not what is considered by some (Stolorow, Atwood, & Brandchaft, 1992) to be "transference compliance" or "pseudo alliance." In these traditional models, the patient identifies with the analyst's stance of inquiry and his theoretical assumptions as well. Rather, I have attempted to demonstrate my reliance on understanding Mark's and his parents' own subjective realities, perceived through sustained empathetic inquiry into their subjective worlds. The parents' values, hopes, and needs were easily discernible. Getting beneath Mark's aggressivity and sense of entitlement posed more challenges. Mark's sharing of his poetry and music ultimately facilitated a rich view of his subjective world, so that this very gifted and creative adolescent emerged out of his heretofore solid armor of narcissistic rage, grandiosity, and rebellion against all that is significant in his parents' world. Affection and regard for his parents and siblings is becoming discernible, and we are beginning to see movement from archaic to more age-appropriate narcissism, side by side and intertwined with a movement from archaic to more age-adequate object love (Kohut, 1984).

REFERENCES

Anderson, J.C. & McGee, R. (1994). Co-morbidity of depression in children and adolescents. In W.M. Reynolds & H.F. Johnston (Eds.), *Handbook of depression in children and adolescents* (pp. 551-601). NY: Plenum Press.

Angold, A. (1993). Depression co-morbidity in children and adolescents: Empirical, theoretical and methodological issues. *American Journal of Psychiatry.* 150: pp. 1779-1791.

Angold, A. & Costello, E.J. (1992). Co-morbidity in children and adolescents with depression. *Child & Adolescent Clinics of North America.* 1: pp. 31-51.

Atwood, G.E. & Stolorow, R.D. (1994). In R.D. Stolorow, G.E. Atwood, & B. Brandchaft (Eds.), *Subjectivity & self psychology.* Northvale, NJ: Jason Aronson.

Bacal, H. (1998). *Optimal responsiveness: How therapists heal their patients.* Northvale, NJ: Jason Aronson.

Balint, M. (1969). *The basic fault: Therapeutic aspects of regression.* London: Tavistock. (Reprinted 1979, Brunner/Mazel, NY).

Basch, M. (1986). How does analysis cure? An appreciation. *Psychoanalytic Inquiry.* 6: pp. 403-428.

Bean, M.H. (1981). Denial and the psychological complications of alcoholism. In M.H. Bean & N.E. Zinberg (Eds.), *Dynamic approaches to the understanding and treatment of alcoholism* (pp. 55-96). New York: Free Press.

Beebe, B. & Lachman, F. (1988). The contribution of the mother-infant mutual influence to the origins of self and object representations. *Psychoanalytic Psychology.* 5: pp. 305-337.

Berkowitz, I. (1981). Feelings of powerlessness and the role of violent actions in adolescents. In S. Feinstein, J. Looney, A. Schwartzberg, & A. Sorosky (Eds.), *Adolescent psychiatry Vol. 9: Developmental & clinical studies* (pp. 477-492). Chicago, IL: University of Chicago Press.

Bettelheim, B. (1976). *The use of enchantment.* New York: Knopf.

Birmaher, B., Ryan, N.D., Williamson, D.E., Brend, D.A. & Kaufman, J. (1996A). *Journal of the American Academy of Child & Adolescent Psychiatry.* 35(11): pp. 1427-1439.

Birmaher, B., Ryan, N.D., Williamson, D.E., Brend, D.A., & Kaufman, J. (1996B). *Journal of the American Academy of Child & Adolescent Psychiatry.* 35(12): pp. 1575-1583.

Carlson, G.A. (1981). The phenomenology of adolescent depression. In *Adolescent psychiatry Vol. 9: Developmental & clinical studies* (pp. 411-421). Chicago, IL: University of Chicago Press.

Director, L. (2000). Understanding and treating adolescent substance abuse: Systems, families and individual meaning. *Journal of Infant, Child & Adolescent Psychotherapy.* 1(1): pp. 97-110.

Essau, C.A. & Petermann, F. (Eds.). (1999). *Depressive disorders in children and adolescents: Epidemiology, risk factors and treatment.* Northvale, NJ: Jason Aronson.

Feinstein, S.C. (1982). Manic-depressive disorder in children and adolescents. In S. Feinstein, J. Looney, A. Schwartzberg, & A. Sorosky (Eds.), *Adolescent psychiatry Vol. 10: Developmental & clinical studies* (pp. 256-272). Chicago, IL: University of Chicago Press.

Freud, A. (1958). Adolescence. *Psychoanalytic study of the child.* 13: pp. 255-278. NY: International Universities Press.

Gardner, R. (1999). *Psychotherapy of anti-social behavior and depression in adolescence.* Northvale, NJ: Jason Aronson.

Hartman, D. (1967). Drug-taking adolescents. *Psychoanalytic study of the child.* 24: pp. 384-398. NY: International Universities Press.

Kazdin, A.E. (1989). Developmental differences in depression. In B. Blahey & A.E. Kazdin (Eds.), *Advances in clinical child psychology Vol. 12* (pp. 193-219). New York: Plenum Press.

Kernberg, O. (1975). *Borderline conditions and pathological narcissism.* Northvale, NJ: Jason Aronson.

Kestenbaum, C. (1982). Children and adolescents at-risk for manic-depressive illness: Introduction and overview. In S. Feinstein, J. Looney, A. Schwartzberg, & A. Sorosky (Eds.), *Adolescent psychiatry Vol. 10: Developmental & clinical studies* (pp. 245-255). Chicago, IL: University of Chicago Press.

Knight, R. (1937). The psychodynamics of chronic alcoholism. *Journal of nervous & mental disease.* 86: pp. 538-548.

Kohut, H. (1972). Thoughts on narcissism and narcissistic rage. *Psychoanalytic study of the child.* 27: pp. 360-400. New Haven, CT: Yale University Press.

Kohut, H. (1984). *How does analysis cure?* A. Goldberg & P. Stepansky (Eds.), Chicago, IL: University of Chicago Press.

Kohut, H. (1971). *The analysis of the self.* New York: International Universities Press.

Kohut, H. (1966). Forms and transformations of narcissism. *Journal of American Psychoanalytic Association.* 14(2): pp. 243-272.

Kronenberger, W.G. & Meyer, R.G. (1996). *The child clinician's handbook.* Boston, MA: Allyn & Bacon.

Lewis, C.S. (1961). *The screwtape letters.* New York: Macmillan.

Mack, J.E. (1981). Alcoholism, A.A. and the governance of the self. In M.H. Bean & N. E. Zinberg (Eds.), *Dynamic approaches to the understanding and treatment of alcoholism* (pp. 128-162). New York: Free Press.

Masterson, J. (1967). The systematic adolescent five years later: He didn't grow out of it. *American journal of psychiatry.* 123: pp. 1338-1345.

Masterson, J. & Washburne, A. (1966). The symptomatic adolescent: Psychiatric illness or adolescent turmoil? *American Journal of Psychiatry.* 122: pp. 1240-1248.

Miller, D. (1986). *Attack on the self: Adolescent behavioral disturbances and their treatment.* Northvale, NJ: Jason Aronson.

Miller, D. (1973). The drug dependent adolescent. In S. Feinstein, J. Looney, A. Schwartzberg, & A. Sorosky (Eds.), *Adolescent psychiatry Vol. 2: Developmental & clinical studies* (pp. 79-97). New York: Basic Books.

Mishne, J. (1993). *The evolution and application of clinical theory: Perspectives from four psychologies.* New York: Free Press.

Mishne, J. (1986). *Clinical work with adolescents.* New York: Free Press.

Mitchell, S. (1988). *The relational concepts in psychoanalysis.* New York: Basic Books.

Model, A. (1984). *Psychoanalysis in a new context.* Madison, CT: International Universities Press.

Morrison, A.P. (1996). Shame, ideal self and narcissism. In A.P. Morrison (Ed.), *Essential papers on narcissism* (pp. 338-371). NY: New York University Press.

Nottelmann, E.D. & Jensen, P.S. (1995). Co-morbidity of disorders in children and adolescents: Developmental perspectives. In T.H. Ollendick & R.J. Prinz (Eds.), *Advances in clinical child psychology* (pp. 109-155). New York: Plenum Press.

Nottelmann, E.D. & Jensen, P.S. (1999). Co-morbidity in depression disorders: Rates, temporal sequencing, course and outcome. In C.A. Essau & F. Petermann (Eds.), *Depressive disorders in children and adolescents: Epidemiology, risk factors and treatment* (pp. 137-191). Northvale, NJ: Jason Aronson.

Offer, D. (1967). Normal adolescents. *Archives of General Psychiatry.* 17: pp. 285-290.

Offer, D. & Offer, J. (1975). *From teenager to young manhood: A psychological study.* New York: Basic Books.

Offer, D. & Sabshin, M. (1963). The psychiatrist and the normal adolescent. *Archives of General Psychiatry.* 9: pp. 427-432.

Offer, D., Sabshin, M. & Marcus, D. (1965). Clinical evaluation of normal adolescents. *American Journal of Psychiatry.* 121: pp. 864-872.

Oldham, D. (1978). Adolescent turmoil: A myth revisited. In S. Feinstein & P. Giovacchini (Eds.), *Adolescent Psychiatry Vol. 6: Developmental & Clinical Studies* (pp. 267-279). Chicago: University of Chicago Press.

Pattison, E.M. (1984). Types of alcoholism reflective of character disorders. In R. Zales (Ed.), *Character pathology: Theory and treatment* (pp. 362-378). New York: American College of Psychiatrists/New York: Brunner/Mazel.

Pearce, J. (1977). Depressive disorder in children. *Journal of child psychology & psychiatry.* 18: pp. 29-82.

Rado, S. (1933). The psychoanalysis of pharmacothymia. *Psychoanalytic quarterly.* 2 pp. 1-23.

Rosenblum, D.S., Daniolos, P., Kass, N., & Martin, A. (1999). Adolescents and the popular culture. In A.J. Solnit, P.B. Neubauer, S. Abrams, & A. Scott Dowling (Eds.), *Psychoanalytic study of the child.* 54: pp. 319-338.

Rutter, M., Graham, D., Chadwick, O.F.D., & Yule, W. (1976). Adolescent turmoil: Fact or fiction. *Journal of child psychology & psychiatry.* 17: pp. 35-36.

Solomon, M.F. (1991). Adults. In H. Jackson (Ed.), *Using self psychology in psychotherapy.* Northvale, NJ: Jason Aronson.

Stanton, M. & Todd, T. (1982). *The family of drug abuse and addiction.* New York: Guilford Press.

Stolorow, R.D. (1984). Aggression in the psychoanalytic situation: An intersubjective viewpoint. *Contemporary Psychoanalysis.* 20: pp. 643-651.

Stolorow, R.D. (1994). Subjectivity and self psychology. In R.D. Stolorow, G. Atwood, & B. Brandchaft (Eds.), *The intersubjective approach* (pp. 31-39). Northvale, NJ: Jason Aronson.

Stolorow, R.D., Atwood, G.E., & Brandchaft, B. (Eds.). (1994). *Subjectivity and self psychology.* Northvale, NJ: Jason Aronson.

Stolorow, R.D., Atwood, G.E., & Brandchaft, B. (Eds.). (1992). Varieties of therapeutic alliance. In *Context of being: The intersubjective foundations of psychological life* (pp. 31-39). Northvale, NJ: Jason Aronson.

Stolorow, R.D., Brandchaft, B., & Atwood, G.E. (1987). *Psychoanalytic treatment: An intersubjective approach.* Hillsdale, NJ: Analytic Press.

Trop, J.L. (1984). Self psychology and intersubjectivity theory. In R.D. Stolorow, G.W. Atwood, & B. Brandchaft (Eds.), *The intersubjective approach.* Northvale, NJ: Jason Aronson.

Vaillant, G.E. (1981). Dangers of psychotherapy in the treatment of alcoholism. In M.H. Bean & N. E. Zinberg (Eds.), *Dynamic approaches to the understanding and treatment of alcoholism* (pp. 36-54). New York: Free Press.

Wieder, H. & Kaplan, E. (1969). Drug use in adolescents: Psychodynamic meaning and pharmacogenic effect. *Psychoanalytic study of the child.* 24: 399-431. New York: International Universities Press.

Winnicott, D.W. (1958). *Through pediatrics to psychoanalysis: Collected papers.* New York: Basic Books.

Woodruff, R.A., Jr., Goodwin, D.W. & Guze, S.B. (1974). *Psychiatric diagnosis.* New York: Oxford University Press.

Wurmser. (1978). *The hidden dimension: Psychodynamics of compulsive drug use.* Northvale, NJ: Jason Aronson.

Zinburg, A. (1975). Addiction and ego function. *Psychoanalytic study of the child.* 30: pp. 567-880. New Haven, CT: Yale University Press.

Two Systems of Self-Regulation

Jack Novick

Kerry Kelly Novick

SUMMARY. Our work on the development and treatment of sadomasochism and its organizing omnipotent beliefs has led us to suggest that there are two distinct kinds of conflict resolution and self-regulation. One, the open system, is attuned to reality and is characterized by joy, competence, and creativity. The other, the closed system, avoids reality and is characterized by sadomasochism, omnipotent beliefs, and stasis. This article places the two-systems model in the framework of single- and dual-track psychoanalytic descriptions of development. We suggest that a dual-track, two-systems model is consistent with Freud's vision of psychoanalysis as a general psychology, as it can encompass both pathological and normal choices throughout development and oscillations between them. Some technical implications of a two-systems model are discussed in relation to the therapeutic alliance. Applications to work with patients of all ages and the parents of child and adolescent patients are included. *[Article copies available for a fee from The Haworth Document Delivery Service: 1-800-342-9678. E-mail address: <getinfo@haworthpressinc.com>*

Jack Novick, PhD, is a Training and Supervising Analyst at the New York Freudian Society, a Child and Adolescent Supervising Analyst at the Michigan Psychoanalytic Institute, and Clinical Associate Professor of Psychiatry at the University of Michigan Medical School.

Kerry Kelly Novick is a Child and Adolescent Supervising Analyst at the Michigan Psychoanalytic Institute and Clinical Director of Allen Creek Preschool.

Address correspondence to: Jack Novick, 617 Stratford Drive, Ann Arbor, MI 48104, USA (E-mail: *jnovick@umich.edu*).

[Haworth co-indexing entry note]: "Two Systems of Self-Regulation." Novick, Jack and Kerry Kelly Novick. Co-published simultaneously in *Psychoanalytic Social Work* (The Haworth Press, Inc.) Vol. 8, No. 3/4, 2001, pp. 95-122; and: *Psychoanalytic Approaches to the Treatment of Children and Adolescents: Tradition and Transformation* (ed: Jerrold R. Brandell) The Haworth Press, Inc., 2001, pp. 95-122. Single or multiple copies of this article are available for a fee from The Haworth Document Delivery Service [1-800-342-9678, 9:00 a.m. - 5:00 p.m. (EST). E-mail address: getinfo@haworthpressinc.com].

KEYWORDS. Development, technique, sadomasochism, psychoanalysis, theory, omnipotence

Our earlier work on sadomasochism and its underlying defensive omnipotent beliefs has led us to the view that there are two distinct kinds of solutions to conflicts throughout development. One is attuned to reality and is characterized by joy, competence, and creativity. The other avoids reality and is characterized by sadomasochism, omnipotence, and stasis. In previous papers (Novick & Novick, 1991, 1996a, 1996b, 1998) we have delineated these alternative solutions to conflict as two systems of self-regulation that we call "open" and "closed." Building on and extending Annie Reich's (1951) clinical descriptions of normal and pathological self-esteem regulation, our goal in this article is to explore in more detail these two systems of self-regulation.

Single- and Dual-Track Models of Development

Psychoanalysis is, above all, a developmental theory and a model of development that informs all therapeutic techniques either implicitly or directly. Freud described various developmental models, but the one that is most used by modern psychoanalysts of all schools is what we term a "single-track" model. In a *single-track model* pathology is understood to be rooted in, and extended to describe, all early development. Adult pathology is explained as fixation or regression to, or persistence or arrest of, what was normal in childhood. In this conceptualization, what was normal in childhood is pathological in adulthood. Frances Tustin, a pioneer in the psychoanalytic treatment of autism, described this as "the mainstream hypothesis . . . to which many psychoanalytic therapists have subscribed, especially in the United States and in Europe" (1994, p. 3). Normal children are routinely described as "autistic," "omnipotent," "paranoid-schizoid," "depressive," "polymorphously perverse," "anal-sadistic," "narcissistic," and so forth, all examples of descriptors of severe pathology in adults. Adult normality is explained as a sublimation or compromise formation on the basis of infantile "perverse" impulses. Tustin wrote a moving paper (referred to above) called "The perpetuation of an error," in an effort to correct what she saw as an untenable clinging to single-track theory. She noted that "this flawed hypothesis, based on faulty premises, has been like an invasive virus in that it has permeated and distorted clinical and theoretical formulations" (ibid, p. 3).

Peterfreund (1978), Silverman (1981), and Gillette (1992) have made similar critiques of single-track developmental theory. Their cogent arguments tend to be ignored, however, and there seems to be a perennial pull, both theoretically and clinically, for psychoanalysts to stress a unitary pathological continuum. This implies neglect of the individual's strengths, capacities, push toward progressive development, and use of the opportunities provided by reality experience, including that of the treatment situation and relationship. Many of the findings of current observational and experimental infant research and of neurobiological studies confirm the existence of motivations and areas of functioning that are outside conflict, and imply motives of competence and mastery (Schore, 1994). There is no indication that normally-endowed infants go through early phases of pathological functioning, only to emerge intact as normally-functioning children. Those individuals who suffer extreme hardship and deprivation in infancy do not uniformly develop later pathology; resiliency and self-righting demand explanation (Werner and Smith; 1982; Moskowitz, 1983; Anthony & Cohler, 1987; Kagan, 1996; Sroufe, 1996).

Freud explicitly delineated an "original reality ego" (1915, p. 136) that preceded the "purified pleasure ego" (ibid, p. 136). Current emphasis on the role of the treatment relationship and patient-therapist interaction presupposes a relation to reality (Renik, 1998), yet single-track, pathology-derived theories of functioning have difficulty integrating these approaches. Levin (1994) has thoughtfully criticized developmental theories that exclude the role of reality and ignore its primacy in Freud's theory. The argument for a dual-track theory is also reflected in Vygotsky's ([1934]1986) critique of Piaget. In contrast to Piaget's description of a developmental progression from autism to egocentric thought to logic, Vygotsky posited that children start with social communicative speech which becomes inner speech, with egocentric speech the transition between the two.

There have been psychoanalytic thinkers who followed Freud's lead in using a *dual-track model of development*, but there seems to be resistance to maintaining such a model, as evinced by the eclipse of the work of Hartmann (1939), Erikson (1950), Anna Freud (1965), and White (1959). Friedman (1999) has suggested a difficulty for analysts in encompassing reality. Nevertheless, there is currently a growing body of literature that is reviving dual-track models within mainstream psychoanalysis, as in the work of Lichtenberg (1989) on different motivational systems and their ramifications for technique (Lichtenberg, Lachmann, & Fosshage, 1992, 1996). From a different theoretical base within psychoanalysis, Grotstein (1986, 1994) comes up with a dual track-theory in which he draws upon the work of Bakhtin (1981) to contrast what he too calls "open" and "closed" systems of development. Emde's (1988) research on early affects has demonstrated the separate development of positive and negative emotions. Current work on "positive psychology" (Peterson, 2000; Seligman, Schulman, DeRubeis, & Hollon, 1999) implies a two-system psychology.

In the emerging interdisciplinary science of developmental psychopathology Cicchetti and Rogosch (1996) draw on the biological and philosophical ideas of Mayr (1988) and von Bertalanffy (1968) to look at two systems of epigenesis, an open system of behavioral and biological plasticity, and a closed system where the initial conditions inevitably determine the end state. Wurmser (1998, 1999) finds a literary source in George Eliot's distinction between "magical" and "tragic transformations." In the allied field of evolutionary psychiatry, the work of Nesse and Berridge (1997) has suggested neurophysiological foundations for two incentive systems, i.e., the "liking" and the "wanting" systems.

The Closed, Sadomasochistic, Omnipotent System and Its Development

We have characterized the two systems in terms of self-regulation, which includes regulation of self-esteem, because of the fundamental nature of the narcissistic economy. Each individual needs to feel safe, that his world is predictable, that his experience is encompassable, that obstacles can be overcome, problems can be solved, and conflicts resolved. Infants can feel pleasure when such conditions can be assumed. Infants faced with overwhelming experiences, whether they originate from internal or external sources, *must* find a way to feel good. If the method they find is through a turn away from reality, safety will continue to reside in an omnipotent solution. Such a learned response can come to feel like the most dependable safeguard, and take on an addictive quality, restricting the baby's attempts to essay other solutions and pathways to problem solving and conflict resolution. Rapaport and Gill (1959) described a structure as a process with a slow rate of change. The sadomasochistic omnipotent system is closed, repetitive, and increasingly resistant to change. In a distorted personality development it can become a structure regulating feelings of control, safety, excitement, enjoyment, power, and self-esteem.

As our ideas about the development and treatment of sadomasochism have evolved (J. Novick & K.K. Novick, 1972, 1991, 1996a, 1996b; K.K. Novick & J. Novick 1987, 1998), we have developed a view that departs from the classical description of "normal infantile omnipotence." In our study on beating fantasies in children (Novick & Novick, 1972), we found it useful to distinguish among wishes, thoughts, and fantasies. Drawing from Schafer (1968), we restricted the usage of "fantasy" to conscious daydreams. Omnipotence is a quality that can be attributed to wishes, thoughts, or daydreams. As such, it can be a harmlessly pleasurable element of play or creativity, so long as awareness of the distinction between real and pretend, between thought and action, is maintained. There can be an illusion of omnipotence accompanying childhood fantasies, including the transitory beating fantasies we found in girls at the oedipal phase (Novick & Novick, 1972). When, however, such ideas meet with external validating factors, such as serious medical conditions, death or other accidents of fate, or psychological trauma stemming from parental inadequacy or pathology, an illusion of omnipotence can be converted into a *delusion*. We have more recently found it helpful to make a further distinction between fantasies and beliefs in order to account for patients' subjective conviction of the reality and truth of their conscious or unconscious ideas (Novick & Novick, 2000; Weiss, 1993, 1998).

In our work we have emphasized that we do not view omnipotent beliefs as part of normal development, nor as equivalent to oceanic feelings, grandiosity, egocentrism, or primary narcissism. Omnipotent beliefs are created in response to reality failures in order to protect the person from physical or psychological trauma. We define such defensive omnipotence as a conscious or unconscious belief in real power to control others, to hurt them, to force them to submit to one's desires, ultimately probably to force the mother to be a "good enough," competent, protective, and loving parent.

Repetitive, resistant, self-defeating functioning, stalling, or impasse in the clinical relationship–these form the arena for most analytic endeavors. Wurmser (1996) has provided several detailed clinical examples of patients who are governed by vicious cycles of repetition. We are suggesting that what is at work in the self-regulation of patients at such times is a closed, omnipotent, sadomasochistic system, in which the active search for pain and suffering has transformed experiences of helplessness into a hostile defense. The organizing *belief* in this defense against overwhelming and even traumatic anxiety, guilt, and helplessness is one of magical power to control the object. Everything the patient does is directed toward control of others. At various times in life, the patient has convinced himself/herself that this defense is effective; indeed, there may have been times when it served as the best or only adaptation to inner and outer circumstances. When the omnipotent defense is consolidated as a solution to conflict over time, it comes to serve multiple functions and motives, which leads in part to its later intractability in treatment.

Rather than seeing sadomasochism as a separate diagnostic entity, we have suggested that sadomasochism, with its core omnipotent beliefs, is present in all cases, in some more visibly and more persistently than others. This dynamic, as opposed to a nosological, approach to omnipotence and sadomasochism is neither radical nor new (A. Freud, 1954). A conscious or unconscious belief in omnipotent power to control, force, or harm others may appear in perfectionism, lack of pleasure in accomplishments, rituals, or a variety of pathological superego manifestations. It is important to connect the underlying omnipotent conviction with the experience of helplessness that gave rise to it. Research support for these clinically-derived formulations is emerging in studies of disorganized attachment (Solomon & George, 1999), a category of functioning that cuts across all types of pathology and modes of attachment and that is dynamically and historically related to experiences of helplessness in the infant-mother dyad.

We have described elsewhere (Novick & Novick, 1996a, 1996b, 1998) how the omnipotent system can contribute to intense resistances at each phase of treatment. Our point has been to emphasize that sadomasochism has determinants from every level of development, and serves multiple functions, and that the omnipotent belief should be seen as an active construction providing a defense against helplessness and overwhelming rage or excitement. In treatment, patient and analyst can discover that, given whatever external circumstances and internal resources were available at any given time, the construction of the omnipotent system may be seen as an achievement. It was the best the individual could then do when the alternatives might have been death, as in marasmus or suicide, or withdrawal into a dehumanized state, such as perhaps depression, alexithymia, or schizoid conditions (Krystal, 1978; Fraiberg, 1982; Sofsky, 1997; Novick & Novick, in press). The delusion of omnipotence in self or others becomes the patient's source of self-regulation. Once constructed and then consolidated in adolescence, it becomes highly resistant to change by experience or analysis. All the ego's capacities and talents are used to defend and preserve the conviction that the individual is an "exception" to reality rules, both social and natural laws, and "entitled," because of his suffering, sadistically to force others to meet his needs (Freud, 1916).

Given the security, safety, and gratification the omnipotent delusion provides to the individual, it is indeed questionable why anyone would give it up. What is the alternative? The patient fears that the only alternative is the primitive state of helplessness, rage, or traumatic guilt that originally gave rise to the defensive omnipotent delusion.

The Open, Competent System and Its Development

At any point in experience or development we discern an alternative possible response, a system of self-regulation that is competent and effective, based on mutually respectful, pleasurable relationships formed through realistic perceptions of the self and others, open to experience from inside and outside and thus generative of creativity in life and work. Elements of description of such an open system can be found scattered in the analytic literature, as in the early idea of the pleasure ego (Freud, 1895), the technical notion of the "unobjectionable transference" (Freud, 1913), and Freud's description of mastery in "Beyond the Pleasure Principle" (1920). It is perhaps most clearly stated in Freud's late conception of Eros and Thanatos ([1938] 1940). Hartmann (1939), with his ideas of primary ego autonomy, posited an innate, separate, non-pathological force in normal development that leads to adaptive rather than neurotic solutions to conflict. Erikson (1950) described polarized possibilities for solution to the conflicts faced at each stage of development in his epigenetic description. Anna Freud (1965) clearly delineated the normal conflicts of the infant and child that can find solutions that are adaptive, as did Bowlby (1969, 1973, 1980) in his discussions of attachment motives. White (1959) summarized this strand of analytic thinking in positing a competence motive that powered ego needs of effectance. Winnicott's (1949a) descriptions of the ordinary mother and her baby vividly portray the possibilities of joyful, progressive development in the context of a loving relationship. Wheelis's (1958) distinction between instrumental and institutional values and processes can be incorporated in our psychoanalytically-derived conceptualization of open and closed systems. Most important, the open system concept makes a place for the inclusion of creativity, love, collaboration, hope, mutuality, and cooperation in the treatment relationship.

Our concept of the two systems of self-esteem regulation is summarized in Table 1. It expands on our previous descriptions of a closed response to the challenges of each developmental phase (Novick & Novick, 1987, 1994, 1996a) and adds specifics of an alternative open system response. Further expansion of the chart would include challenges for each subphase of adulthood (Colarusso & Nemiroff, 1987). The table is useful in summarizing characteristics of different responses to developmental phase challenges at any point in development. Derivatives of conflicts around these phase challenges appear in clinical material at all ages, and the table may assist the clinician both in identifying the derivatives and in fashioning appropriate technical interventions.

Beyond the phase challenges listed would be the internal and external factors that can turn ordinary difficulties into traumata. Children faced with any of the myriad mischances of life may feel unable to manage without recourse to magical, omnipotent defenses against the helplessness and rage engendered by circumstances beyond their control or mastery. By deferred action, a later event or the developmental conflicts of a later stage may raise the earlier experience to traumatic intensity and evoke an omnipotent response (Novick & Novick, 1994, 2001a; Novick, J., 1999). Response to a trauma need not be based on an omnipotent defense. If the parent or child is helped to draw upon

TABLE 1. Two Systems of Self-Regulation

Phase challenge	Open, adaptive, competent response	Closed, omnipotent, sadomasochistic response
Mother during pregnancy Parental helplessness re. physical changes, intactness, and safety of baby.	Helplessness evokes parents' finding areas of realistic effectiveness and sources of support; Conscious planning to avoid repetition of own infantile experience.	Helplessness leads to parental fantasy of baby as controller, devourer, savior; Transference to baby from old relationships; externalization of devalued/feared/wished for aspects of self on to baby.
Infancy Infant's failure to evoke needed response; Transient parental loss of attunement.	Mismatch followed by repair. This is root of positive feelings of competence, effectance, and reality-based self-regard. Positive feelings instigate and represent effectance and basic object tie. Signs include predominance of positive affect, secure attachment, psychophysiological harmony.	Parent fails child, and infant is left in helpless rage, frustration, and traumatic overwhelming; turn away from reality and competence; reliance on magical controls; attachment through pain. Symptoms may include gaze aversion, failure to thrive, hairpulling, head-banging, biting.
Toddlerhood Exploration, independence, and assertion frustrated.	Child's aggression is absorbed in constancy of parental love; exploration and assertion protected and enjoyed; autonomy and independence a source of pride, with positive attachment strengthened at new level. Ambivalence can be tolerated with aggression increasingly separated from assertion. Anger and aggressive impulses a useful signal, calling into play ego capacities and realistic use of object. Signs include preponderance of joy, swift recovery from negative affects, capacity to accept help of others, to negotiate resolution of conflicts, concern for others.	Assertion defined as aggression, parents helpless to absorb aggression, modulate excitement; separation experienced as attack; wishes given stamp of reality–assertion becomes aggression becomes sadism; self-esteem derived from control of others; externalization by parents; identification with externalizing defense of parents. Symptoms may include rages, sleep disturbances, separation problems, attacking other children, interference with development of speech, toilet mastery, bodily control, mastery of feelings (tantrums, inconsolability).

Phase challenge	Open, adaptive, competent response	Closed, omnipotent, sadomasochistic response
Phallic-Oedipal Reality of gender and generational differences (exclusion from adult activities).	Turn to reality gratifications, internal sources of self-esteem. Development of autonomous superego with both affirming and prohibiting characteristics, open to reality corrections. Signs include curiosity in service of growing reality sense, development of independent friendships, capacity to use adults as resources.	Parental failure to protect from overwhelming experiences (primal scene, frightening films, TV, etc.). Child's response to trauma by sexualization, denial, and externalization. Parental collusion with child's fantasies promotes formation of omnipotent delusion; sadomasochistic fantasy substituted for superego, which is tyrannical, divorced from reality, unmodified by experience. Symptoms include persistence of earlier problems, inability to give up transitional object, bossiness and controlling behavior, provoking attack, obsessional rituals, bedwetting
Latency Negotiate rules, rewards, demands, and controls of external world.	Good feelings from image of self as competent, effective, capable of learning, playing, negotiating, socializing, controlling self, and changing. Signs include successful mastery of impulses, tolerance of ambivalence, development of complex relationships, capacity for pleasure in work.	Self-esteem based main y on fantasy control of others; real talents and capacities co-opted to maintain fantasy image of omnipotent self (entitlement, exception). Symptoms include persistence of earlier problems, intensification of obsessional rituals altering with wild "hyper" anxiety-driven behavior, lack of pleasure in real achievements, learning problems, bullying, victimization, inability to play, social isolation.
Adolescence Real changes in body, mind, and social expectations.	Ownership of mature sexual body; consolidation of gender identity, realistic self- and object-representations. Signs include pleasure in appearance and functioning of body, increase in capacity to parent self, constant relationships with peer and adults, pleasure in work.	Maintence of omniptent fantasies by means of increasingly desperate self-destructive actions. Symptoms include pathological use of the body (eating disorders, self-mutilation, suicide, substance abuse, pregnancy, repeated abortion, rapid repeat pregnancy, promiscuity), delinquency, depression, fragmentation of personality, low achievement, grandiosity, social isolation.

Jack Novick, PhD and Kerry Kelly Novick © 1997

open system, competent resources, the trauma can be mastered. This helps explain the mystery of children developing well despite traumatic beginnings, for example, the young concentration camp victims followed by Moskowitz (1983). We assume, however, that repeated use throughout development of an open system of conflict resolution, and hence of self-regulation, strengthens the child's capacity to deal with difficult experiences in a realistic, adaptive way.

Technical Applications

The conceptualization of two different types of conflict resolution, which are used by the individual in constructing characteristic modes of self-regulation, must make a demonstrable contribution to theory and clinical practice to be worth retaining. We would like to turn to technical applications of our conceptualization of two systems in the treatment of patients of all ages. We do not believe that our two-system model leads to any radical innovations in technique. In fact, we think that most experienced clinicians do much of what we will outline. But without a theoretical framework and vocabulary, they may be uncertain or unwilling to describe it.

In "The Ego and the Id," Freud said, ". . . analysis does not set out to make pathological reactions impossible, but to give the patient's ego *freedom* to decide one way or the other" (1923, p. 50n). Nearly fifty years later, Rangell (1982) reiterated that the goal of analysis is choice. Yet, in discussions in the literature and in clinical practice, our field seems to have lost sight of this simple goal or criterion for termination. Analysts have also neglected to elaborate on the implications of the idea of the ego's capacity to choose. First, this statement seems to refer to an ongoing possibility of choice throughout life, despite the persistent availability of pathology. Secondly, we should note that Freud referred to the *ego's* choice, not to the superego's moral alternatives. How can clinical work be directed to those aspects of the ego's functioning that are involved in choice? Finally, what can increase the freedom of choice? How does analysis contribute to such a process?

Two Systems and the Therapeutic Alliance

In papers on a revised concept of the therapeutic alliance (Novick & Novick 1996b, 1998), we have suggested that our developmentally based theory of the therapeutic alliance gives clinicians a road map for working with defensive omnipotent resistances. We suggested that the closed, omnipotent system is in the "borderland." In order to travel safely in such difficult and dangerous territory, the analyst needs to be supported by concepts that allow him to track the journey of the treatment. The tasks of the therapeutic alliance at each phase of treatment constitute such an aid. In the context of this article, it becomes apparent that the accomplishment of therapeutic alliance tasks at each phase of treatment is a manifestation of open or competent system functioning for both patient and analyst. There is a convergence between the concept of the therapeutic alliance tasks and the idea of two systems of self-regulation. Each contributes to the overarching treatment goal of restoring the patient to the path of progressive development, so that there is a real choice about how to proceed with life.

As we discuss the phases of treatment, we will not focus primarily on work directed to elucidating the closed, omnipotent system of self-esteem regulation. This we have described elsewhere (Novick & Novick, 1996a, 1996b, 1998). Here we will try to indicate some techniques designed to address conflicts over using the open system. These techniques, in turn, contribute to the possibility of a genuine choice for the patient. They also contribute to the *therapist's* conviction that there are alternatives, which maintains hope in the treatment. As we go through the phases of treatment we will look at the application of our ideas about the therapeutic alliance and two systems to work with children, adolescents, and adults. The general ideas apply to work with all ages, and each group can highlight particular aspects of our technical approach.

EVALUATION PHASE

In our work we tend to extend the evaluation longer than many other practitioners. This is partly due to our using the evaluation to discern and verbalize material related to open functioning. Open-system functioning is attuned to reality, so reality considerations are included in the evaluation. This is particularly evident in work with children and adolescents. A single-track theory of development can lead to technique that will minimize or ignore the role of parents, both in development and treatment of young people. We have written elsewhere in great detail about our assumption that work with parents is not only crucial to restoring child or adolescent patients to the path of progressive development (Novick & Novick, 2001b, in press), but it also includes restoration of the parent-child relationship and parental development in the phase of parenthood. Work with parents is directed toward moving them from closed-system to open-system functioning. Awareness of the two potential systems of self-regulation suggests that analysts should undertake a treatment only when they can find in themselves the potential for what Winnicott (1949b) called "objective love" of the patient. This involves recognition of the analyst's own potential for functioning in both open and closed systems and the search for elements in the patient that will aid the development of a strong therapeutic alliance. The analyst can use the evaluation period to discover in both adult and child patients, as well as in parents, unique individuals with strengths, courage, and capacities that are worthy of respect, genuine interest, and even admiration.

In relation to looking at the open, competent system of self-regulation in the patient at the time of evaluation, it is important to have a long enough period to discern areas of past and current functioning that point to achievements, talents, moments of pleasure and joy, and possibly even genuine satisfaction in the process of work and creativity. We seek to know where and when the patient experiences pleasure and whether it can be maintained. Often pointing out to the prospective patient his or her difficulties in experiencing ordinary pleasure or satisfaction provides a crucial initial motivation and defines an important shared goal of treatment. With parents it is important to get beyond their negative feelings for the child and find or renew respect and primary parental love.

BEGINNING PHASE

At the beginning of analysis with adults the therapist often has first to live through and empathize with the patient's conscious feelings of victimization and righteous anger. This is the patient's way of being with the analyst. Eventually, however, the positive aspects of the patient's construction should be verbalized. Adaptation is the operative idea, for the patient has used talents and skills to find the best solution possible, given childhood limitations and the overwhelming nature of external events. We start by verbalizing the need *all* children feel for attachment, protection, safety, control, predictability, affect regulation, and mastery of internal and external demands. The analyst can emphasize that these are legitimate needs, not only for all infants, but for everyone throughout life. For many patients, this is a revolutionary idea; making it explicit may open up new areas of conflict, especially around dependency needs.

In this context one can appreciate and verbalize the achievement of finding a way, *any* way, to regulate feelings in a situation where no other ways seemed possible. Validating past and current needs links the patient to reality and allows for extending beyond experiencing the analyst as a transference object to include the analyst's functions as auxiliary ego, an interpreter of reality (A. Freud, 1965), a transformative object (Bollas, 1987), a developmental object (Tahka, 1993; Hurry, 1998). Acknowledging the validity of self-regulation and self-esteem needs and appreciating the achievement of a construction, however pathological its current functioning, springs from an understanding of and leads to early inclusion of the potential for open, competent functioning.

We introduce here the idea that ego capacities can be co-opted by the closed, omnipotent system and that part of the analytic work will be to disentangle them. An omnipotent defensive solution can make use of the ego's perceptiveness and intelligence, and then the patient comes to associate these qualities with stereotyped magical, omnipotent thinking. Patients and analysts all grapple with the problem that patients may be very high-functioning, skilled, and successful in age-appropriate ways, and yet cannot retain good feelings about themselves. Momentary pleasure from triumph is swiftly followed by fear of exposure as a fraud, so that the individual needs to seek constant reassurance from external sources (Novick & Novick, 1996c).

This work is arduous, as the patient operates on the basis of his long-standing conviction that this is the only way to feel good. To the patient, this is so self-evident that it operates like procedural memory; in other words, it represents a systemically unconscious belief. Drawing joint attention to repetitions of this pattern in the treatment, the analyst can begin to delineate the distinction between alternative systems of self-regulation and lay the foundation for the idea that there are other ways to feel good about the self than the lifelong, repetitive, pain-seeking, defensive adaptations of the sadomasochistic, omnipotent system. This is highlighted in work with adults, but applies equally to work with children, adolescents, and parents. In work with parents, for example, it is important to show them how the child has come to depend on pathological closed-system adaptations. Parents are then less likely to respond to a child's misbehavior with punitive or sadistic aggression, and can be helped to offer the child alternatives. For instance, when a parent of an adolescent talks angrily about a youngster's antisocial behavior, we find it helpful to explain the co-opting of good ego functions like creativity, intelligence, ingenuity, leadership, and so forth.

Analysts can also be vulnerable to dissatisfaction with the achievement of ordinary good feelings in the work, seeking instead more dramatic anguish and deeper id derivatives (Busch, 1995, 1999). The patient who complains that therapy has not achieved anything can be helped to appreciate, only if the analyst also can, pleasure in being listened to and understood, in being able to come regularly, pride in participation, growing facility in expressing feelings, reflecting on events, and so forth. During the beginning phase, the therapist also has the opportunity to differentiate modes of self-regulation and sources of self-esteem and its regulation in him or herself. When we accept that we, too, strive to defend against helplessness and that our own self-esteem depends on feelings of safety, control, gratification, and predictability, then we can recognize our vulnerability to functioning within the closed, omnipotent system.

The excitement of being idealized, venerated, indispensable is highly seductive, and patients can be very practiced and subtle in titrating the amount of masochistic enthrallment necessary to hook the particular therapist. We are using the imagery of addiction, because being the object of a patient's enthralled submission is a rush to which a therapist can become addicted. The opposite experience can have a similar effect, as when the therapist experiences himself as able to contain, absorb, and tolerate more abuse and intense affect than any other therapist. Some clinical presentations can sound like the famous Monty Python skit, "Who had the worst childhood." The intense excitement and pleasure of sadomasochism is one among many reasons for clinging to omnipotent functioning, whether by patient or analyst (Coen, 1992; Novick & Novick, 1996a, 1996b).

As much as the analyst inevitably engages with and is transiently drawn into the patient's sadomasochistic functioning, an alternative can be sought in the open, reality-oriented, competent system of self-regulation. To that end we notice and comment on, with conviction, those moments, past and present, in the patient's life, in and out of the treatment, that appear to have characteristics of the open system. We focus on the range of relatively quieter, reality-based emotions that often get swamped by the overwhelming and intense affects associated with the magical functioning of the closed system. Panicky or overexcited children, moody or withdrawn adolescents, and miserable adults have come to depend on their intense affective states. Patients may experience themselves as constantly under threat of being flooded by overwhelming feelings of rage, despair, emptiness, elation, excitement, and so forth. They find it hard to notice or appreciate feelings of annoyance, contentment, peace, satisfaction, creative joy, harmonious integration, mutuality, and affection. The work of Tomkins (1991, 1992) and others has made clear the availability of the full range of affects from birth. Thus we can conclude that difficulties in experiencing and maintaining *all* one's feelings involve defensive adaptations that have been achieved in the course of development. These characteristic ways of dealing with inner and outer experience, the ways individuals come to regulate their feelings, must be accessed and addressed in treatment of patients of all ages (Holinger, 1998).

Material comes in words, paraverbal functioning, actions, and enactments by patient and analyst in the context of the therapeutic relationship. The two-system framework enables us to appreciate and reaffirm the centrality of verbal communication in development and analytic treatment. The current shift in psychoanalytic thinking to emphasis on early object relations has led to a focus on what is called the preverbal period and, with that, a diminution of the importance accorded to words. Infant research on the role of touch (Brazelton & Cramer, 1991), vision and affect mirroring (Stern, 1985), and neurobiological emphasis on the preverbal, affect-linked development of the suborbital regions of the right hemisphere (Schore, 1994, 1997) has reinforced the view that words are a late addition to other modalities of interaction. What is thereby neglected is that words are a major carrier of maternal affect and attachment, even from pregnancy. In our work with infants and toddlers we encourage parents to talk, explain, and sing to their children, and we note with them the very early onset of receptive language. Putting feelings into words for toddlers is a major method of fostering internalization of self-control, mastery, and symbol formation, and hence of promoting the development of an open system of self-regulation (A. Katan, 1961; K.K. Novick, 1986; Segal, 1998).

Words are also important in the development and operation of a closed, omnipotent system, where they can be used to abuse, control others, maintain magical beliefs, and avoid reality. Verbalization by the analyst in the beginning phase focuses joint attention on the patient's use of words to engage with or avoid reality. It increases the patient's self-observing skills, which promotes the transition into the middle phase of analysis. Even very small children can be helped to appreciate the power of words in creating an adaptive alternative to a magical solution. In this way, young children can be explicitly enlisted in the work of the analysis, entering into an open-system, collaborative relationship within the therapeutic alliance.

MIDDLE PHASE

The long middle phase of analysis is where the analyst and patient address issues about the patient's mind–how it works, and how it joins with other minds, particularly the therapist's, in working together toward a goal. Without a focus on and shift to an interest in the patient's mind and how it engages with reality, creates solutions to conflict, and maintains self-esteem, the therapy can stalemate.

In previous work, we have emphasized the omnipotent, sadomasochistic solution as a defense that patients will do anything to protect, including self-injury or suicide. Without the open competent system as a viable alternative, patients have little incentive to change the adaptation they have clung to, perhaps from earliest childhood. Patients usually come for help because omnipotent solutions are not working well enough. They then press to cast the therapist as another omnipotent figure they can control by sadomasochistic means.

One of the goals of the middle phase is to help the patient experience an alternative in the affects associated with the open competent system of self-regulation. These affects encompass:

- *attachment* through objective love, rather than through fantasies of control,
- the use of affects such as anger, anxiety, or excitement as *signals* for reality engagement rather than means to overwhelm and control the object,
- the lower-keyed, but sustained and dependable, *pleasure* of effective work together with the analyst and alone, and
- joy in the *creative* use of one's mind, rather than the rush of excited apparent fulfillment of a wish for omnipotence.

We have noted that Freud (1914) described analysis as providing a playground in which the transference can be allowed to expand in complete freedom (Novick & Novick, 2000). With adult patients locked in sadomasochistic solutions, we have found that their childhoods were marked by an inability to play. Child patients who are unable to play are often denying the distinction between real and pretend. A hallmark of open-system functioning is the capacity to encompass and address the realities of one's own feelings and impulses, relationships, and the outside world. A major goal of the middle phase, highlighted by work with children, is movement into open-system pleasure in play.

We point out these aspects of competent open-system functioning as they arise in child or adult patients. This is not done by education or exhortation, but by consistent focus on how the open system functions effectively to resolve conflicts, thereby sustaining self-esteem, and on the interferences that arise to block this process. As we do this, it becomes apparent that the patient feels threatened by this work, for the closed system is bolstered by the conviction that there is no alternative to omnipotence but helplessness and annihilation. As the patient becomes aware that there are other and more sustainable ways to maintain good feelings, an *internal conflict* develops between the two modes of self-esteem regulation, the old, closed omnipotent system and the newly-rediscovered system of open, competent functioning. With this internal change, there is increased motivation for change and additional leverage to address the range of superego pathology, with its underpinnings of clinging to omnipotent beliefs.

Treatment usually contains derivatives of the patient's past responses to the developmental phase challenges of exploratory impulses, reality, and the demands of work, as described in Table 1. First, the analyst has the task of understanding and assessing the nature of the patient's past and current adaptations or compromise formations, that is, whether the response relates to open or closed system functioning. Second is the question of choice of intervention.

The idea of two systems of conflict resolution and self-regulation can lead to a conceptualization of *two kinds of technique,* one that elucidates closed-system functioning, another that enhances open-system functioning. Technical interventions have differing impacts on phenomena relating to the two systems. Closed-system phenomena require the classical approach of transference and resistance analysis, with the aim of putting the patient in the active center of his pathology. But defense and transference interpretations of open-system functioning can pathologize and drive away competence. Mirroring, empathy, reconstruction, validation, support, and developmental education, to list but a few, link open-system phenomena with the analyst's functions beyond serving only as a transference object. These techniques applied to closed-system functioning, however, may be, at best, a palliative waste of time and, at worst, may serve to reinforce a passive, helpless, victimized stance on the part of the patient. Thus, we have to think in terms of expanded and alternative technical options to encompass the open-system dimensions of our patients' personalities and the opportunities of the treatment situation.

Parents of children and adolescents also seek help when their solutions to problems, often pathological, have failed. Because there has been no coherent model for parent work in child treatments, many child treatments never get started, and those that do often back away from parent work in the middle phase. We suggest that the middle phase brings with it a series of important tasks in the alliance with parents. Engagement with these tasks can consolidate the adult in the phase of parenthood and open-system functioning, allow for dealing with subtle parental resistances that would otherwise stalemate the child's treatment, and help ensure that the therapy will proceed to a useful termination with continued positive growth beyond the end of treatment.

By the middle of a treatment, parents who have worked consistently with the child or adolescent's therapist through the earlier phases have addressed their extreme feelings of failure and transformed their guilt into usable concern. They have begun to regain a sense of competence as parents, and can begin to see their children as separate from themselves, which allows for starting to master the tasks of psychological separation from the child, allowing the child patient to be with another adult and to begin to form a significant relationship.

Allowing for psychological separation, individuation, and autonomy is the primary therapeutic alliance task for parents during the middle phase, accomplished by working collaboratively with the therapist. But this also brings with it specific anxieties, conflicts, and defenses in the parents, which can give rise to resistances, stalemates, and premature termination. At this point in the treatment of children, the analyst works to help parents move toward the possibility of more open-system functioning. We have many techniques available for this work. There are *educative* interventions, such as explaining the difference between an authoritarian stance, in which a parent arbitrarily exercises the power of his age and strength, and an authoritative one, in which he uses his knowledge to explain and teach the child about the situation. *Support* and *validation* are central needs of parents that therapists meet by empathic *verbalization* of feelings, and *tracking* of emerging open-system functioning, as when a parent shows pleasure in the child. *Modeling* different ways to think about the child's behavior and feelings, and to talk with the child, provides parents with powerful examples of effective relating. *Facilitating* parents' efforts to find more adaptive ways to respond to and interact with the child involves fostering realistic mutual identifications in place of relationships based on externalizations.

Child and adolescent therapists have always used these techniques with parents, but have suffered from the lack of a conceptual framework and, therefore, a sense of permission to be explicit about it. Even more vexing and little discussed is the substantive therapeutic dimension of parent work. Despite the ubiquity of therapeutic interventions with parents in practice, child analysts and therapists have no coherent theoretical model to encompass this work. We suggest that the concepts of two systems, the therapeutic alliance tasks, and the treatment goals of parental restoration to the path of progressive adult development within the context of their child's or adolescent's treatment provide the beginning of such a model.

This brings us then to the application of the whole repertoire of clinical techniques in parent work. In order to address both closed- and open-system functioning in parents of child patients, we need to be able to use both kinds of techniques discussed above. The two-systems framework gives us theoretical support in using classical technique for parental closed-system functioning, and the other interventions to foster open-system capacities.

Work in the middle phase can be long, painful, and often frustrating for the analyst, as the patient clings to the closed system and tries to provoke the therapist to act in such a way as to justify what Steiner (1993) has called a "psychic retreat." We have pointed out that an omnipotent delusion cannot be created or maintained without the participation of the external world (Novick & Novick, 1996a). The analyst's feelings and conscious and unconscious responses are part of the patient's external reality. Patients may retreat from the risks of realistic functioning for their own internal reasons, but if this reaction is too frequent or too prolonged, analysts should examine themselves to see if they are contributing to the difficulty. The analyst may be reacting to the patient's new pleasure and creativity with envy; he/she may be reacting to the patient's growing self-analytic competence with feelings of rejection, uselessness, or loss; the thought of impending termination may evoke worries ranging from loss of income to fears of abandonment and depression. If these feelings are not worked through by analysts, patients may feel, perhaps in repetition of earlier childhood experiences, unable to sustain a sense of "true self" (Winnicott, 1960). The true self encompasses the capacities of the open system, while a "false self " is part of a defensive wish for an omnipotent capacity to care for and control a depressed or unavailable or abusive or lost parent. If the analyst can work through his own psychic retreat from conflicts about the patient's progression, he will be available to help the patient consolidate the possibility of an open system of self-esteem regulation and move forward from the static timelessness of omnipotent beliefs into the pretermination phase of treatment.

PRETERMINATION PHASE

The pretermination phase is seldom written about in the psychoanalytic literature, and it is rarely conceptualized as having its own specific features, tasks, anxieties, or conflicts. We have described the importance of defining a pretermination phase of treatment in which both patient and analyst can explore whether they are ready to enter into and make maximum use of the termination period. Criteria for *starting* a termination phase differ significantly from the criteria used at the end of treatment to assess the relative success of the work (Novick, 1982, 1988; Novick & Novick, 1996b). Making the judgment tends to be intuitive, with criteria based on a sense of movement or momentum, that is, a sense that progressive development is reinstated. In patients of all ages we note an increase in pleasure, joy, creativity, and autonomous, independent use of capacities, all hallmarks of open-system functioning. Either the patient, the analyst, or both begin to think that an ending might be possible. These criteria derive from the idea of the overarching child analytic goal of restoration to the path of progressive development; we have extended the goal to encompass adult treatment and work with parents of child and adolescent patients (A. Freud, 1965; Novick, 1990; Novick & Novick, 1996b, 2001b).

Without setting a date, the therapist and patient discuss what will be involved, with the analyst describing in general terms how this part of the work can be structured and what can be accomplished. The analyst emphasizes the termination period as one of hard work that can bring great benefits. It is a time of consolidating therapeutic gains and internalizing the accomplishment of the therapeutic alliance tasks in the context of saying goodbye. This description prompts a joint assessment of work accomplished, work remaining, and a catalogue of capacities that will be called upon to do the work of termination. During the pretermination phase, both analyst and patient work to consolidate open-system functioning and to address remaining wishes and beliefs that protect the closed, omnipotent system. This is accomplished by mastery of the therapeutic alliance tasks for the patient, whether child or adult, for the analyst, and for the significant other or parents of the patient. The idea of extending therapeutic criteria to parents is a major application of the two-systems framework, as it allows for concrete goals of movement from closed- to open-system functioning in the parent-child relationship in the context of child and adolescent treatments.

Considering termination implies assessment of results, which often reveals a search for perfection. Perfection is a magical, omnipotent ideal that serves to perpetuate sadomasochistic misery and disappointment in self and others, often defensively maintained to protect against rage at the shortcomings of a damaged or inadequate parent. Nearing the end of treatment both patient and analyst have the opportunity to face the imperfections of the results. It can be helpful to hold on to the awareness that perfection constitutes a hostile, unrealistic demand on self and others, and thus has no place in an open, creative system, with its integration of good-enough functioning and realistic standards. As we illustrate in our study of interferences with creativity and performance (Novick & Novick, 1996c), the creative artist experiences joy in the process rather than expectation of a perfect product. A dual-track developmental conception, such as that of two systems of self-regulation, is related to the emphasis found in Gedo (1996) and Greenacre (1957) on the centrality of the artist's sense of competence, rather than the Romantic notion of the need to suffer. The inclusion of the open system as a focus of attention through the middle phase has brought the patient's conflicts over creativity to the center of the analytic work. By the pretermination phase, the patient has come to realize that creativity, and its attendant joy, are dependably rooted in competence and are interfered with by omnipotent functioning. For the analyst, excessive therapeutic ambition can represent an omnipotent, perfectionistic interference with his/her own competence and creativity. It is a form of "soul blindness" (Wurmser, 1994, 1996; Novick & Novick, in press), wherein analysts deny the true nature and characteristics of the patient in favor of their own image.

A related conceptualization, enshrined in single-track psychoanalytic models of development, is that omnipotent convictions are a leftover of childhood that must be relinquished, mourned, and then, like a dead person, be gone forever. Here the idea of two systems as potential responses present in everyone *throughout development* has important application. Common observation, for instance, of people faced with serious illness, or death, or disaster, that is, situations of realistic helplessness, indicates that many reach for an omnipotent, magical response, as in attempts at quack remedies, mystical practices, or sudden conversions to religion. These may be individuals who otherwise function very well; there is no guarantee that the best-analyzed patient will not also be prone under certain circumstances to attempts at self-regulation and conflict resolution by recourse to defensive, sadomasochistic, omnipotent beliefs.

Another is the idea that one can operate in both systems at the same time: that one can be omnipotent, sadomasochistic and "soul blind," while being caring, loving and sensitive to others. We have identified the belief that one need not choose, that one can deny the incompatibility of irreconcilable systems, as the *adolescent* developmental contribution to the formation of a closed, omnipotent system (Novick & Novick, 1996b). As the analysis nears the end, both analyst and patient have to confront the "ineluctable reality of existence" (James Joyce, 1916, p. 253). As noted earlier, the goal of analysis is the possibility of choice. But before this can be truly faced and accepted during the termination phase, some pretermination work can usefully be done on the denial of the necessity to choose between the two systems of self-regulation.

A termination phase cannot be started without work during pretermination on the patient's objective or realistic love for the analyst (Novick & Novick, 1997, 1998). Here we would emphasize that objective love, in contrast to sadomasochistic enthrallment, is part of an open system of functioning. We have detailed elsewhere (Novick & Novick, 2000) how objective love grows through the phases of treatment. By the termination phase, it is important for a true leave-taking that analyst and patient love each other. Otherwise, termination can be a further expression of hostile dominance and submission, or angry abandonment and rejection.

It is important for the analyst to acknowledge internally and explicitly that it is not only with the child or adolescent patient that there is an important attachment; equally, parents of child patients and the therapist have a deep and significant bond. Saying goodbye to each other will evoke the complex feelings, anxieties and defenses associated with separation and loss. We say to parents that we adults need a goodbye time just as much as the child does.

The open system, by definition, is open to experience and to objective love, and, therefore, in touch with reality; so fantasies can be monitored, used or enjoyed *as fantasies,* but not believed or acted upon. Everyone has transient *wishes* for omnipotence when faced with the helplessness of frustrations or thwarting, but we learn the illusory nature of such wishes. In the open system, analysts learn to differentiate between omnipotent therapeutic wishes and realistic possibilities.

TERMINATION PHASE

Setting the termination date together creates a real life stressor, that of separation. Both patient and analyst may respond with either omnipotent sadomasochistic or competent solutions. The model of two systems is helpful in this arena. The open and closed responses to the phase challenges of the phallic-oedipal phase, latency and adolescence, summarized in Table 1, can aid the therapist in assessing changes and keeping in mind open-system, competent, alternative responses to the stresses of ending treatment. With children and parents we take up the omnipotent belief that life can be trouble-free, and that, therefore, treatment should ensure a future smooth passage by introducing the idea that what they and their child have developed in treatment is "emotional muscle," a tolerance for ordinary stresses and strains.

Termination is usually thought of as a time of mourning, but it has not been made explicit in the literature what or who is being mourned, or how this relates to sadness, depression, or the ability to choose. Analysts tend to speak about mourning the loss of a person, a phase of life, or a fantasy. In a single-track psychoanalytic theory of development, much is made of how "normal" omnipotence has to be mourned and then relinquished. With a dual-track, two-system model, we can posit that a belief is never mourned or gone, but rather it is set aside. Sadomasochism and omnipotent beliefs remain a potential response, but the work has helped the patient find competent alternatives and so transform a pathological belief into a wish or fantasy, a delusion into an illusion. Setting aside organizing convictions may be painful, but the pain may be likened to the withdrawal from an addictive substance. It is a process different from mourning, in that there is no subsequent internalization and identification. In the closed, omnipotent system, separation represents loss of control of the object and of feelings, and, therefore, a depressive response in defense against rage and helplessness may be an expected reaction when the patient reverts to attempts at omnipotent control.

The crucial issue is that of sadness. Sadness is present only when there is love, when there is a genuine loss. Thus sadness exists in the realm of the open system, with its connection to real experience. We can only mourn the loss of someone we love, and, through the mourning, internalize aspects of the person and qualities of the relationship. What is truly mourned by child and adult patients and their parents, and the analyst, at termination is the unique working and loving relationship that has enhanced each person (Kantrowitz, 1997) and will now persist internally as they separate. What each can internalize and identify with is a greater understanding of the realistic interdependence and independence to be found in a mutually respectful relationship of autonomous individuals.

The role of the analyst during the termination phase is not to be a cheerleader for either system, not to take sides in the patient's or the parents' conflict, although it may be clear that our choice for ourselves is the open system. Our role is to keep the fact of ego choice open to the patient. First, we work on our own unconscious wishes to keep the patient enmeshed in a sadomasochistic power relationship. Second, we interpret the patient's reversion to closed, omnipotent-system reality distortions, secret destruction of genuine appreciation and love, or co-opting of competent aspects of ego functioning in an attempt to protect and maintain a delusion of omnipotence.

CONCLUSIONS

We have tried in this article to begin to describe the utility of a dual-track psychoanalytic model of development that encompasses two kinds of solutions to conflicts and systems of self-regulation. Such a conceptualization allows for inclusion of normality and pathology, internal and external reality, wishes, fantasies and beliefs, and earlier and later determinants of pathology in psychoanalysis as a general psychology. The two-systems approach allows us to make crucial distinctions within important psychoanalytic concepts that otherwise tend to be blurred. For example, idealization, sexuality, aggression, dependence, superego, regression, sublimation, to name but a few, merit further examination.

For example, in our application of two-systems concepts to creating a conceptual framework for parent work in child treatments, we elucidated a significant distinction between guilt and remorse:

> Remorse is a feeling that accompanies open-system functioning, in that it recognizes the reality of our helplessness to undo the past. Guilt, on the other hand, includes an omnipotent assumption of responsibility and denial of the reality of time. With a setting aside of the omnipotent quality of the feeling of guilt, a person is left with remorse. With remorse, reparation becomes possible. In a family context of the reality of sins of omission or commission in the past, reparation can be considered in terms of what can actually be done currently. Despite the limitations of reality, parents can be helped to take a series of reparative steps. First there has to be an acknowledgement to the child of past wrongdoing. For instance, we can help a parent to recognize that even being a passive bystander while someone else was abusive allowed the abuse to occur. A further reparative step that the analyst can encourage is parental awareness of the continuing impact in the present of past events and sensitivity to related current difficulties. Then parents can do something ameliorative in the present. (Novick & Novick, in press)

This distinction, here applied to parents, holds equally with individual patients of any age, and thus the two-systems base allows for far-reaching revision of clinical and technical understanding. In relation to technique, the two-systems idea expands the analyst's repertoire and enhances the ego of the patient. This model integrates many technical approaches, which otherwise may appear antagonistic or have been prematurely discarded from the analyst's repertoire of interventions. A classical "one-person" focus on the patient's defenses, conflicts and resistances may hereby be combined with a "two-person" focus on the therapeutic relationship and the forms of interaction between analyst and patients. Individual work with children and adolescents can then include intensive work with parents.

The two-system formulation leads to delineating two kinds of technique, one that elucidates closed-system functioning, the other that enhances open-system functioning. Expanding our repertoire of interventions is an important benefit of this rethinking of a psychoanalytic developmental model.

Convergence and integration of a variety of approaches takes place in practical terms through the application of the framework of our revised theory of the therapeutic alliance, with its phase-specific tasks for each party to a treatment. By the end of analysis, the mastery of therapeutic alliance tasks contributes to movement out of closed-system functioning to open-system functioning. The mourning process of the termination phase allows children, adolescents, adults, and parents to internalize and consolidate a loving, trusting, and mutually enhancing relation with the self and others. The ego functions freed for use in the therapeutic alliance become available for the choice of creative living and self-analysis when necessary.

REFERENCES

Anthony, J. and Cohler, B. (1987). *The Invulnerable Child*. New York and London: Guilford.

Bakhtin, M. (1981). *The Dialogic Imagination: Four Essays of M.M. Bakhtin*. C. Emerson and M. Holquist, trans. Austin: University of Texas.

Bollas, C. (1987). *The Shadow of the Object: Psychoanalysis of the Unthought Known*. London: Free Association Press.

Bowlby, J. (1969). *Attachment and Loss, Vol. 1 Attachment*. New York: Hogarth Press.

———(1973). *Attachment and Loss, Vol. 2 Separation: Anxiety and Anger*. New York: Basic Books.

———(1980). *Attachment and Loss, Vol. 3 Sadness and Depression*. London: Hogarth Press.

Brazelton, T.B. and Cramer, B.G. (1991). *The Earliest Relationship*. London: Karnac.

Busch, F. (1995). *The Ego at the Center of Clinical Technique*. Northvale, NJ: Jason Aronson.

———(1999). *Rethinking Clinical Technique*. Northvale, NJ: Jason Aronson, Inc.

Cicchetti, D. and Rogosch, F. (1996). Equifinality and multifinality in developmental psychopathology. *Development and Psychopathology* 8: 597-600.

Coen, S. (1992). *The Misuse of Persons: Analyzing Pathological Dependency*. Hillsdale, NJ: The Analytic Press.

Colarusso, C.A. and Nemiroff, R.A. (1987). *Adult Development*. New York: Plenum Press.

Emde, R. (1988). The Interpersonal World of the Infant: A View from Psychoanalysis and Developmental Psychology. *Journal of the American Psychoanalytic Association* 36: 228.

Erikson, E. (1950). *Childhood and Society*. New York: Norton

Fraiberg, S. (1982). Pathological defense in infancy. *Psychoanalytic Quarterly* 51: 612-635.

Freud, A. (1954). Discussion of the "widening scope of analysis." *Collected Writings of Anna Freud*, 4: 356-376.

———(1965). Normality and Pathology in Childhood. *Collected Writings of Anna Freud* 6: 3-273. New York: International Universities Press.

Freud, S.(1895). Studies in hysteria. *Standard Edition of the Complete Psychological Works of Sigmund Freud* (S.E.) 2: 3-335.

———(1913). On beginning the treatment (Further recommendations on the technique of psycho-analysis I). S.E. 12:123-144.

———(1914). Remembering, repeating and working through. S.E. 12: 147-156.

———(1915). Instincts and their vicissitudes. S.E.14: 117-140.

———(1916). Some character-types met with in psychoanalytic work. S.E. 14: 311-336.

———(1920). Beyond the pleasure principle. S.E. 18: 3-64.

———(1923). The ego and the id. S.E. 19: 3-66.

———(1940 [1938]). An outline of psychoanalysis. S.E. 23: 141-207.

Friedman, L. (1999). Why is reality a troubling concept? *Journal of the American Psychoanalytic Association* 47: 401-425.

Gedo, J. (1996). *The Artist and the Emotional World: Creativity and Personality*. New York: Columbia University Press.

Gillette, E. (1992). Psychoanalysis' resistance to new ideas. Journal of the American Psychoanalytic Association 40: 1232-1235.

Greenacre, P. (1957). The childhood of the artist. *Emotional Growth* 2: 479-504.

Grotstein, J. (1986). The psychology of powerlessness: disorders of self-regulation and interactional regulation as a newer paradigm for psychopathology. *Psychoanalytic Inquiry* 6: 93-118.

———(1994). Foreword to: *Affect Regulation and the Origin of the Self*, by Allan N. Schore. Hillsdale, NJ: Lawrence Erlbaum Associates. pp. xxi-xxviii.

Hartmann, H. (1939). *Ego Psychology and the Problem of Adaptation*. New York: International Universities Press (1958).

Holinger, P.C. (1998). Early intervention and prevention in psychoanalysis and psychiatry: Toward a "usable" affect theory. Unpublished manuscript.

Hurry, A. (1998). Psychoanalysis and developmental therapy. In: *Psychoanalysis and developmental therapy*, ed. A. Hurry. London: Karnac Books. pp. 32-73.

Joyce, J. (1916). *Portrait of the Artist as a Young Man*. New York: Penguin Books.

Kagan, J. (1996). Three pleasing ideas. *American Psychologist* 51: 901-907.

Kantrowitz, J. (1997). *The Patient's Impact on the Analyst*. New York: The Analytic Press.

Katan, A. (1961). Some thoughts about the role of verbalization in early childhood. *Psychoanalytic Study of the Child* 16: 184-188. New York: International Universities Press.

Krystal, H. (1978). Trauma and affects. *Psychoanalytic Study of the Child* 33: 81-116. New Haven: Yale University Press.

Levin, C. (1994). Containing the container: The structure of narcissistic fantasy and the problem of "primary undifferentation." Unpublished manuscript.

Lichtenberg, J. (1989). *Psychoanalysis and Motivation*. Hillsdale, NJ : Analytic Press.

Lichtenberg, J., Lachmann, F., and Fosshage, J. (1992). *Self and Motivational Systems: Toward A Theory of Technique*. Hillsdale, NJ: Analytic Press.

—————(1996). *The Clinical Exchange: Techniques Derived from Self and Motivational Systems*. Hillsdale, NJ: Analytic Press.

Mayr, E. (1988). *Toward a New Philosophy of Biology*. Cambridge, MA: Harvard University Press.

Moskowitz, S. (1983). *Love Despite Hate*. New York: Schocken.

Nesse, R.M. and Berridge, K.C. (1997). Psychoactive drug use in evolutionary perspective. *Science* 278: 63-66.

Novick, J. (1982). Termination: Themes and issues. *Psychoanalytic Inquiry* 2: 329-365.

—————(1988). Timing of termination. *International Review of Psychoanalysis* 69: 307-318.

—————(1990). Comments on termination in child, adolescent, and adult analysis. *Psychoanalytic Study of the Child* 45: 419-436.

—————(1999). Deferred action and recovered memory: The Transformation of memory in the reality of adolescence. *Child Analysis* 10: 65-93.

Novick, J. and Novick, K.K. (1972). Beating fantasies in children. *International Journal of Psycho-Analysis* 53: 237-242.

—————(1991). Some comments on masochism and the delusion of omnipotence from a developmental perspective. *Journal of the American Psychoanalytic Association* 39: 307-321.

—————(1996a). A developmental perspective on omnipotence. *Journal of Clinical Psychoanalysis* 5: 129-173.

—————(1996b). *Fearful Symmetry*. Northvale, NJ: Jason Aronson.

—————(in press). Soul blindness: A child must be seen to be heard. In: *Divorce and Custody: Contemporary Developmental Psychoanalytic Perspectives*. Ed: L. Gunsberg and P. Hymowitz. Washington, D.C.: American Psychological Association Books. Ch. 8 (in press).

—————(2000). Love in the therapeutic alliance. *Journal of the American Psychoanalytic Association* 48: 189-218.

—————(2001a). Trauma and deferred action in the reality of adolescence. *American Journal of Psychoanalysis* 61: 43-61.

—————(2001b). Parent work in analysis: Children, adolescents and adults. Part one: The evaluation phase. *Journal of Infant, Child, and Adolescent Psychotherapy* 1: 55-77.

—————(in press). Parent work in analysis: Children, adolescents, and adults. Part three: Middle and pretermination phases. *Journal of Infant, Child, and Adolescent Psychotherapy*.

Novick, K.K. (1986). Talking with toddlers. *Psychoanalytic Study of the Child* 41: 277-286.

Novick, K.K. and Novick, J. (1987). The essence of masochism. *Psychoanalytic Study of the Child* 42: 353-384. New Haven: Yale University Press.

————(1994). Postoedipal transformations: Latency, adolescence, and pathogenesis. *Journal of the American Psychoanalytic Association* 42:143-170.

————(1996c). I won't dance: A psychoanalytic approach to interferences with performance. Unpublished manuscript.

————(1998). An application of the concept of the therapeutic alliance to sadomasochistic pathology. *Journal of the American Psychoanalytic Association* 46: 813-846.

————(in press). Parent work in analysis: Children, adolescents and adults. Part two: Recommendation, beginning and middle phases of treatment. *Journal of Infant, Child, and Adolescent Psychotherapy.*

————(in press). Parent work in analysis: Children, adolescents and adults. Part four: Termination and post-termination phases. *Journal of Infant, Child, and Adolescent Psychotherapy.*

Peterfreund, E. (1978). Some critical comments on psychoanalytic conceptualizations in infancy. *International Journal of Psycho-Analysis* 59: 427-441.

Peterson, C. (2000). The future of optimism. *American Psychologist* 55: 44-55.

Rangell, L. (1982). Some thoughts on termination. *Psychoanalytic Inquiry* 2: 367-392.

Rapaport, D. and Gill, M.M. (1959). The points of view and assumptions of metapsychology. In: *The Collected Papers of David Rapaport*, ed. M Gill. New York: Basic Books. pp. 795-811.

Reich, A. (1951). Normal and pathological forms of self-esteem regulation. *Psychoanalytic Study of the Child*. 15: 215-232.

Renik, O. (1998). Getting real in analysis. *Psychoanalytic Quarterly* 67: 566-593.

Schafer, R. (1968). *Aspects of Internalization*. New York: International Universities Press.

Schore, A.N. (1994). *Affect Regulation and the Origins of the Self: The Neurobiology of Emotional Development*. Hillsdale, NJ: Lawrence Erlbaum.

————(1997). Interdisciplinary developmental research as a source of clinical models. In: *The Neurobiological and Developmental Basis for Psychotherapeutic Intervention*. Northvale, NJ: Jason Aronson. pp. 1-71.

Segal, H. (1998). "The importance of symbol-formation in the development of the ego"–in context. *Journal of Child Psychotherapy* 24: 349-357.

Seligman, M., Schulman, P., De Rubeis, R., and Hollon, S. (1999). The prevention of depression and anxiety. *Prevention and Treatment* 2: article 8.

Silverman, D.K. (1981). Some proposed modifications of psychoanalytic theories of early childhood development. In: J. Maslin, (ed.): *Empirical Studies of Psychoanalytic Theories*, vol. 2. Hillsdale, NJ: Analytic Press. pp. 49-71.

Sofsky, W. (1997). *The Order of Terror: The Concentration Camp*. Princeton, NJ: Princeton University Press.

Solomon, J. and George, C. (1999). *Attachment Disorganization*. New York: Guilford Press.

Sroufe, L.A. (1996). *Emotional Development*. New York: Cambridge University Press.

Steiner, J. (1993). *Psychic Retreats*. London: Routledge.

Stern, D. (1985). *The Interpersonal World of the Infant*. New York: Basic Books.

Tahka, V. (1993). *Mind and Its Treatment: A Psychoanalytic Approach*. Madison, CT: Int. Univ. Press.

Tomkins, S.S. (1991). *Affect Imagery Consciousness. Volume III. The Negative Affects: Anger and Fear*. New York: Springer.

————(1992). *Affect Imagery Consciousness. Volume IV. Cognition: Duplication and Transformation of Information*. New York: Springer.

Tustin, F. (1994). The perpetuation of an error. *Journal of Child Psychotherapy* 20: 3-23.

von Bertalanffy, L. (1968). *General Systems Theory*. New York: Braziller.

Vygotsky, L. (1986[1934]). *Thought and Language*. Translated and edited: A. Kozulin. Cambridge, MA: The MIT Press.

Weiss, J. (1993). *How Psychotherapy Works: Process and Technique*. New York: Guilford Press.

————(1998). Bondage fantasies and beating fantasies. *Psychoanalytic Quarterly* 67: 626-644.

Werner, E.E. and Smith, R.L. (1982). *Vulnerable But Invincible*. New York: Morrow-Hill.

Wheelis, A. (1958). *The Quest for Identity*. New York: W.W. Norton and Co.

White, R.W. (1959). Motivation reconsidered: The concept of competence. *Psychological Review*, vol. 66, 5: 297-333.

Winnicott, D.W. (1949a). The ordinary devoted mother and her baby. In: *The Child, the Family, and the Outside World*. Middlesex, England: Penguin Books. 1964, pp. 15-18.

————(1949b). Hate in the countertransference. Reprinted in: *In One's Bones: The Clinical Genius of Winnicott*. Ed. D. Goldman. Northvale, NJ: Jason Aronson. pp. 15-24.

————(1960). Ego distortion in terms of true and false self. In: *The Maturational Processes and the Facilitating Environment*. London: Hogarth Press. pp. 140-152.

Wurmser, L. (1994). A time of questioning: The severely disturbed patient within classical analysis. *The Annual of Psychoanalysis*, ed. J.A.Winer. Chicago Institute for Psychoanalysis. pp. 173-207.

————(1996). Trauma, inner conflict, and the vicious cycles of repetition. *Scandinavian Psychoanalytic Review* 19: 17-45.

————(1998). "Magical Transformation" and "Tragic Transformation": Comments to Tolstoy's Novel *Resurrection*. Unpublished manuscript.

————(1999). Traumatic shame, shame-guilt conflicts and magic transformation. Panel at Meetings of the American Psychoanalytic Association, Washington, D.C. May 1999.

A Two-Systems Approach to the Treatment of a Disturbed Adolescent

Howard D. Lerner

SUMMARY. This article is based upon the rich conceptual and technical framework for understanding and treating sadomasochistic psychopathology presented by the Novicks (this volume). Specifically, the Novicks' "two-systems" approach to self-regulation is applied to the treatment of a disturbed adolescent boy. Examples of "open" and "closed" functioning are presented as well as the role of underlying defensive omnipotent beliefs and fantasies. The clinical utility of this model, the pivotal role of the therapeutic alliance, and the significance of clinical work with the family through all stages of the treatment process are illustrated. *[Article copies available for a fee from The Haworth Document Delivery Service: 1-800-342-9678. E-mail address: <getinfo@haworthpressinc.com> Website: <http://www.HaworthPress.com> © 2001 by The Haworth Press, Inc. All rights reserved.]*

KEYWORDS. Sadomasochism, omnipotent, therapeutic alliance

Anna Freud (1958) was one of the first to point out that the very developmental position of the adolescent conflicts with fundamental aspects of the

Howard D. Lerner, PhD, ABPP, is Assistant Clinical Professor of Psychology in the Department of Psychiatry, University of Michigan Medical School.

Address correspondence to: Howard D. Lerner, PhD, 555 E. William St., #20L, Ann Arbor, MI 48104 U.S.A. (E-mail: *hdlerner@umich.edu*).

[Haworth co-indexing entry note]: "A Two-Systems Approach to the Treatment of a Disturbed Adolescent." Lerner, Howard D. Co-published simultaneously in *Psychoanalytic Social Work* (The Haworth Press, Inc.) Vol. 8, No. 3/4, 2001, pp. 123-142; and: *Psychoanalytic Approaches to the Treatment of Children and Adolescents: Tradition and Transformation* (ed: Jerrold R. Brandell) The Haworth Press, Inc., 2001, pp. 123-142. Single or multiple copies of this article are available for a fee from The Haworth Document Delivery Service [1-800-342-9678, 9:00 a.m. - 5:00 p.m. (EST). E-mail address: getinfo@haworthpressinc.com].

123

psychoanalytic situation. The adolescent's need to modify or weaken attachment to parental figures tends to undermine the establishment of a therapeutic alliance and alters the transference; rising internal pressures propel the teen to action rather than reflection; the fragility of self-esteem predisposes the adolescent to tenaciously externalize rather than self-observe. Perhaps the most vexing problem in the treatment of a disturbed adolescent is that of finding a channel for the establishment of a therapeutic relationship. Too old for the play techniques of early childhood, the adolescent has not yet fully evolved the cognitive and self-observing capacities that permit the free association approach of adult analysis and is in any case a frequently unwilling patient leading the family and, at times, the community to be active participants in the treatment. The task of providing assistance to adolescents is further complicated by a number of factors–some residing in the patient, many residing in the family, and those residing in the therapist. Among those factors residing in the patient are a reluctance to acknowledge distress, the propensity of externalization and the frequent shifting character of mental organization. Complicating factors residing in the family revolve around the powerful forces of denial and the intergenerational transmission of psychopathology. Complicating factors in therapists revolve around a lack of clarity about developmental norms and expectations and a clear conceptual framework for understanding adolescent psychopathology that at once informs technique and facilitates clinical work with families. A third major complicating factor in working with disturbed adolescents is the cultural context. Adolescent psychopathology cannot be fully understood without a consideration of the ecology of American high schools today. In what follows, I will first address the cultural context of adolescents today, a culture that in many ways breeds omnipotent, quick-fix solutions to adolescent developmental problems, then briefly outline the rich conceptual and technical framework for understanding and treating adolescents presented by the Novicks (this volume), and, finally, illustrate the clinical utility of the Novicks' two-system model with an in-depth report on the treatment of a very disturbed adolescent boy. I will emphasize, utilizing this clinical model, the pivotal role of the therapeutic alliance throughout treatment, and clinical work with the family.

THE CONTEXT

One can conceptualize passage through the American education system in the following manner. Upon entry, beginning in preschool or nursery school, students are given a certain amount of credit, which can be thought of as being deposited at the principal's office. When students respond well to their teachers and make few demands, they receive credit that moves them more swiftly toward graduation to a less restrictive and confining environment. On the other hand, when youngsters act out and wreak havoc, when they are bullies or chronic targets of bullies, or are deemed "weird," there is often an initially subtle and subsequently not so subtle movement within the community to marginalize them. Initially, buzzwords, such as ADD, conduct disorder, troublemaker, learning disabled, creep into administrative discussions and only vaguely conceal the wish to extrude. This is often a signal for the initiation of more intrusive, invasive interventions such as detention, special classes, recommendations for medications or higher dosages of medications, and, eventually, transfer to a more restrictive, invasive environment, such as a private school, residential treatment facility, or a juvenile detention center. Nowadays, with the pressure of tightened budgets, managed care, the misreading of psychological literature to state that all feelings should be expressed rather then mastered, and with the increased abdication of parental responsibilities, young people in the past who would have been excluded from the system are increasingly marginalized within the system. In a sense, these marginalized groups provide an important function for the majority culture as they become a repository for disavowed, unwanted, and externalized self-images, ideas, and feelings. Being marginalized within the high school caste system leaves many of these students with deep-seated feelings of helplessness, hopelessness, and rage. Out of these feelings they seek magical, omnipotent solutions. Our own feelings of hopelessness and helplessness in relationship to troubled adolescents to some extent reflect the feelings of a hopeless, helpless, and enraged teenager. In any human relationship, the study of one individual, no matter which one, is likely to illuminate the behavior of the other.

Cultures, totally determined by a peer group, isolated and cut off from the world of reality can become dangerous. The American high school culture can be likened to William Golding's *Lord of the Flies*–an allegorical novel about a group of boys stranded on an island after a plane crash. In the absence of adults and in spite of the efforts of a few leaders to form an organized society, the boys revert to savagery complete with primitive rites and ritual murder. Not unlike Golding's island or prison, the system of social interaction in American high schools is reduced to a primitive tribe and a physical pecking order in which violence or the threat of violence dominates. Competence, skills, and personal sensitivity are demeaned and denigrated. An isolated mentality ensues in which there is a cultural push for easy solutions. A primitive hierarchy is formed in small tribal organizations which do not require sensitivity or competent, complex skills. Without competence, one has self-esteem regulated by primitive qualities such as physical strength, power, the threat of violence, and the provision of physical pleasure. This becomes an easy and readily accessible way of regulating self-esteem. This is a characteristic of closed institutions and is intensified in adolescence, allowing for the acting out of omnipotent fantasies.

Today we see in many teenagers an acceleration of omnipotent, out-of-control behavior with little check or counterbalance. Because of the complex tasks they have and the demands on them, many adolescents are left with feelings of helplessness and hopelessness. One way of dealing with this is through an omnipotent fantasy–"I can do what I want to do, when I want to do it and with 100% efficiency." Confronted with the developmental issues of time and gender, most competent, reality-based adolescents can cope effectively. Many adolescents, especially those prone to seek quick-fix solutions through violence, drugs, or promiscuous sexuality, attempt to deny the constraints and limitations of reality and involve themselves in destructive activities. These activities are readily available to adolescents all the time. Unfortunately, many teenagers deal with it through omnipotent denial, often with the statement, "I can handle it." The need for omnipotent fantasies and solutions escalates when these beliefs are assailed by reality. Increasingly faced with the reality of time, of gender, of limitation and constraint, or of mortality, there comes an increasing need to validate omnipotence. Recklessness and death-defying acts ensue. Increasingly, faced with reality, there comes a need for absolute control of others. A characteristic of teenage omnipotence involves using the body in pathological ways. While suicide represents an extreme, eating disorders, substance abuse, and body piercing (cutting) represent the enactment of omnipotent fantasies through the body. Unfortunately, because adolescence is both a turbulent and exciting phase, there is a tendency to tolerate and normalize everything as "just adolescence" or part of "normal adolescent experimentation."

The Two-Systems Approach to Adolescence

In a number of important publications, Novick and Novick (1991, 1996a, 1996b, 1998, this volume) have extended their earlier work on sadomasochism and defensive omnipotent fantasies and organized it into a larger and broader conceptual model which encompasses a dual-track model of development, revolving around two kinds of solutions to conflict and two systems of self-esteem regulation. This formulation permits the inclusion of normality and pathology, internal and external reality, fantasies and beliefs, as well as both earlier and later determinants of psychopathology. What is increasingly becoming known as the "two-systems approach" has both conceptual and technical implications. This model brings together technical approaches which have often been thought of as antagonistic, such as the "one-person" emphasis on defenses, or conflicts and resistances with the "two-person" focus on the therapeutic relationship and clinical interaction. The Novicks (1996b, 1998, this volume) have also offered a revised concept of the therapeutic alliance that is developmentally based and offers clinicians a road map for working with defensive omnipotent resistances. It is the therapeutic alliance that bridges the two systems of competence and omnipotence through each phase of treatment. The revised concept of the therapeutic alliance tasks and the notion of two systems of self-esteem regulation both contribute to the treatment goal of restoring the patient to a path of progressive development so that real choice can be exercised freely.

Core to the two-systems approach is the important connection of underlying omnipotent beliefs with the experience of helplessness and hopelessness that give rise to it. Research support for this clinically derived formulation has emerged in studies of disorganized attachment (Solomon & George, 1999) as well as the developmental literature on competence and effectance (Tronick & Gianino, 1986; Papousek & Papousek, 1975; Stern, 1985).

In contrast to the dominant view within psychoanalysis that omnipotence is part of normal development, the Novicks (this volume) regard omnipotent beliefs as issuing from real failures on the part of caretakers to protect the individual from physical or psychological trauma. Omnipotence is thus seen as a defense, a conscious or unconscious belief in the real power to control others, to inflict pain upon them, to force them to submit to one's will. It is an ill-fated attempt to force the mother to be "good enough," that is, competent, protective and loving. Self-regulation and self-esteem governed by this closed, omnipotent system is highly sadomasochistic, as the active quest for pain and suffering transforms experiences of helplessness and hopelessness into a hostile defense. What organizes the omnipotent belief as a defense against traumatic anxiety is the magical power to control objects. While at one time this defense may have been adaptive and even validated by reality, over time it becomes consolidated as a maladaptive solution to conflict which serves multiple functions and motives. In contrast, and as an alternative to the closed omnipotent system, is what can be thought of as an open, competent system of self-regulation which utilizes ego skills and talents, which is based on mutually respectful, pleasurable relationships formed through realistic perceptions of the self and others. Functioning within this open system revolves around the utilization of ego capacities to experience real pleasure in the exercise of those capacities as well as realistic self-esteem.

The developmental phase of adolescence is ushered in by real changes in the body, mind, and sociocultural expectations. The potential for closed, omnipotent, sadomasochistic responses to the phase challenges to omnipotence are accessible to the individual as are open, adaptive, competent responses. Teenagers who have often experienced sadomasochistic events develop destructive, omnipotent fantasies of swift hostile victories over others and are unable to integrate these fantasies with the reality of a changing body and changing reality demands. Adolescent development, with the potential to put wishes into action, demands transformation of earlier fantasy solutions. On the other hand, individuals who have experienced the consolidation and enhancement of ego skills, talents, and pleasure in competent interactions eagerly greet the growing capacities of body and mind that accompany adolescence and actively engage in opportunities to increase self-esteem. While adolescence, not unlike any other phase, contains disappointment, failure, and the realization of limitation, teenagers who have experienced "good-enough" parenting are in a far better position to master the ordinary obstacles they encounter. The following case report will illustrate the clinical utility of the two-system model in the treatment of a disturbed adolescent boy. Both the conceptual and technical implications of the two-system model will be outlined through the course of this youngster's treatment.

CASE ILLUSTRATION

Evaluation Phase

According to the Novicks' (2001b) reformulation of the therapeutic alliance concept within the framework of the two-systems approach (Novick & Novick, this volume), the aim of child, as well as adolescent, analysis is the restoration of the patient's progressive development *and* the restoration of the parent-child relationship to its fullest potential as a lifelong positive resource for both. Clinical work is directed toward moving all participants from closed- to open-system functioning. The Novicks conceptualize the therapeutic alliance in terms of multiple tasks which can ". . . allow for heightened attention to the capacities and motivations, conscious and unconscious, from all levels of personalities and all stages of development that enter into the specific collaborative tasks of each phase of treatment, and to the resistances and conflicts that arise around these tasks" (p. 8). These tasks apply to both adolescents and their parents and are crucially important during the evaluation phase. The evaluation phase should be open-ended with a view toward achieving a number of transformation tasks for both patient and parents. The therapist engages and facilitates all parties in transforming self-help to collaborative work, apparent crisis to order and meaning, fantasies to realistic goals, and external complaints to therapeutically amenable internal conflicts.

Chris, a 14-year-old high school freshman at the time, was initially referred to treatment by his school guidance counselor, parents, and local police. Both the parents and the police began to accumulate evidence that Chris was responsible for stealing over $23,000 from an elderly uncle (maternal grandmother's brother) and neighbors through a series of break-ins. He was also suspected of dealing and using drugs. Interestingly, these allegations were always difficult to prove conclusively despite large deposits into his bank accounts. Chris's criminal behavior only recently had come to the attention of his parents. Chris's history revealed that he was adopted at 6 weeks of age. His mother recalled that he had had severe diaper rash and never smiled. Chris experienced many traumas. At age 6, during a visit to a paternal uncle and aunt, his uncle, shortly after showing Chris his gun collection, shot himself in the head and died. The very next year, Chris was deposited with his infamously perverted maternal grandfather and over a period of 10 days was sexually abused.

Indeed, upon meeting Chris, I was struck by how sad, depressed, and apathetic he appeared. The little that he did have to say was that he felt he had no problems, was doing fine in school, and really had no interest in anything. He was the picture of detachment and indifference. According to his parents, despite good social skills, high intelligence, and good looks, he preferred to be alone, and, at every step along the way, would recklessly sabotage his own achievements and skills. For example, he used his lucrative baseball card collection as a front for stolen money. Once this was uncovered, he lost any interest he had in collecting baseball cards. The parents were exasperated, and my office was the last stop before admission to a long-term residential treatment center. Previous stops included frequent visits to the principal's office, two short-term psychotherapies at ages 8 and 9, before the sexual abuse was even detected, a regimen of behavior modification with a view toward rearranging reinforcement contingencies to improve school performance, and the recommendation of a 12-step program based upon a sexual addiction model. While closed-system functioning was blatantly obvious, it became crucially important to assess open-system capacities for pleasure and realistic self-esteem.

Chris's parents, the Smiths, came from lower middle-class backgrounds. Mrs. Smith, a frenetic-looking woman in her mid-40s at the time, was an only child. On her side, what stood out in the evaluation is how her own mother was supposedly in love with the father and then discovered on the wedding day–seeing her husband at the other end of the church–that he had "hate in his eyes." It was a troubled marriage from the very beginning. Mrs. Smith was conceived right away, the father feeling that she had been conceived by another man. He developed severe alcohol problems. She was born prematurely and slept in her parents' bedroom for the first six years of her life, which she felt she was working through in her own analysis because she was subjected from six months on to child abuse, about which not even her husband knew the details. This abusive relationship only stopped, it seemed, when the mother, after yearly miscarriages, was told by her physician to take care of the one daughter she did have. The father left the home on the night of Mrs. Smith's high school graduation. She excelled in high school, where she earned high honors. She was unable to conceive children due to complications from Dilantin, which she was given for trouble with her periods. After several major surgeries, she eventually had her ovaries removed. Despite training as a librarian, Mrs. Smith remained a housewife. Carol, the oldest daughter by three years, was also adopted and at the time of the evaluation was a senior in a parochial high school, preparing for college.

Mr. Smith came from a working class area where his father was a mechanic. He was the next-to-youngest child in a sib-ship of seven. Mr. Smith always did well in school and was able to use school to get away from the father's "volatile temper," although he went to great lengths to say how he experienced his family as caring and supportive. He totally immersed himself in high school to withdraw from his family. After obtaining an MA degree in business, he took a job with an airline, where he headed a major department. His wife characterized his position as "high up." In talking about Chris, the parents emphasized the "bad condition" he was in when they adopted him at age six weeks. They had minimal information about the biological parents, knowing only that they were local, that the father was around 6'3" and was 17 years old and that the mother was 15. After birth and until he was adopted, Chris resided with a foster family. The Smiths emphasized how Chris was not a happy baby; he was gloomy and "serious" from the very start. At age 7 or 8, in an ill-fated attempt to reconcile with her father, Mrs. Smith sent Chris and his sister to visit the grandfather. Shortly thereafter, Chris, according to the mother, attempted to hang himself in the backyard. This led to his first psychotherapy referral. Only later did Chris reveal that he was sexually molested by his grandfather, but never revealed the details. The mother was concerned with Chris's "deviant sexuality," which she related to the abuse. Deviant sexuality carried the meaning of Chris being homosexual, with thoughts that he looked feminine, that he showed little interest in girls, and that there were references in his yearbook to him being "perverted." I referred Chris for psychological testing aimed at evaluating his capacity to form a treatment alliance, as well as to assess the degree of internalized superego formation and the capacity to tolerate and verbalize conflict and affects associated with conflict. Testing revealed a near-superior IQ, but a massive emphasis on disengagement, "slippery thinking," little capacity for affect tolerance, massive constriction, and an overall impression of a "paranoid character in its formative stages."

EARLY PHASE

Despite a history of the mother supporting treatment and the father opposing it, both parents accepted my recommendation for psychoanalysis involving four sessions per week with Chris and one family session. In terms of establishing a therapeutic alliance, I was aware that there was nothing that I could say or do–this is to say that there was nothing in my power that could prevent Chris from stealing, dealing and using drugs, or failing in school. I recognized that if I attempted to do so, I would be engaging in a power struggle which would replicate, in fantasy and symbolic action, the uncle's suicide and abuse which he had experienced. I conveyed to Chris that I was there neither to break him, persuade him of the errors of his ways, uncover memories, nor penetrate his deep secrets. I saw the focus of our work as helping him understand how his mind worked, to help Chris understand himself and reflect upon his actions and those of others, as well as to assist him in growing up. As such, I saw any problem or conflict which he touched upon as a potential treatment lever. Anything that bothered Chris immediately became a topic of our interest. He approached treatment in a detached and sullen way. I observed with Chris that he attempted to be cool and calm about everything. I wondered if anything bothered him, and he noted that he was not happy with his grades in school. I commented that given his level of intelligence, he could be getting at least B's. I then connected his coolness with his grades. I concurred that there was certainly something beneficial about staying cool and calm and that I would certainly like to help him with that, but his way of staying cool involved turning himself into an iceberg, i.e., to stay cool meant turning his brains off. The goal of our work then became staying cool but turning his brains on.

It was important that we set up a therapeutic task that Chris could comprehend. What was of utmost importance was helping him to feel understood. I closely monitored how comfortable Chris was with being with me. I continually focused on how it was important to turn the eye inward and capitalize on any piece of curiosity or worry that he experienced. During silences, I pointed out to Chris how the mind never stops working and that silences have to do with not wanting to see or know me, or even have feelings toward me. I attempted to give him a sense of the complexity and intrigue of the mind and assured him that when we finished he would really know how his mind and the minds of other people worked, how knowing yourself helps you to know others. I tried to continually get across to him the idea that the mind is in charge of everything, and when he is connected to it, he does better and feels better, and when his mind is not in charge, he cannot learn or get better. I pointed out how the mind helps you get better and better, even in areas such as biking and skiing, two activities he enjoyed. When we talked about stereos or computers, I likened the components to ego functions, such as memory, thinking, and the modulation of feelings. One day he forgot his sunglasses, and we examined it in terms of why he "turned off" his memory. He seemed intrigued. Our aim, then, became developing a map of his mind, likening it to a computer. We needed to know the components to understand better why, at times, he did not use his full brainpower. One day we needed to reschedule a session, and he felt he needed to talk to his parents first. I likened this to his turning off his brain in order to ask his parents. I conveyed that I was there neither to nag or hound him (like his mother) but to assist him in getting interested in his own mind and how he inhibits it, as well as things that he could do with it, and how good feelings came directly from using his competencies. Citing intense conflicts with his mother and misunderstandings with his friends, we slowly came to understand how he turned his brain off in order to protect himself from intense, hurtful feelings. We searched for better ways to protect himself and, in so doing, better ways to cope with his parents, school, and friends.

After several months of work with Chris and his parents, it became increasingly clear that what resided in deeper layers of the parents' minds was a view of Chris as a murderer and sexual abuser. A task of treatment was to move Chris from being a basic target of blaming. Chris made himself an easy target by lying and avoiding responsibility, especially in terms of bringing home school reports and informing his parents of his own activities. The parents' idealization of me swiftly turned family sessions into a court in which I presided over Chris being accused of daily felonies and misdemeanors. My work with Chris at this time focused on helping him to see his own role in the process and pathology. The process at this time revolved around assisting Chris to internalize various structures. It was clear that I represented the superego for the family and Chris as well as various ego functions for Chris. Chris did not exist separately from his family. The mother was the worrywart and the father the fixer. Chris quickly sensed his father's initial ambivalence toward treatment and his mother's idealization of me as a way of taking it over, with me seen as an extension of her wishes. The early resistance involved both parents overtly supporting treatment as long as I carried out their wishes, and Chris contending the treatment was not his. A goal became making the treatment Chris's alone. Family sessions increasingly revealed that Chris got between his parents and formed pathological alliances described by the family as "two-being" (tubing). The focus of the family work became to better understand the "two-being" in terms not only of how Chris used it in order to gratify his own wishes, but also with it, to examine chronic problems in the marriage.

Certain issues deepened the therapeutic relationship. As Chris was better able to make treatment his own and to see me as an ally of his, he began to talk more openly about his history of stealing, including the $23,000 from his uncle; his use of drugs, including growing a pot plant in his room under his parents' nose; and his experience of being molested by his grandfather and the meaning it held for him. I was able to point out to Chris how his thinking actually became sharper and more focused when he took on more affectively charged topics such as adoption or molestation. Chris experienced a great deal of pride in sharing how he could crack locks, less in terms of being able to steal and get away with things, but more in terms of the skill and finesse it took. He came to better appreciate the working of his mind through long discussions about the existence of God, the nature of government, and the effects of THC on the central nervous system. Work with Chris increasingly focused on stealing and the link of stealing to long-term feelings of deprivation. Chris and I spoke for months about stealing $23,000 from his uncle, how he did it, and the feelings of guilt which accompanied it. It became increasingly clear to both of us that his uncle, a priest, had also stolen the money from the church. As these sessions wove their way into family sessions, they became linked to adoption, and how the $23,000 Chris stole from his uncle was following a "script" initially written by the maternal grandmother and orchestrated by Chris's mother that men are wild, unruly, and messy–her early image of Chris. The mother talked about how her own mother harangued Mrs. Smith for having a boy–"Why would you want one?" I was able to point out in a family session how Chris's uncle, a priest, of all people, appeared to have stolen the $23,000 from the church. Defensively, the mother argued that Chris's problems began and were determined by the first six weeks of his life in which she claimed he was seriously abused and deprived by foster parents, as evidenced by his severe diaper rash, early head banging, and serious ear infections. These externalizations became obvious to everyone. In turn, Chris became more curious about his adoption and shared fantasies about his biological parents, including how they named him Travis, an orphan and central character in the movie *Paris, Texas,* whose father was psychotically depressed and whose mother was a prostitute. The improvement in Chris's overall functioning was seen in school performance, around separation and autonomy issues, and in how he was making treatment increasingly his own. This generated a family crisis between the parents. Chris, no longer enacting their externalizations, on the one hand, posed a danger to the treatment itself, on the other hand. The mother became enraged at me, and the father tended to follow her commands. On my part, countertransferentially, I became increasingly identified with Chris against his parents. At this time the parents entered couples therapy and the father, after several ill-fated starts, finally began his own treatment. Around this time, Chris became involved with Mary, one year older, whose image, values, and need to control were very reminiscent of his mother. As the relationship deepened and was punctuated by starts and stops, issues of separations and loss, as they reactivated adoption issues, surfaced in increasingly clear ways.

Key dynamic issues emerged in this phase of the treatment. The transference became less externalized and revolved increasingly around ways Chris used and did not use his own ego functions. As he became sexually involved with Mary, his mother's view of men as wild and unruly, as well as her own need to control sexuality, became increasingly evident. The sexual relationship with Mary initially blew his parents apart. Chris could better see his mother's pathology when she misheard Mary and him "fooling around" as him raping her. With greater utilization of his ego functions came a growing depression. As his object relations became more differentiated in the transference and his ego functions became more focused, powerful feelings of depression, loss, inadequacy, and envy surfaced. The task became one of helping Chris keep these affects within non-overwhelming bounds. Chris repeatedly complained of "giving in" to Mary, in part as a way of avoiding conflict and in part as a way of assuming a passive role. We were able to see how the relationship with Mary, an older woman, had a quality of abuse in terms of "being taken over by her." At times, he tended to cede his higher-level ego functions to Mary.

MIDDLE PHASE

The major therapeutic alliance tasks of this phase of treatment revolved around working together with Chris and assisting him to make maximum use of his ego functions. The work with the parents was to further facilitate separation-individuation. A disturbing pattern became increasingly evident to both of us; that is, as Chris made progress in terms of school performance, separation, and autonomy, he continuously sabotaged himself and, in turn, established an earlier-type sadomasochistic relationship with his mother. This was seen in terms of having his driver's license suspended for "driving under the influence," a positive drug test for cocaine, and the continued appearance of involvement in delinquent activity. With this came increased intrusions into the treatment by the mother, a binding view of Chris, on her part, as a "bad kid," and engagement in intense, sadomasochistic interactions between mother and son, all of which posed a major threat to the continuation of treatment. As Chris's high school graduation loomed in the background, family sessions were reinstituted as the work shifted from treatment to management. Chris's proneness to discouragement and with it a frantic search for shortcuts, led us to focus on a core conflict within Chris between his competencies (intelligence, social skills, and capacity for reparations) and his quest for magical, omnipotent solutions (perfectionism, clean slates, and entitlement). Within this, core family dynamics were clarified and a significant intervention involving separating Chris from his mother was initiated.

A positive drug test for cocaine occasioned a stormy family session in which both parents were prepared on the spot to remove Chris from treatment, with the feeling that I had colluded with him in denial of his drug activities. Underlying their rage at me were powerful feelings of hopelessness around taking control of their son's behaviors, which in many ways they supported. Countertransferentially, I felt defensive and both empathic with and angry at Chris for sabotaging our work together. The main task of our work became saving the treatment. At a moment in which treatment seemed to be at its darkest point, Chris made an impassioned plea to his parents to continue treatment, feeling that it was the most important relationship he had ever had. He went on to list a number of ways that he had changed. I attempted to deal with both Chris and his family concerning the drug issue as both a pathological source of self-esteem for Chris, as well as demonstrating the multifaceted ways in which the parents themselves colluded with those very behaviors on Chris's part which they condemned. In our sessions together, I made it clear that Chris faced a choice as to whether or not he wanted to view himself as a "loser," linked to his mother's image of him, or as a person with potential for success through the development of his competencies. I was able to point out to Chris that it had been successes in reality which had occasioned a number of recent crises. Chris's view of himself as a "loser" was seen as the image of the "younger Chris" who because of punishments could never leave home, confirming his mother's worst fears and deepest wishes.

What became clear is that during a period when Chris was functioning more separately and autonomously, his mother got involved in the theater, family sessions ended, and the father began to travel more. The link between his own autonomous functioning and his mother's departure recapitulated earlier feelings of rejection and loss. Chris and I began to understand how he became a character (the bad kid) in his mother's script. Unconsciously, Chris invited rejection as a means of controlling it. With high school graduation approaching and after several breakups with Mary, choices that Chris experienced internally were increasingly clear–that is, between shortcut, quick-fix solutions, or more hard-earned attempts to connect to his mind and to apply himself in school. With that came the experience of feeling vulnerable in the service of long term gain. This conflict became alive for Chris, which indicated less denial, and with it increased narcissistic vulnerability.

Chris and his mother continued to engage in intense sadomasochistic interactions, which not only increased when the father was gone, but also excluded me. These interactions consisted of punishments and restrictions, which kept both Chris and his mother at home fighting and isolated from the rest of the world. It appeared that the mother was using the time when the father was gone to once again pathologically reclaim her son. This early dynamic, referred to us as "two-beings/tubing," became increasingly sexualized. In essence, it was not only the father, but also the analyst who was being excluded, and Chris had arranged, through his delinquent, drugged-appearing behavior, to set things up so that he was alone with his mother all day.

Within the context of breaking up with Mary and saying goodbye to high school, adolescence, and childhood, Chris experienced being "betrayed" and "stabbed in the back" and once again rekindled thoughts and fantasies of his adoption–did his biological parents "leave [him] anything?" Chris could "play with" fantasies about his biological parents, including his father being a basketball star and his mother being a brilliant student. He always appeared to have a need to justify the adoption in terms of his parents not being prepared to assume the responsibility of parenthood. Although accurate, Chris could also entertain the notion that this was a rationalization that he would prefer to believe rather than to experience feelings of betrayal and rejection linked to the very origin of his life.

The family matrix of omnipotence born out of victimization continued to intensify and was thematized by Chris responding to his mother's intrusion into one of his therapy sessions by shoplifting immediately after the session and under her nose. The mother insisted that the store call the police. Feelings of victimization linked Chris with his mother and created the ambiance in which she maintained that he could do whatever he wanted. This created a vicious circle which enraged the mother and provided further justification for Chris's rule breaking. His omnipotent sense of entitlement created the situation which made the parents feel they could not let him go–that is, he was a "little boy." Unconsciously, this is what Chris and his mother wanted. In essence, the family dynamic was that Chris's rage provided the justification for breaking rules, yet invariably he got caught because of unconscious guilt and conflict, though his mother's unremitting anger relieved the guilt and further justified anger on his part and further rule breaking. The outcome was that he turned his home into a prison in which he was alone with his mother, like a baby.

It became increasingly clear that Chris's capacity to bring analysis to a successful conclusion hinged greatly on his ability to separate from his mother's image and script for him. Further, it was apparent that Chris was not going to have the grades to graduate from high school and had little in the way of viable plans for the immediate future. Following a very successful spring vacation as well as exhibiting creativity in the classroom and with it a growing sense of maturity on Chris's part, it became abundantly clear how well he functioned when separated from his mother. Chris needed to achieve relative independence from his mother; he needed to continue treatment and to gain support for separation from his father. An intervention was planned in which I suggested to Chris and his parents that his best interest would be served if he moved to Ann Arbor. Much of this need was captured in Chris's statement about his mother–"She makes me crazy!" As I interpreted, his stealing and delinquent behavior could be seen as a way of saying, "Mom, you're right, I am a criminal." Chris, on his part, was excited by the suggestion, viewing Ann Arbor as a "sanctuary for the mind." He became realistically anxious and wondered if he was capable of being independent and successful because a voice inside of him said "once a crook, always a crook," which I interpreted as the voice of his mother and the need to separate himself from that. His thinking became increasingly more lucid or in his words, "fluid." He noted how "crazy" he was in relationship to her and how she induced chaos within him by "twisting things." What surfaced on Chris's part were developmentally appropriate anxieties and concerns about separation and the future. Surprisingly and uncharacteristically, both parents were fully approving of the suggestion and moved swiftly and effectively to support their son during this most crucial time in his development.

PRE-TERMINATION PHASE

Adjusting to life in Ann Arbor, attaining gainful employment, and working intermittently toward a high school diploma in a community college ushered in the pre-termination phase. Pre-termination tasks for Chris involved consolidating the progress he had made, attempting to assume greater responsibility for his own treatment, and, most importantly, an attempt to translate insight in what he had learned about himself into effective action. Putting insight and awareness into constructive action became a major task and source of resistance for Chris, because it challenged his omnipotent system of magical power and quick-fix solutions, such as becoming a rock star and striking it rich. The incompatibility between the systems of omnipotence and competence became Chris's fundamental and ongoing conflict. Chris getting an apartment in the neighborhood of my office appeared to symbolize my becoming a developmental object for him. His move to Ann Arbor was productive in a number of ways; for example, he was able to stay clear of involvement with the police, he did not go overboard on drugs or alcohol, he maintained jobs, worked out a cooperative and facilitating relationship with his parents (especially his father), and was able to look toward the future, particularly a career in culinary arts. The major source of resistance for Chris during this time involved missing sessions with me, secondary to a pattern of relationships with women in which he gave himself over to them.

There was a tension within Chris knowing, on the one hand, that coming to treatment was good for him, that he benefited, and that he saw me as an "asset," whereas, on the other hand, it also became important that he could do things and manage on his own. Discussion of this conflict led to Chris recognizing his problem of giving himself over to women. He felt in a non-motivational state because, in part, he felt stagnant in terms of his future. I interpreted to Chris that it was as if he needed to give himself up to be with a woman, that is, he ceded his masculinity and competence as a way of staying his "mommy's little boy." Becoming an independent, masculine individual, like his father or me, made him fearful about being able to get a woman. As we later talked, it appeared that he was following a script written by his mother who did not like competent men. I interpreted that it was as if he could not have both a girlfriend and me. It was clear to both of us that in his relationships with women he tended to replay his infancy with his mother. There appeared to be a clash within Chris of two worlds–a new world in which he got hints of trusting himself, of being able to figure things out, an ability to feel good and competent, versus an old magical world in which mother would love him more than father because he was a failure. Chris became incompetent by giving himself over, initially to his mother and subsequently to girlfriends. The unconscious illusion was that this was what women needed; and in exchange, they would not leave him. The unconscious assumption was that by becoming a little baby and making himself useless, a woman would take over and would take care of him.

I helped Chris better appreciate the need to translate impulses and wishes into constructive action. Chris increasingly became aware that something inside of him was stopping him and that it was self-destructive. I attempted to point out how I represented his mother in the transference, and how he used his parents to bail him out. I presented myself as a developmental object and attempted to show how he could be connected to me by being for himself, that is, coming to his sessions could be a way of him beginning to rescue himself. It was as if Chris felt he had to give me up as the father, representing masculinity, growth, and competence to be able to connect to mother and others who in the past bailed him out. I attempted to show Chris that he could have both mother and father, relate to them both, and at the same time take care of himself; but he had to learn a new language of success, real relationships, and achievement. I helped him better appreciate the constant availability and access to the old language consisting of old wishes and omnipotent fantasies. I emphasized that he could not speak both languages simultaneously. Chris, in turn, became increasingly aware of how the intense sadomasochistic interactions he had with girlfriends, the experience of being controlled and devalued by them, the attempts to leave and subsequently the experience of loneliness and return, represented a pattern he had with many women that in important ways linked him to his mother. It was as if separation, independence, and growth were destructive things for Chris because he was so powerful that leaving women was tantamount to killing them. This rekindled thoughts and associations to adoption. Chris appeared less interested in whether or not his birth parents "left [him] anything" and more curious in who they were.

I continually pointed out Chris's use of omnipotence as a way of avoiding growing up and dealing with reality. In turn, Chris increasingly struggled with depression and anxiety as he attempted to deal with the realities of not being ready for marriage and the need to make important choices having to do with a career. Despite these struggles, Chris painted and wrote poetry. He could gain some realistic esteem by recognizing that he had maintained his restaurant job for well over a year and a half. His major struggle through this period continued to involve coming to his sessions, which was increasingly seen as an avoidance of setting aside and relinquishing his omnipotent system and committing to reality.

TERMINATION PHASE

It gradually became clear that Chris's conditions for love involved rescue and ceding his competence. This struggle increasingly entered the transference. His underlying fear was that by becoming competent he would have to stop treatment–i.e., if he functioned well and became more independent he would be abandoned. Feeling helpless, incompetent, and unable became a way of making me love him. This was a powerful fantasy which tied Chris to his mother, to girlfriends, and to me. The task of termination became clear: relinquishing his omnipotent fantasies and Chris being able to leave me. A major focus of the termination phase involved further fostering of open-system functioning through the internalization of the therapeutic alliance. Just as the intervention resulting in Chris's move to Ann Arbor and fostering a separation from his mother ushered in the pre-termination stage, my assistance in actively helping Chris receive a high school diploma appeared to usher in the termination phase. Chris remained one language course short of a high school diploma. Looking dejected, Chris and I once again reviewed his history of language courses, calculating that he had taken and failed five. He was able to acknowledge that early on he did not try, but in the past three courses he really had tried his hardest and just was not able to do it. I pointed out how hard he had worked in taking a second language and to his credit he had really stuck with it rather than throwing in the towel. I explained that I did not think that failing these courses was a reflection of his intelligence, but rather that he had a specific disability in the area of second language acquisition that was quite unfortunate in the sense that it had impeded, in his own words, "moving on in life." Associating to how he would like to apply to a culinary school, I noted with him that I would be glad to be of help. He wondered if I could write a letter for him after he met with his former high school guidance counselor. Chris and I together recognized that he had passed at least four classes on the college level and were able to integrate this into a number of reasons why the high school language requirement should be waived. In the very next session, Chris had arranged for his guidance counselor to call me, which she did. The counselor was quick to agree that Chris had the capacity to do well in school; he showed that in high school. She was more than happy to grant him a diploma if he could document the language courses he had taken and failed. I then shared the news with Chris, who was at once ecstatic and appreciative. He immediately caught his tendency, particularly in the past, to be carried away with grandiose ideas about his future. In fact, he tried so hard to control those tendencies that he had been reluctant to even talk about a career with people because now it was the time for doing rather than talking. He came to the very next session with diploma in hand. He was profusely thankful and appreciative as we talked about plans to apply to a training program for culinary arts.

The goal of termination became one of saying goodbye in a different, non-adolescent way. The shift in our sessions was toward reality and a more realistic consideration of his strengths and weaknesses with a view toward strengthening his competent, realistic side. We attempted to utilize Chris's strength to look at his life more realistically and to be able to say goodbye in a growth enhancing way. This was in marked contrast to his long history of rejections and his tendency to seek quick-fix, omnipotent solutions. At this time Chris's father became much more actively involved in Chris's career planning.

The termination became increasingly real when Chris was accepted at a culinary institute in California. This became a time of taking stock of himself, his friends, and his accomplishments. This led into his feelings about leaving me, his feelings of indebtedness to me, as well as how his real accomplishments paled in comparison with his omnipotent fantasies.

During the termination phase many issues came up for the last time, not the least of which was Chris's adoption within the context of his 23rd birthday. Chris declared that he really wanted to grow up and become an adult, yet his immediate yearnings were also to be a juvenile. I said that he could not be both. He then asked me directly if I felt, on the basis of knowing him as well as I did, that being adopted had a big effect on him. I wondered what he thought and essentially he said that he was not as close to his parents as other people, that his childhood was "weird," "different than other kids." We talked about the adoption in terms of feelings of rejection as well as how the parents who adopted him had feelings about not being able to conceive their own child, and hang-ups, especially his mother, in terms of feelings she had toward men and traumas that she had experienced in her own childhood. Many of the explanations and understandings about adoption that Chris developed earlier in his life were being reassessed now and found, perhaps, not to fit as well as they used to. For example, the notion that at least his birth parents had him rather than aborting him, that his parents weren't ready to be parents and did the right thing, that the parents he had were good enough. All of these were true, but I encouraged Chris to also think of the adoption not just from the perspective of ideas he developed growing up but perhaps also the way a child might see it. He had always felt "different and weird." Recognizing that his birthday was coming up, his thoughts were drawn to issues of freedom and responsibility. He could acknowledge wanting to have some of the freedoms and privileges of a child, but as I continually pointed out, he could not have both, and there were greater pleasures and opportunities for real self-esteem in being an adult. It was clear that Chris was struggling to assess himself more realistically, recognizing that he had often in the past gotten by in school by cheating, that he was not as smart as he thought he was, that he had never really fully applied himself to find out, and yet his very next associations were to a movie in which someone from a background not much different than his was a genius and could answer all questions and figure out all things. Chris voiced that to accept limitations of adulthood meant that life had no meaning, that it was a "purposeless journey." I noted with him that meaning and purpose came from his mind, from the inside, and that to find your own meaning and your own purpose was a positive part of being an adult. Both Chris and I mutually recognized that we had had a very interesting therapeutic journey together. I commented to Chris that I always found him a very interesting person, and Chris said that I have always said that about him and that he appreciated it.

Following termination in the celebratory meeting with his parents, who thanked me for "saving Chris's life," I received some phone calls from Chris telling me about his experience in the culinary institute. Essentially he was doing very well, in fact, much better than he ever expected, especially academically. He was working hard and appropriately concerned about his future with thoughts about pursuing more training in the culinary arts. He reported feeling a bit lonely but more focused and stable. At this point, the post-termination alliance tasks pointed toward being available to Chris as his analyst and assisting the parents to allow for continued growth in their son and the capacity to grow along with him.

REFERENCES

Freud, A. (1958). Adolescence. *Writings.* 5:136-166. New York: International Universities Press.

Novick, J. and Novick, K.K. (1991). Some comments on masochism and the delusion of omnipotence from a developmental perspective. *Journal of the American Psychoanalytic Association.* 39:307-321.

Novick, J. and Novick, K.K. (1996a). A developmental perspective on omnipotence. *Journal of Clinical Psychoanalysis.* 5:129-173.

Novick, J. and Novick, K.K. (1996b). *Fearful symmetry.* Northvale, NJ: Jason Aronson.

Novick, J. and Novick, K.K. (2001a). Parent work in analysis: Children, adolescence, and adults. Part One: The evaluation phase. *Journal of Infant, Child, and Adolescent Psychotherapy. 1*:55-77.

Novick, J. and Novick, K.K. (2001b). Two systems of self-regulation. *Psychoanalytic Social Work. 8,* nos. 3 & 4.

Novick, K.K. and Novick, J. (1998). An application of the concept of the therapeutic alliance to sadomasochistic pathology. *Journal of the American Psychoanalytic Association.* 6:813-846.

Papousek, H. and Papousek, M. (1975). Cognitive aspects of preverbal social interaction between human infants and adults. In *Parent-infant interactions.* New York: Associated Scientific Publishers.

Solomon, W. and George, C. (1999). *Attachment disorganization.* New York: Guilford Press.

Stern, D. (1985). *The interpersonal world of the infant.* New York: Basic Books.

Tronick, E.Z. and Gianino, A. (1986). Interactive mismatch and repair. *Zero to Three.* 6:1-6.

The Therapeutic Process with Children with Learning Disorders

Joseph Palombo

SUMMARY. Clinicians who work with children and adolescents with learning disorders must be aware of the relationship between the learning disorder and the psychopathology the children present. This article offers a conceptual framework, based on psychoanalytic self psychology, to understand the modifications that are necessary in the treatment of this population. The author suggests that, in contrast to other approaches, it is not possible to conceptualize the treatment of these children as having a beginning, a middle, and an end. Rather, the therapeutic process is open-ended and conceived as occurring during a series of moments. The moments may be categorized as concordant, complementary, or disjunctive. During concordant moments a holding environment is created; during complementary moments the transference and countertransference is addressed; and during disjunctive moments the ruptures that inevitably occur during treatment are dealt with. *[Article copies available for a fee from The Haworth Document Delivery Service: 1-800-342-9678. E-mail address: <getinfo@haworthpressinc.com> Website: <http://www.HaworthPress.com> © 2001 by The Haworth Press, Inc. All rights reserved.]*

Joseph Palombo is Founding Dean and faculty member of the Institute for Clinical Social Work, Chicago, faculty member of the Child and Adolescent Psychoanalytic Therapy Program, Chicago Institute for Psychoanalysis, and Research Coordinator, Rush Neurobehavioral Center, Rush Children's Hospital, and the Department of Pediatrics, Rush-Presbyterian-St. Luke's Medical Center, Chicago.

This article extracts from chapters in Joseph Palombo's book, *Learning Disorders and Disorders of the Self in Children and Adolescents,* published by W.W. Norton, 2001. (Published by permission.)

[Haworth co-indexing entry note]: "The Therapeutic Process with Children with Learning Disorders." Palombo, Joseph. Co-published simultaneously in *Psychoanalytic Social Work* (The Haworth Press, Inc.) Vol. 8, No. 3/4, 2001, pp. 143-168; and: *Psychoanalytic Approaches to the Treatment of Children and Adolescents: Tradition and Transformation* (ed: Jerrold R. Brandell) The Haworth Press, Inc., 2001, pp. 143-168. Single or multiple copies of this article are available for a fee from The Haworth Document Delivery Service [1-800-342-9678, 9:00 a.m. - 5:00 p.m. (EST). E-mail address: getinfo@haworthpressinc.com].

143

KEYWORDS. Self psychology, child psychotherapy, learning disorders, learning disabilities

In some respects, all children are alike, yet in other respects each child is unique and different from every other child. In this article, the focus is on the *differences* between children rather than on their similarities. Specifically, it is on the differences that result from having a learning disorder and on the way these differences influence the treatment process. By a learning disorder, I mean a neuropsychological deficit or weakness in one or more of the domains of perception, attention, memory, executive function, verbal and nonverbal language, affect regulation, or social functioning.

The profile of an individual child's neuropsychological strengths and weaknesses is analogous to the topography of a landscape. For some children, the terrain is fairly flat; that is, their competencies are evenly distributed. Other children's profiles look like a terrain filled with prominent peaks. These children are gifted in multiple areas. Yet the valleys between the ridges indicate that their gifts are rarely uniformly distributed across the entire terrain. Gifted children may also have learning disorders (Vail, 1989). For children with learning disorders, the terrain is highly variable. There are peaks and valleys that are notable for the contrast they present. The valleys between the peaks are much deeper than one would expect, indicating a great disparity between the areas of strength and those of weakness.

Some children appear unaffected by their learning disorders. In fact, the presence of a deficit may remain undetected, either because the child has learned to compensate for it or because the environment has not placed a demand on her[1] to demonstrate competence in that area. However, for those children who manifest symptoms, the learning disorder produces academic underachievement, psychological disturbances, or both. I refer to these psychological disturbances as disorders of the self. Such disorders of the self may manifest as failures to attain or maintain a sense of self-cohesion or as an inability to construct a coherent self-narrative or both.

A disorder of the self may manifest as dysfunctional behaviors or emotional problems, or may appear in combination. The dysfunctional behaviors may range from the absence of motivation to perform academically to disruptive behaviors at home and in the classroom. The children's emotional problems may present as low self-esteem, depression, anxiety, or difficulties in affect regulation. Dysfunctional behaviors may manifest as an inability to cope with the environment or an impairment in the ability to form positive relationships to caregivers, to respond appropriately to peers, or to function in school settings. For some children the emotional problems manifest as intense shame, because they feel that they cannot be as successful as they want to be. They realize that they are smart but find themselves unable to demonstrate their competence in academic work. Their self-image is deeply affected. The net result of these dysfunctional behaviors and emotional problems is that these children's development takes a different course than it would have taken had they not been impaired. The extent to which children are affected, as I will discuss, depends on many factors. Among these is the severity of the learning disorder, the demands and expectations made of the child, the child's capacity to compensate for the disorder, opportunities and resources available to the child for the remediation of the disorder, and the parents' responses to the problems the child presents, which in circular fashion affect how the child will react and respond.

Learning disorders do not occur in a vacuum. Children with learning disorders exist in an environment that has a significant impact on their functioning. I refer to that environment as the *context* in which the child is found. My preference for the term "context" instead of "environment" grows out of my desire to emphasize the child's social and emotional milieu rather than simply the physical location in which the child is raised. Caregivers, as well as other aspects of the context, provide psychological nurture that is as important as the physical care the child receives. This context may complement deficits in endowment by providing protective factors, which may explain how the context can, at times, mitigate the impact of deficits in endowment (Cohler, 1987). At the other extreme, the context may amplify the effects of a deficit and overwhelm the child. While endowment may help overcome the deprivations that exist in some contexts, endowment can also act as a constraint that limits the child's development in a way for which no context can compensate.

The relationship between learning disorders and disorders of the self is complex. Disorders of the self may interfere with the acquisition of knowledge, but they do not cause learning disorders, since the latter are neurologically based. The impression derived from clinical experience is that children with learning disorders appear to suffer psychologically more than their peers who do not have learning disorders. As many children do not display psychological symptoms, their suffering cannot be measured through manifest symptoms alone. Epidemiological data, which look at overt symptoms, do not deal with the children's subjective responses to their learning disorder. Most of the children seen clinically seem to suffer at a minimum from self-esteem problems, anxiety, or depression. Some have, in addition, psychiatric problems–comorbid conditions such as mood disorders, anxiety disorders, obsessive-compulsive disorders, and adjustment problems. But no single pattern of problems is associated with all learning disorders. Some subtypes of learning disorders produce specific identifiable configurations of behavioral and emotional problems, while others do not seem to be associated with any pattern of such problems (Brown, 2000; Rourke & Furerst, 1991).

The complex interplay among the neuropsychological deficits or strengths and weaknesses, the context, and the compensations a child utilizes lead to a variety of outcomes. While it is probable that no one is totally unaffected by the presence of a learning disorder, the manifestation of the impairment in the form of successful or unsuccessful adaptation or functioning can range from mild to severe. In the milder cases, the mark left may take the form of personality traits that uniquely identify the person. In the middle range, the combination of factors may lead to self-esteem problems or to narcissistic vulnerabilities to particular situations. In the severe cases, the child's functioning can be seriously impaired. (See also Palombo, 1979; Palombo, 1985a, 1985b; Palombo, 1987; Palombo, 1991; Palombo, 1992; Palombo, 1993; Palombo, 1994; Palombo & Feigon, 1984.)

Therapy with children and adolescents with learning disorders is, in some respects, no different from therapy with any child. In other respects it is quite different. The major difference is that the therapist brings to the process a perspective that is informed by the contributions the context and the child's competencies make to the child's psychodynamics. In this article, I do not undertake to develop a model of the therapeutic process. A model implies a set of standard techniques that are applicable to all patients. While such techniques may exist, the creative aspect of the therapeutic process cannot be captured by such an approach. This is especially true for work with children with learning disorders, where the modes of interaction involve play, drawing, fantasy games, and an entire repertoire of nonverbal modes of communication. In addition, treatment with these children necessitates work with their parents, their teachers, tutors, and other professionals who are closely involved with them.

The goal of the therapeutic process is twofold: (a) *To engage the child in an experience* in which she can either relive an old pattern of interaction and create a new pattern in which feelings are deeply engaged and made more meaningful, (b) *to cocreate a narrative with the child* that helps her understand her strengths and weaknesses, what happened to her historically, and how to use that knowledge in dealing with future situations. The first set of transactions is directed at strengthening the cohesiveness of the child's sense of self, while the second is intended to help her integrate past experiences into her self-narrative. Experience without understanding may be beneficial but is limited because it leaves the person in the dark as to what exactly occurred and what strategies to consciously bring to bear in future situations. Understanding without an experience in which to anchor the understanding is pure intellectual knowledge.

Such knowledge may be helpful, but it may not immunize the child from responding, both affectively and behaviorally, in old ways to current situations.

In the transference, the child unconsciously relives old patterns with little understanding of the motives for her conduct. As new experiences occur between the therapist and child, the therapist has an opportunity to reframe the child's understanding of her narrative and can help her create an entirely new self-narrative. Having an understanding for her conduct–that is, having a narrative interpretation that ties disparate events together–provides a road map that serves as a guide for the child. This is a necessary component of the therapeutic process. The therapist's interpretations or explanations serve to reveal the nature of the patterns and help the child begin to build new patterns for conduct. As the child informs the therapist of the narrative themes that shape the enactments, the therapist gains an understanding of the explanation the child has given to herself for her conduct.

In order to understand the treatment process with these children, I introduce the term *moments*[2] to describe nodal aspects of the process at different phases of the treatment. These moments consist of specific interactions in the dialogue between therapist and child. During this dialogue, feelings associated with past experiences and narrative themes emerge. These moments do not necessarily occur sequentially but arise episodically; they become organizing events that capture for the therapist the essence of the issues with which the child is struggling. As such, they present opportunities for the therapist to intervene through supportive statements, interpretations, or other interventions.

MOMENTS

The therapeutic dialogue with children with learning disorders may be deconstructed as series of moments (Pine, 1985) in which nodal occurrences are in the foreground of the interaction. By "foreground" I mean that the dialogue is experienced as having an ebb and flow during which attention gets focused on a particular set of affect-laden and meaningful interactions. Therapists often theorize that the therapeutic process unfolds in an orderly sequential way and that the movement is from one phase to another–from beginning to middle to termination phase. This sequential approach does not sufficiently appreciate the fluid, dynamic and untidy nature of the dialogue with a child with a learning disorder. In speaking of different *moments* it is possible to view the process as malleable, oscillating from one position to another. The three moments to which I will refer are *concordant moments, complementary moments,* and *disjunctive moments* (Palombo, 1985b; Racker, 1968).

Concordant moments are episodes that occur when the foreground issues are related to the therapist's efforts at maintaining a connection with the child and at creating an environment of safety and confidence. Under the concordant moments, I subsume those issues that have traditionally been classified as pertaining to the therapist's empathy for the child, the creation and maintenance of a holding environment, and the fostering of a working alliance between child and therapist.

Complementary moments are episodes that occur when the foreground is occupied by the *transference* or *non-transference* dimensions of the process. In those moments when the transference elements are activated, the themes of the child's narrative emerge to shape the interaction between the child and the therapist. The therapist must be open to experiencing those themes and understanding the impact they have had on the child's life. Themes from the therapist's narrative also arise within the therapist in response to the child's themes. These inevitably intrude into the process: they are part and parcel of the exchanges. They cannot be understood as undesirable; rather, it is through the interplay between the two sets of themes that a better understanding of the child's communications occurs. At times, nontransferential elements related to the child's neuropsychological deficits are activated. In those moments, the child may be seeking adjunctive functions from the therapist. Adjunctive functions are psychological or cognitive functions that reflect the child's neuropsychological weaknesses. The search for complementarity is motivated by the child's inability to function adequately without that assistance. The therapeutic dilemma for the therapist lies in how to respond to what the child perceives that she needs.

Disjunctive moments are episodes during which disruptions in the dialogue occur. The disruptions may be due to factors related to the therapist or the child. When such a disjunction occurs, the treatment is in crisis. It is essential that the therapist heal the rupture and reestablish the concordance between himself and the child. It is my view that, in those moments, the therapeutic process engages both child and therapist at the deepest levels of their senses of self. Countertransference reactions that stem from the therapist's own problems are subsumed under disjunctions; however, the concept is meant to include a much broader set of contributors to the disruptions that occur between child and therapist.

Concordant Moments: Immersion into the Child's Experience and Narrative

The therapeutic process begins with the establishment of concordant moments in which the therapist's efforts are directed at understanding either the child's psychic reality, or the meanings of what she reports. By becoming immersed in the child's view of the world and resonating with the child's experiences, thoughts, feelings, and memories, the therapist enters that reality. The child must experience the therapist as being attuned to her feelings and responsively appreciative of their significance. Through his attuned responsiveness, the therapist begins to understand the meanings to the child of what she brings to the sessions. As the therapist experiences what the child experiences, he conveys, directly or indirectly, the assurance to the child that the clinical setting is a safe place in which no intentional harm will be inflicted.

EMPATHY

Kohut defined empathy as the tool through which we vicariously introspect our way into a patient's experience (Kohut, 1959). Stern enlarged the definition to include the experience of affect attunement (Stern, 1984). Stolorow emphasized the more cognitive aspect of understanding the meaning of an experience to a patient (Stolorow, Brandchaft, & Atwood, 1987). Each of these definitions underscores the role of nonverbal communication in the clinical process. When we attune ourselves to patients or resonate with their emotional state, we use nonverbal clues to guide us in our understanding of their experience. We listen to patients' verbalizations, but we also note their facial expressions, the direction of their gaze, their prosody, body posture, and other cues that enhance our capacity to enter into their experience. We form impressions of the child's self state through reading these nonverbal cues and respond to them with appropriate verbal and nonverbal interventions.

Empathy, as a tool for gathering data about the child's experience, is used to read nonverbal communications while experiencing with the child what she feels. We do not need to translate the child's nonverbal feelings into words for us to understand what the child is communicating. Through empathy we can tap into areas of the personality to which the child's verbalization may not give us access. Understanding a child's experience occurs through an understanding of the personal and shared meanings she derived from those experiences.

An important step in the empathic process is that of matching affective states. The concepts of attunement, alignment, and resonance describe a process by which caregivers attempt to match the affective state of an infant. This capacity to grasp or to understand is rooted not simply in cognition, but also in the contextual relations experienced by the child, and affective states evoked in her. One determinant of the meaning of an utterance is the context. The therapist's alignment with the child's affect state while grasping the meaning of the experience to the child defines an act of empathy.

The reliability of any information acquired through empathic observation is constrained by the limits of the therapist's capacity to be attuned to and understand another person's experiences. Therapists face a difficult problem in their attempts to empathize with the experience of a child with a neuropsychological deficit. If the therapist has no knowledge of learning disorders, he may grasp intuitively the source of some of the child's struggles but will not understand their origins as related to neuropsychological deficits.

During the decades when psychodynamically oriented therapists had no knowledge of neuropsychological deficits, much good therapeutic work occurred. However, the work was incomplete because the paradigm did not account for these deficits. A detailed understanding of the nature of those deficits is essential to gaining an empathic understanding of the child's struggles. Empathizing with the child who has dyslexia presents therapists with a very different experience from empathizing with the child who has Asperger's disorder. Neglecting to incorporate an understanding of each of those disorders will lead to a failure to understand the child.

I am reminded of an adolescent with severe dyslexia who was failing most of his high school subjects. He often came to sessions angry that he had to be in treatment for his problems. He would open the sessions with contemptuous remarks about my waiting room magazine selection, the office furniture, or even my car. He compared me to his father's therapist, who had a larger office, more expensive furniture, and an expensive car. It was hard for me not to feel annoyed and injured by these contemptuous remarks. The temptation to respond defensively or to retaliate because of the child's attacks was also hard to control. Only after I could take these assaults in stride could I point out to the adolescent how badly he must be feeling due to his failures and how he dealt with his disappointment in himself by directing his anger at me. The contrast he drew between his father's therapist and me paralleled how he felt. He felt that others were much better endowed and more competent than he was. Had I not known of his dyslexia, I might have interpreted his comments as motivated by other dynamics, such as oedipal competitiveness or narcissistic self-centeredness.

During concordant moments, the therapist seeks to establish an environment in which the child can feel safe and understood. A number of factors enter into the creation of such an environment. The therapist conveys a sense of caring and concern by his demeanor and attitude, as well as a readiness to be responsive and helpful. Such a stance is characteristic of the "holding environment" (Winnicott, 1965, p. 240). This position has also been described as a "working relationship" (Keith, 1975). By being nonjudgmental, by assuring the child of the confidentiality of all transactions, and by consistently trying to maintain a perspective that is from within the child's experience, the therapist establishes an alliance with the child. By being open and receptive to feelings, the therapist strives to permit the child to experience an optimal level of intimacy. The therapist's depth of understanding is related to his knowledge of the effects of the learning disorder on the child's development and personality and his ability to convey that understanding to the child. A therapist who lacks that knowledge is prevented from fully empathizing with the child and understanding her psychodynamics (Ornstein, 1976; Ornstein, 1981; Ornstein, 1986).

The atmosphere created in the clinical setting is always dictated by the standards of social propriety consistent with the cultural context in which the therapy is conducted. It assumes unqualified acceptance of and respect for the child. This demeanor is not just part of the empathic stance that is proper for the conduct of the therapy but also implied by the code of conduct to which society and the professional code of ethics subscribe. Deviations from such standards can, in more serious forms, represent a betrayal of the child's trust. At times minor deviations from social propriety, such as not acknowledging a significant event in the child's life or refusing to respond to questions but not explaining why, insert into the setting an element of artificiality that cannot help but bring discomfort or embarrassment or both to the child. The deviations may be perceived as reflective of the therapist's detachment or wish to exert power. Since the therapist owes the child safety and respect as a condition of therapy, these deviations should be explained to her. Failure to adhere to these standards may introduce an iatrogenic element that will add to the child's suffering.

Finally, maintaining a concordant position is at times equivalent to being available to share meaningful affective experiences. Such responses raise the hope in the child that the therapist will acknowledge and respond to her unsatisfied longings. For the therapist to allow himself to be so experienced requires the discipline of keeping his own longings into the background. This disciplined self-denial constitutes the essence of professional integrity.

CONCORDANT RESPONSES

It is possible to conceptualize a variety of *concordant responses* that constitute therapeutic interventions. These are primarily either supportive remarks, indicating to the child that the therapist understands, or remarks directed at the enhancement of the alliance. Most children with learning disorders begin treatment with some initial resistances that must be recognized and worked through. These resistances are often motivated by the fear that their problems will be dealt with much as they have been by others. The empathic atmosphere may raise children's hopes and transference expectations, although they are likely to remain wary that their fear will be realized. Time and acquaintance with the therapist can help work through some of these resistances. Articula-

tion of these resistances through interpretations that convey a general understanding of their source may speed the process along.

Occasionally interpretations of a child's resistance to the establishment of a
concordant position might also be made. Adolescents, for example, are often
resistive to the process itself, experiencing the therapist's attempt to be empathic with their experience as intrusive. They seem to actively repel any effort
at being understood. Such patients drag their heels into treatment, resentfully
complying with caregivers' wishes. Their engagement is initially quite difficult. Rather than responding to these patients in an adversarial way, therapists
might think of them as one would of children who are burn victims and require
physical therapy in order to be rehabilitated. The therapeutic process itself is
agonizingly painful and may even appear to be traumatizing. Keeping their
distress in mind makes it easier to respond with gentle firmness, rather than
harshly and punitively. The resistance must be addressed with the utmost sensitivity. General interpretations consisting of no more than a comment about
the distrust of adults may be more effective than other means.

Once these initial resistances are addressed, the process may unfold. Some
of the archaic selfobject needs begin to surface as the transference develops,
and what Ornstein call the "curative fantasy" (1981, 1983, 1986) becomes activated. This fantasy, which is often unconscious, embodies within it the unful-
filled longings contained within the deficient self. Another way to think of this
fantasy is to understand it as the activation of the child's hope for self-restora-
tion. The hope is that, at last, relief from the chronic suffering is in sight–something will change things radically for the better.

Complementary Moments

Complementary functions are psychological functions children with learning disorders use to maintain a sense of self-cohesion. I refer to selfobject as
well as adjunctive functions. In the context of the treatment process, I return to
the construct of complementarity and extend its meaning to describe part of
what occurs between the child and the therapist. The application of this construct to the therapeutic process highlights the parallels between therapy and
the functions that parents perform to enhance the child's growth and development. It also sheds light on the replication of those patterns in the transference.

A complementary moment may be said to occur when the therapist repli-
cates the childhood context as the child experienced it. One set of complementary moments is related to the *transference of self-object functions and
narrative themes*; the other is related to the performance of adjunctive functions by the therapist, which I designate as a *nontransference reaction.* Let me
first discuss those moments that are related to the transference dimension, and

then deal with those that are related to the nontransference dimension or the search for adjunctive functions.

SELFOBJECT TRANSFERENCES AND NARRATIVE THEMES

Broadly speaking, transference is the perception of the present from a particular perspective in the past. It is the arena in which the child reenacts, and reexperiences old selfobject needs and themes from his narrative.

With regard to selfobject needs, if we were to contrast Kohut's view with Freud's, we might say that Freud understood patients as wanting something forbidden in the transference (the oedipal object), while Kohut saw them as wanting something they needed (selfobject functions). Selfobject transference then is the evocation of the early experiences that resulted from the frustration of selfobject needs. The revival is the reawakening of the uncompleted developmental sequence, not the reemergence or reenactment of an unresolved conflict.

What is recreated is not the selfobject deficit itself–it would make no sense to speak of the rearousal of something that does not exist–but the desire for particular kinds of responses or the disavowed feelings related to the deficit. The positive transference produces an expectation that the new relationship will in some magical fashion provide the patient with the longed-for selfobject functions, that the current relationship will provide what was missed or will repair the injury produced by past events. The negative transference is the expectation that the therapist will respond as others had responded in the past. The child will then be retraumatized. I will deal with this aspect of the transference in the section on disjunctive moments.

From the perspective of the child's self-narrative, the transference represents the enactment of the themes that have organized her experiences. The form the enactment takes reflects the way in which the incoherences in the narrative organized the child's life historically. The clinical setting is, then, a microcosm of the child's current life. It reflects the child's organizing themes in the here-and-now. Those dynamics reflect the unintegrated personal meanings the child has retained. Enactments often represent the best integration the child has made of her experiences. They represent the psychic reality or the narrative interpretation of the child's past. In this sense the historical reality may not have been distorted, because the experience was integrated within the cognitive-affective givens of the child. What makes these experiences problematic now is not that they are fantasies, but rather that they represent a view of reality that has remained walled off from the rest of the child's system of meanings and so has not been integrated with them into a coherent view. The walling-off itself may have been due to an attempt at either repression or of disavowal of the affects associated with the experiences.

Two particular narrative themes I have frequently encountered in the transferences of children with learning disorders are emplotment and conventionalization.

EMPLOTMENT

The concept of emplotment (Kerby, 1991) is used in narrative theory to delineate the ways in which patients become characters in other people's narratives or become engulfed by their own expectations of how their self-narrative ought to unfold. Children can become emploted in their caregivers' narratives when they try to conform to their expectations. They may take on the themes of the narratives of those they wish to please. Caregivers' self-narratives include the meaning the child has for them as well as the role the child is to play in their lives. In effect, the parents experience their infant as a character in their own plot. If the child appropriates these attitudes and behaviors and includes them as subplots within her narrative, she thus becomes emploted into the caregivers' narrative characterizations of her.

Emplotments occur when the child finds it necessary to conform to the narrative themes of others in her context. Children with learning disorders have a great need for others to complement their deficits. At times, the price they have to pay is high; not only must they perform selfobject functions for others, but they must also conform to their expectations. While it is true that many children resist such expectations by rebelling against those who require them, some collapse into compliant conformity. Those who rebel come to the notice of adults more frequently because of their noisy protests. But the compliant ones often fade into the background and are written off as lazy, unmotivated, or simply not bright enough to perform the tasks demanded of them. These children accommodate to their context by trying to become as invisible as possible.

Not all emplotments involve such withdrawals. Some children act out a parent's unconscious assignment of a particular role. A parent may identify the child with a sibling who died young or was a childhood rival. The child's behavior then appears to mimic that of the assigned surrogate.

The sources of these behaviors are often obscured by the fact that they are subtly shaped by the caregivers' unconscious expectations. For example, an eight-year-old child with dyslexia whose testing placed him within the average range of intelligence was referred because his school performance was so much lower than his capacities. His second grade teacher thought he was retarded. During an extended evaluation, the mother revealed that she had a younger brother who had Down Syndrome. This brother had required much attention from her parents, who were determined to give him every opportunity to feel valued. My patient's mother interpreted their behavior as disinterest in her and a sign that the parents favored her brother. Her resentment toward her brother, however, was fraught with guilt. When she was assigned duties for his care, she felt both responsible to act as a caring older sister and deeply resentful that she had to give of herself to this rival for her parents' attention.

When her son was born, she was unambivalent in her love for him. But as developmental deficits emerged and he required more and more of her, her old ambivalent feelings toward her brother began to surface. She struggled against these feelings with increasing guilt; in spite of her best efforts, however, she began to treat her child as she had treated her retarded brother. For the boy's part, he needed his mother to fulfill complementary functions, and the only way he felt he could stay connected to her was through close compliance with what he perceived to be her expectations. The net result was that he became emploted in his mother's narrative by representing his mother's brother, whom he unconsciously mimicked by presenting himself as less smart than he actually was.

In the transference, this child seemed desperate to find a role he could play in the therapist's life. He persistently asked for details about the therapist's family. When given a few facts, he tried to fit himself into the family constellation. He imagined that my other patients were my children and that he was their sibling. He would ask me if I prefer them to him, and were they smarter than he. My responses were that he wished he could be as loved by his mother as he imagined me to love my other patients. I also pointed out that he could not imagine himself to be smarter than my other patients, a comment that he met with disbelief. It was only after his parents could integrate the fact that the dyslexia stood in the way of his accomplishing more academically that their perceptions of him changed. He was then able to integrate the understanding of having a reading problem as not being equated with being retarded. As the family dynamics shifted, his self-perception changed, and he could begin to use tutorial help to learn to read.

CONVENTIONALIZATION

Society presents each individual with a set of "predesigned" narrative themes and expects its members to embrace them. Each patient must integrate some social norms, expectations, and behaviors into her self-narrative or suffer some consequence for defying. Children feel pressured to conventionalize their narratives by making them approximate the normative narrative, that is, the canonical narrative of the social/cultural milieu (Bruner, 1990). The child is confronted with the task of integrating the shared meanings of the context into her self-narrative. In order to maintain selfobject ties to the members of the larger social group, she must embrace or reject the values that the group maintains. She must modify her narrative to bring it closer to the expectations of those whose opinions are valued.

The issue of conventionalization is closely related to alter-ego selfobject functions. Children with learning disorders often feel themselves to be foreigners in the context in which they are raised; yet they desperately wish to be part of the peer group. They see acceptance by the group as minimizing their sense of strangeness. The desire to conventionalize their narratives leads them to try to be as others expect them to be. There are numerous ways in which children manifest the desire to conventionalize their narratives. By conforming to how others dress, how they talk, the activities in which they engage, or even the drugs they use, they try to join a group of peers that is considered "cool." Acceptance by that group erases the sense of difference and normalizes their behavior.

CASE ILLUSTRATION: JIM

Jim was an obese high school freshman who had a history of receptive language problems and impairments in auditory memory and auditory processing. His ability to understand verbal communications was impaired, as was his ability to extract information from reading, although he did not have dyslexia. While he heard clearly what was said to him and could process simple verbal communications, he had difficulty fully understanding other people's spoken words if they were not couched in simple sentences. Even with the assistance of a tutor, he struggled to get C's in courses that involved listening to teachers' lectures. In math, or in subjects that did not involve reading, he consistently got high grades. His perception of himself, in his high-achieving family, was that of someone who would never attain the level of success reached by his parents and siblings. Consequently, he was chronically depressed and had lapsed into a passive stance in which he took no initiative in any activity. His preferred form of entertainment was playing video games, at which he had become quite expert. In addition, he had resorted to eating as a way to comfort himself and was unable to control his food intake. He was more than 60 lbs. overweight, although his large frame masked his obesity so that he looked like an ideal football player.

Jim's father, who had a similar physique, came from a large family in which he had to fend for himself. He was able to become highly successful by being aggressively competitive. While he intellectually understood his son's problems, he felt utterly frustrated by Jim's passivity. He would become enraged whenever he saw Jim watching TV, munching on snacks, or playing video games. To him, Jim was a lazy slug who would never amount to much. He developed the approach of "motivating" Jim by berating him, presenting him with the image of failure unless he did something with himself now to become like other kids. He constantly compared Jim with his high-achieving siblings, tried to restrict his food intake and TV watching, and pushed him to engage in sports. Jim inevitably responded by increasing his food intake and putting even less effort into homework than usual.

When Jim entered high school, his father decided that the solution to the problem was for Jim to try out for football. He felt that participation in football would not only involve him in a healthy athletic program but also encourage him to become more assertive. Jim hated the idea. Being fearful of body contact and not well coordinated, he saw only failure and humiliation ahead of him. However, he felt caught between his own desire to remain regressed and his desire to please his father and gain his approval and affection. For his part, his father dangled the prospect of more fun times together should Jim comply; he threatened to withdraw altogether from Jim if he did not. Finally, Jim's resistance was overcome by the gains he felt he would be making in pleasing his father.

Football turned out to be a painful but bearable experience for Jim. The coach was impressed by Jim's size and saw him as a promising linebacker who could contribute to the team's success. He took a great interest in Jim's training, praised him for the efforts he made, and rewarded him by publicly recognizing any success on the field. The rest of the team became equally invested in Jim's success since they needed him; they made him an integral part of the group and accepted him as one of their own. Jim began to make efforts to be like the others. He saw his salvation as lying in the direction of conventionalizing his behavior so that he appeared to be more "normal." He began to daydream of being a star on the football team, thereby shaping his identity into one that would conform to others' expectations of him.

By embracing a conventionalized theme, that of the heroic football player, Jim was able to find an avenue of success that helped restore a measure of self-esteem in an activity into which he had been pushed. While the initial impetus for his trying out for football was a desire to please his father, his involvement was transformed by the responses he got from his coach and teammates. The desire to be like others and to be accepted as part of the group became a powerful force for his continued involvement in football, in spite of his initial fearfulness and his lack of aggressiveness.

Jim was desperate to attain a conventionalized self-narrative. This included an adamant refusal to involve himself in therapy, because that would have accentuated his sense of difference.

We might speculate as to the type of transference that would have developed had Jim become engaged in treatment. We would expect that Jim's resistance would be in the forefront of the initial work. He would need to be engaged at a level that was acceptable to him. The first priority would be to establish an alliance with him in which he could see the therapist as understanding and supportive. One way such a relationship could have been achieved would have been by focusing on the difficulties Jim was having in his academic work. In this connection, it would be important to find out how well he understood the limitation his learning disorder imposed on his capacity to achieve. Addressing this issue would be complicated by his receptive language problem. Care would be needed in communicating with him verbally, to make sure he understood what was said.

In time, it might have been possible to develop an alliance. The hard work would come with the unfolding of the transference. Expecting the therapist to be as critical and deprecating of him as his father had been, Jim would be acutely sensitive to any negative overtones he might pick up from the therapist's interventions. At the same time, he would be wondering what he needed to do to please the therapist so as to be perceived as a "normal kid."

In the positive transference, the therapist would be responding to Jim's desire to "not have any problems." The issue would be engaged around the meaning Jim attached to having a learning disorder. If he could come to accept that, could he then feel that it did not detract from who he was, and could he feel himself to be different from others without seeing that as a stigma? If those questions could be answered positively, he would escape from the need to seek acceptance by conventionalizing his self-narrative and be freed to find his own path in life.

NONTRANSFERENCES

Not all conduct by a child in the clinical setting is motivated by unconscious factors. Some conduct is the product of the child's neuropsychological deficit. In treating children with learning disorders, therapists confront a major confounding factor, that of making a distinction between a child's responses based on transference and those based on the child's search for adjunctive functions. While sharp differentiations cannot be made, some distinctions are possible that will help therapists in making interventions. These children have emotional *and* learning disorders. They suffer from two types of deficits that often cannot be distinguished: selfobject deficits and neurocognitive deficits. Each has its own history and its own associated set of symptoms. Each leads the child to look to others to fill in these deficits. Neurocognitive deficits do not result from disruption in relationships but from the child's endowment or innate givens. Selfobject deficits arise from the complex interplay between what the child brings to the relationship and the responses of significant others to what they experience the child as expressing. In addition, the child, through her innate givens, contributes significantly to the shape of the relationship with caregivers. Unaware of the child's deficits, caregivers respond to her from the belief that their responses address what the child requires. The failure in the dialogue results in the child's experiencing the parents as unempathic. The therapist must be attuned to the subtle or not so subtle miscommunications that inevitably arise in the transference and that replicate these patterns.

Since, as therapists, our focus is always on the transference, the question can be posed as follows: Can we as therapists distinguish between behaviors that are "brain driven" (hence, unmotivated) from behaviors that are motivated by conscious or unconscious factors and, hence, will manifest as transference reactions? If we were able to answer this question, we would be well on our way to defining appropriate interventions and gaining a better understanding of these children.

At times therapists modify their techniques to respond to specific needs of children with learning disorders. A dilemma is created for the therapist when the child's request requires a departure from what is considered acceptable. For example, a child with a handwriting problem may bring her homework to the session and wish to dictate her work to the therapist. Or, a child may ask that the therapist write a note excusing her from a gym activity that is particularly embarrassing because the child feels exposed and humiliated. The response to these requests must take into account the child's struggles and the issues being addressed. It is not inappropriate to comply with such demands if they serve to demonstrate to the child that the therapist understands the difficulties she is facing.

The child has little or no awareness of her own deficits; therefore, the burden falls upon the therapist to make the distinction and to make a response based on the child's needs. Problems arise less at the extremes than in the middle ground. When a child clearly transfers onto the therapist attitudes that were not invoked by the therapist and manifests patterns of interaction that occurred with significant others, such episodes bear the clear imprint of transference. But when a child asks the therapist to accompany her to the bathroom door because the corridors the child has to negotiate to get to the destination are totally disorienting, it is an injustice to the child to attribute such a request to regressive motives or transference. The request does have meanings to the child based on past interactions, but in most situations these meanings are not clear-cut. The therapist's focus and the context must help determine the proper intervention. Ultimately, observing the results of the interpretations of such behaviors permits the therapist to differentiate between transference and nontransference requests. An interpretation may attenuate the effects of selfobject deficits, but it cannot modify the cognitive deficits–only compensations or new skills can do that.

Disjunctive Moments

A disjunction may be said to occur when the child ceases to feel understood by the therapist. The therapist may also feel that he does not understand the child. The situation need not be symmetrical. At such points the child may withdraw, become enraged, express disillusionment with the progress of the therapy, or actively seek to reengage the therapist in the process. For the therapist, these indicators are flags that something is seriously amiss in the dialogue. While the reactions may be part of the larger transference, they cannot be ignored. The repair of the disruption must take precedence over the reconstruction of the pattern of response. (See also Atwood & Stolorow, 1984, p. 47 on *intersubjective disjunctions*.)

Several factors contribute to the creation of disjunctions or derailments in the dialogue. These may emanate from three sources:

1. *Negative transference reactions* result from the nature of the child's dynamics and recreate experiences in the child's past.
2. *Transferences of the therapist to the child* are the traditional countertransferences that have been discussed at length in the literature and which I will address in relation to the special problems that occur in the treatment of children with learning disorders.
3. *Nontransferential areas of the therapist's functioning* are disruptions created by the therapist's theoretical orientation, lack of experience, interferences due to supervision, personal life events, neuropsychological strengths and weaknesses, and other factors.

NEGATIVE TRANSFERENCES

Children tend to anticipate that a retraumatization will occur in the therapeutic relationship. The negative transference becomes activated when the child experiences the therapist as the embodiment of past negative relationships. The conditions for such a reactivation are often found in a seed of reality in the interaction with the therapist, the result of some small, inadvertent responses on the part of the therapist. Such responses are experienced by the child as intentional or even maliciously inflicted injuries, the concrete manifestations of her fear of retraumatization.

In the complementary interplay, a nucleus of reality is embedded in the activity or the personality of the therapist, to which the child attaches great meaning. This sets off negative expectations. Since such incidents are an inevitable part of the process and reflect the child's dynamics, they provide an opportunity for therapeutic work. What is required is that the therapist acknowledge his contribution to the disjunction. This affirmation of the nucleus of reality in what occurred allows the empathic bridge to be rebuilt. Following that reconnection it may then be possible to comment to the child about the intensity of her response and its possible transference character. Usually what emerges is that the episode represents a reenactment of a segment of the child's past experience that is now available for possible interpretation. This ebb and flow in the process is one of the major components of the curative dimension. The therapist shifts from a disjunctive to a concordant position back to a complementary one. The shifts are an inevitable part of the treatment process. Healing the disjunction is essential to the treatment.

A disjunction may be triggered when the therapist is perceived as threatening, assaultive, or destructive. The therapist may experience the attribution of such feelings as threatening to his own sense of cohesion. The feelings are alien, not in keeping with the view the therapist has of himself. The therapist may then make a concerted effort to disabuse the child of her notions by pointing out the reality that the attributions are not correct. The child experiences these efforts as evidence that the therapist does not understand. The disjunctive gap widens. It is then not even necessary for the therapist to do anything that conforms to the child's expectations for the child to feel misunderstood.

CASE ILLUSTRATION: ASHLEY

A therapist came to consult me about a case with which he was having difficulty. He described Ashley as an attractive, angelic-looking eight-year-old child, who had been referred because of serious behavior problems at school, although her behavior at home seemed to be well within acceptable bounds. She was diagnosed with AD/HD. The parents had a terrible marital relationship; they had been feuding with each other for years. They seemed unable or unwilling to break the impasse by either working on their relationship or separating.

In the course of twice-a-week treatment, Ashley became more and more contemptuous of her therapist. She ordered him around like a slave, demeaning him by her humiliating insistence that the messes she created be cleaned up by him as she gleefully watched. She developed the disconcerting habit of walking into the office and greeting the therapist by giving him the finger and saying, "Hello, you f–." The therapist felt helpless and bewildered as to how to respond to the greeting and to the disrespect. If he did not comply with Ashley's wishes, she would throw a tantrum by screaming, kicking, and spiting in his face. Yet if he did comply he felt totally devastated at being placed in such an abject position. When at one point he complained about her name-calling, she responded that names are only words and can hurt no one. Wouldn't he rather be called names than be kicked or spat upon? While he recognized that Ashley was replicating with him what she probably witnessed at home, the therapist's rage at the constant injury suffered at the hands of this child mounted until he felt his therapeutic effectiveness was totally defeated. He eventually requested that treatment be terminated since he could not see how he could be of help to this child.

In consultation to discuss the impasse, we determined that the concordant position could not be maintained because the therapist's vulnerability to the assaults would not permit him to resolve the child's negative transference. As the consultant, I recommended that the case be transferred to another therapist. What the therapist discovered during the course of the consultation was that Ashley's assaultive behaviors brought up the teasing and taunting he himself had suffered from peers in grade school because of his poor coordination. He had never worked through his embarrassment or his rage at his peers for these assaults. Ashley's parents had dealt with her hyperactivity as misbehavior that required strong reprimands and punishment to control. In the therapy, she replicated the way she had been treated. Unfortunately, rather than responding therapeutically, the therapist became enraged and paralyzed in dealing with the negative transference.

COUNTERTRANSFERENCE

A different type of disjunction occurs when the child's own internal chaos produces a contagious anxiety in the therapist. The therapist may feel assaulted and overwhelmed. Because he feels alone and unable to help the child, he may cast about for measures other than those the relationship provides, such as medication, or possible hospitalization. It may not always be clear which, if any, of these measures are, in fact, indicated. What confuses the issue is the helplessness the therapist feels and the effect it has in clouding his therapeutic judgment. Some therapists tend to respond with resentment and rage, as though the child is intentionally tormenting them and making them feel inadequate. Other therapists find their grandiosity stimulated and take charge of such situations with alacrity and zeal; they become directive and intrusive in the child's life. Obviously, in these instances the burden falls on the therapist to deal with the feelings the child has stimulated.

CASE ILLUSTRATION: KEVIN

Kevin was a sturdy seven-year-old boy who had been referred because of serious behavior problems. He was diagnosed with AD/HD, for which he was on Ritalin and in a special education class in his school. He was impulsive, disorganized, and, at times, intensely provocative. He seemed to know his therapist's vulnerabilities and had acquired the knack of provoking instantaneous rage reactions. At one point in the course of treatment, Kevin would walk by the therapist and then, unexpectedly, lunge toward him and hit him in the genitals. Although the therapist tried to anticipate these assaults, he was not always quick enough to fend them off or defend himself against them. He was repeatedly exposed to both humiliation and physical pain. On occasion he became so enraged at Kevin that he grabbed him and could feel himself almost enough out of control to have hit him. Fortunately, the therapist was able to observe the process closely enough to realize that these assaults were not totally unexpected. Instead, they occurred most often when the child felt on the verge of disintegrative anxiety caused by something that had occurred either in the prior session or in his environment. The complementary positions of the therapist were leading to disjunctive responses.

In consultation, the therapist realized that his own helplessness was reminiscent of physical abuse he had suffered as a child at the hands of an older brother. He became aware of his countertransference and was able to maintain a therapeutic stance. His realization led to an exploration of the management of Kevin's disruptive behavior at home. After several sessions with the parents, they were able to reveal that between the ages of two and five Kevin was cared for by a housekeeper while his mother was working. The parents began to suspect that she might be either physically or sexually abusing him when his behavior grew increasingly out of control. When they discovered a bruise on Kevin's arm, they immediately dismissed her. Kevin never talked or complained about her, which they surmised was because she might have threatened him if he reported what she did to him.

After these revelations, the therapist was able to empathize with Kevin's victimization. Kevin was doing to the therapist what he experienced as having been done to him. It was then possible for the therapist to share with Kevin his parents' suspicion and to have the parents also talk to Kevin, expressing their concern and sadness at what might have happened. While Kevin never could talk about any of this, the assaultive behavior stopped.

Trying to explain to the child the contribution of the learning disorder to the disruptive pattern without making the child feel that he is being blamed for what occurred requires considerable tact. In Kevin's case, there is no doubt that his overactivity made him a very difficult child to control. While this did not justify physical abuse, it raised the question of how to help him understand that his behavior had an impact on others and that others' responses were in part related to that impact.

The therapist began by explaining to Kevin that when he got out of control, bad things happened–people did not like it and could not be nice to him. Once he understood that, his therapist was able to discuss with him the internal disruption caused by his overactivity, that is, while he felt excited and stimulated when he got "hyper," it was difficult for him to settle down and feel good after that. Kevin could then acknowledge that it was difficult for him to stop himself, especially after the medication wore off. At that point, the therapist engaged him and his mother in a discussion of how she could intervene to stop things from escalating without his getting enraged at her. Since he could now accept her interventions without associating them with the physical assaults of the housekeeper, it became possible to restore a measure of calm to his life.

OTHER DISJUNCTIONS

Some authors have written about difficult patients (Groves, 1978; Martin, 1975; Winnicott, 1949) to illustrate the fact that some patients are capable of evoking exceptionally intense positive or negative feelings in therapists. With them the threat of a disjunctive response always seems imminent. These are patients whom therapists come to dislike or even hate. Some children produce anxiety at the prospect of their arrival: they are physically or verbally assaultive; they heap invectives and obscenities; they are obnoxious, contemptuous, and disrespectful. These children provoke, enrage, and push therapists to the limit of their tolerance. They also have the capacity to distort what occurs in the treatment and, adding insult to injury, report the distortions to their parents under the guise that the therapist is mistreating them. With these children, therapists find themselves trapped between desires to retaliate or to terminate the treatment.

When therapists attempt to treat such hostile or neglected children, they reach the very limits of their capacities for concordant responses. Serious ruptures inevitably occur, and the boundaries of what is usually considered appropriate are overstepped. It is as though therapists leave the safe confines of traditional technique and habitual responses and jump into the turbulent reality of the child's life, responding as others do in the child's life.

One question these cases raise is how much of the disjunction is caused by the child's difficult behaviors and how much results from the therapist's failure to understand the child, who in turn rages at the therapist. While this may not be true of all difficult patients, among several cases of children and adults referred to me because their therapy had failed, a common reason for the failure was that the therapists did not understand the nature of their patients' disorders. To those therapists, the patients were difficult, impossible to treat, or could not benefit from treatment. The therapists appeared to have little insight into the motives behind their patients' conduct. This is not to say that the patients did not have personality problems that made them difficult to treat. I only want to emphasize that when patients are not understood, they will, at times, respond with rage at the therapist and appear not amenable to treatment.

Child therapists who hold onto psychoanalytic theories that fail to take into account the effects of neuropsychological deficits on development often arrive at an impasse with their patients. They are handicapped by their incomplete understanding of the psychodynamics of their patients. The disjunctions that result are caused by an outdated or deficient paradigm.

As therapists, we must look not only at patients' contributions to the process, but also at our own. The sources of our contributions are not limited to our personalities but extend to our theoretical orientation, our belief system, and our self-narratives. Ignoring the significance of these factors in the therapeutic process is as detrimental to the process as ignoring the contribution of the context to the child's adjustment.

As therapists, we are imperfect beings, not unlike our patients. We have our share of difficulties, and some of us have learning disorders similar to those of our patients. The empathy we confer on patients ought also to be turned back onto ourselves. We, too, are in need of others to complement us and to serve as adjuncts. What we cannot do is turn to our patients for these.

Ruptures in the therapeutic process invariably occur. Once they occur and the child's rage is mobilized, the therapist must focus on the interventions that will bridge the chasm that has been created. The tasks of healing the rupture, of remaining available as a selfobject, and of restoring the capacity to listen to the child are crucial. Ultimately, the flow of empathy between the child and therapist must be reestablished if treatment is to continue.

In summary, in this article I have attempted to illustrate a perspective through which to understand the treatment process with children with learning disorders. Treatment is an encounter between a child whose personal narrative inadequately organizes her responses to the world and a therapist who attempts to understand and modify the child's narrative. This goal is achieved through a process in which the child experiences being understood and has validation for her perceptions. Once there is a set of shared experiences, it becomes possible for the child to experience the differences between the therapist's responses and those of others. A set of shared meanings is created that helps the child reframe her understanding of the problems. Evidence for greater integration of the child's experiences is found in the greater coherence of her self-narrative. Themes that formerly reflected the assignment of personal meanings to some experiences now encompass shared meanings that have grown out of the child's maturation and experiences in therapy. The child's rehabilitation and restoration to better function can be credited to the combination of greater parental understanding, appropriate school programming, improved social functioning, and the therapist's educative, corrective, and interpretive efforts.

NOTES

1. Where the child's gender is unspecified, I refer to her as feminine. Since I was the therapist in most of these cases, I refer to therapist as male.
2. I borrowed the term *moments* from Pine (1985) (see his Chapter 4, Moments and Backgrounds in the Developmental Process, pp. 38-53), although I give the concept a different interpretation from his. The term is currently being used by the Process of Change Study Group, Boston, of which Daniel Stern and Louis Sander, among others, are members. This group (Sander, 1998) uses the term "moments of meeting." Their use of the term is different from either Pine's or mine.

REFERENCES

Atwood, G. E., & Stolorow, R. D. (1984). *Structures of subjectivity: Explorations in psychoanalytic phenomenology.* New York: The Analytic Press.

Brown, T. E. (Ed.). (2000). *Attention-Deficit Disorders and Comorbidities in Children, Adolescents, and Adults.* Washington, DC: American Psychiatric Press, Inc.

Bruner, J. S. (1990). *Acts of Meaning.* Cambridge: Harvard University Press.

Cohler, B. J. (1987). Adversity, resilience, and the study of lives. In E. J. Anthony & B. J. Cohler (Eds.), *The Invulnerable Child* (pp. 363-424). New York: The Guilford Press.

Groves, J. E. (1978). Taking care of the hateful patient. *The New England Journal of Medicine* (April), pp. 883-887.

Keith, C. R. (1975). The therapeutic alliance in child psychotherapy. *Journal of Child Psychiatry, 7,* 31-43.

Kerby, A. P. (1991). *Narrative and the Self.* Bloomington: Indiana University Press.

Kohut, H. (1959). Introspection, empathy and psychoanalysis. *Journal of the American Psychoanalytic Association, 7,* 459-483.

Martin, P. A. (1975). The obnoxious patient. In P. L. Giovacchini (Ed.), *Tactics & Techniques in Psychoanalytic Therapy* (Vol. 2, pp. 96-204). New York: Jason Aronson.

Ornstein, A. (1976). Making contact with the inner world of the child: Toward a theory of psychoanalytic psychotherapy with children. *Comprehensive Psychiatry, 7*(1), 3-36.

Ornstein, A. (1981). Self-pathology in childhood: Developmental and clinical considerations. *Psychiatric Clinics of North America, 4*(3), 435-453.

Ornstein, A. (1983). An idealizing transference of the oedipal phase. In J. D. Lichtenberg & S. Kaplan (Eds.), *Reflections on Self Psychology* (pp. 135-148). Hillsdale, NJ: The Analytic Press.

Ornstein, A. (1986). Supportive psychotherapy: A contemporary view. *Clinical Social Work Journal, 14*(1), 14-30.

Palombo, J. (1979). Perceptual deficits and self-esteem in adolescence. *Clinical Social Work Journal, 7*(1), 34-61.

Palombo, J. (1985a). Book Review: The borderline child: Approaches to etiology, diagnosis and treatment, Kenneth S. Robson (Ed.). *Child & Adolescent Social Work Journal, 2*(4), 272-273.

Palombo, J. (1985b). The treatment of borderline neurocognitively impaired children: A perspective from self psychology. *Clinical Social Work Journal, 13*(2), 117-128.

Palombo, J. (1987). Selfobject transferences in the treatment of borderline neurocognitively impaired children. In J. S. Grotstein, M. F. Solomon, & J. A. Lang (Eds.), *The Borderline Patient* (pp. 317-346). Hillsdale, NJ: The Analytic Press.

Palombo, J. (1991). Neurocognitive differences, self cohesion, and incoherent self narratives. *Child & Adolescent Social Work Journal, 8*(6), 449-472.

Palombo, J. (1992). *Learning Disabilities in Children: Developmental, Diagnostic And Treatment Considerations.* Paper presented at the Fourth National Health Policy Forum, Healthy children 2000: Obstacles & Opportunities, April 24-25, 1992, Washington, D.C.

Palombo, J. (1993). Neurocognitive deficits, developmental distortions, and incoherent narratives. *Psychoanalytic Inquiry, 13*(1), 85-102.

Palombo, J. (1994). Incoherent self-narratives and disorders of the self in children with learning disabilities. *Smith College Studies in Social Work, 64*(2), 129-152.

Palombo, J., & Feigon, J. (1984). Borderline personality in childhood and its relationship to neurocognitive deficits. *Child & Adolescent Social Work Journal, 1*(1), 18-33.

Pine, F. (1985). *Developmental theory and clinical practice.* New Haven: Yale University Press.

Racker, H. (1968). *Transference and countertransference.* New York: International Universities Press.

Rourke, B. P., & Furerst, D. R. (1991). *Learning disabilities and psychosocial functions: A neuropsychological perspective.* New York: The Guilford Press.

Sander, L. (1998). Intervention that effect change in psychotherapy: A model based on infant research. *Infant Mental Health Journal, 19*(3), 280-281.

Stern, D. N. (1984). Affect attunement. In J. D. Call, E. Galenson, & R. L. Tyson (Eds.), *Frontiers of Infant Psychiatry* (pp. 3-14). New York: Basic Books.

Stolorow, R. D., Brandchaft, B., & Atwood, G. (1987). *Psychoanalytic treatment: An intersubjective approach.* Hillsdale, NJ: The Analytic Press.

Vail, P. L. (1989). The gifted learning disabled child. In L. B. Silver (Ed.), *The assessment of learning disabilities: Preschool through adulthood. College* (pp. 135-159). New York: Hill Publication: Little, Brown Co.

Winnicott, D. W. (1949). Hate in the countertransference. *International Journal of Psycho-Analysis, 30,* 69-74.

Winnicott, D. W. (1965). *The maturational processes and the facilitating environment.* New York: International Universities Press.

Attention Deficit Disorder, Anxiety Disorder, and Learning Disabilities: Preliminary Results of an Object-Relational/Psychoeducational Treatment Approach with an Eight-Year-Old Girl

Vivian Farmery

SUMMARY. This article details an individualized psychoeducational model designed to treat a child with interrelated psychological and developmental issues whose psychic functioning was deteriorating within the traditional educational system. The team had leeway to function outside of the educational system to create an individualized, remedial, psychoeducational program. At the time we began the program, her diagnostic picture included: Anxiety Disorder, Attention Deficit/Hyperactivity Disorder, and Learning Disabilities. The treatment team consisted of an education specialist, two additional part-time teachers, a clinical social worker, an occupational therapist, a consulting senior child psychoanalyst, and the child's mother. The results at the close of the first school year are examined. Perspectives informing the psychoanalytic as-

---

Vivian Farmery, CSW, is a psychotherapist in private practice in New York City. She is a doctoral candidate and Adjunct Professor at the New York University School of Social Work and co-founder of the Center for Individualized Education.

[Haworth co-indexing entry note]: "Attention Deficit Disorder, Anxiety Disorder, and Learning Disabilities: Preliminary Results of an Object-Relational/Psychoeducational Treatment Approach with an Eight-Year-Old Girl." Farmery, Vivian. Co-published simultaneously in *Psychoanalytic Social Work* (The Haworth Press, Inc.) Vol. 8, No. 3/4, 2001, pp. 169-192; and: *Psychoanalytic Approaches to the Treatment of Children and Adolescents: Tradition and Transformation* (ed: Jerrold R. Brandell) The Haworth Press, Inc., 2001, pp. 169-192. Single or multiple copies of this article are available for a fee from The Haworth Document Delivery Service [1-800-342-9678, 9:00 a.m. - 5:00 p.m. (EST). E-mail address: getinfo@haworthpressinc.com].

169

pects of this case include Winnicottian and Fairbairnian Object Relations Theory and therapeutic milieu model. *[Article copies available for a fee from The Haworth Document Delivery Service: 1-800-342-9678. E-mail address: <getinfo@haworthpressinc.com> Website: <http://www.HaworthPress.com> © 2001 by The Haworth Press, Inc. All rights reserved.]*

KEYWORDS. Special education, therapeutic milieu, holding environment, AD/HD, anxiety disorder, learning disabilities

INTRODUCTION

Children are typically asked to adjust themselves to existing systems, adapting to their environments as best they can regardless of the psychic price they pay. We rarely alter systems to meet an individual's requirements. When children and systems do not integrate well together, the system doesn't acknowledge that it is poorly equipped to meet the child's needs. Instead, we attempt to put round pegs into square holes while we treat with psychotherapy and medication the obvious signs of disenfranchisement. Even though we may believe the child's emotional pathology to be the direct result of that poor fit, there is seldom anything that we as clinicians are able to do to ameliorate his/her unhappiness.

The case of Emily represents a child who was in considerable emotional distress as a result of her unhappy experiences within the educational system. A new psychoeducational program was created specifically to serve her educational and emotional needs. This is an exceptional case with respect to its handling although it appears to represent a common diagnostic situation, and, while it is too early to say that gains have been or will be consolidated, it appears that the approach is having significant success. It remains to be seen whether there is solid ground upon which to build a model to generalize this approach for the treatment of other children. There may be value in a future attempt to extrapolate useful theoretical, clinical, and programmatic principles from our experience with Emily.

The team's psychoanalytic and psychoeducational interventions are intended to reposition a developmental picture that had moved off an optimal track. The treatment approach was designed to alleviate the psychic distress that resulted from her unhappy experiences within both the traditional and special education school systems. The treatment goal is to help Emily become less anxious in the face of academic tasks so that she might resume learning and develop according to her highest intellectual and psychological capacities. By easing her psychological distress and restoring her previous characteristic level of happiness, it is hoped that we can optimize her future functioning within society.

Seven-year-old Emily was initially recommended for typical interventions within the system. These included psychotropic medication, special education school, and traditional psychotherapy. Subsequent difficulties and the lack of relief afforded by these interventions are discussed and a rationale provided for the alternative treatment plan created. Some preliminary results at the end of the first year are also discussed.

Considerable developmental history relevant to the issues involved will be presented to illustrate the relationships between Emily's preexisting developmental weaknesses and the iatrogenic psychopathology to which her schooling and medication experiences gave rise.

The Diagnosis of Attention Deficit/Hyperactivity Disorder

While a discussion of the issues involved in these diagnoses is not the purpose of this article, a few comments may highlight the controversies involved. Emily was diagnosed at age seven with both Attention Deficit/Hyperactivity Disorder, Predominantly Inattentive Type (AD/HD) and Generalized Anxiety Disorder. We know that both of the diagnoses are increasingly common in our society today and that they frequently overlap (Barkley, 1998). According to the *Fourth Diagnostic and Statistical Manual* (DSM-IV), approximately three to five percent of all school-aged children are diagnosed with AD/HD (American Psychiatric Association, 1994).

Emily suffered birth trauma, an occurrence causally linked to Attention Deficit Disorders in the DSM-II, where it was referred to as Minimal Brain Dysfunction (American Psychiatric Association, 1968). In addition, it appears likely that Emily's father suffers from adult AD/HD. This and her difficult birth are the known genetic and traumatic factors that may have predisposed her to the vulnerabilities which were then exacerbated by her formal school experiences. Although a discussion of the etiology of AD/HD is beyond the scope of this article, it is important to acknowledge that controversies around etiology and nosology (Barkley, 1998) and even the very existence of the syndrome (Breggin, 1998) pervade the literature.

Emily is, and apparently has always been, the preternatural dreamy artistic child. She appears to be somewhat unrelated to time and space. Time of day, day of the week, months of the year, and seasons of the year all remained beyond her grasp until quite recently. Whether we speak of this as AD/HD or as an artistic temperament, the fact remains that her dealings with the educational system were unproductive and psychically harmful to her.

EARLY DEVELOPMENTAL HISTORY

Emily was very much a wanted child. Her parents spent eight months trying to conceive her. Although the pregnancy was reportedly normal, Emily's mother was in hard labor for 30 hours, and both Pitocin and high forceps were employed in the child's delivery. Apparently, Emily was stuck in the birth canal, although, according to the fetal monitor, she was not in distress. At birth, her head was misshapen from the protracted pushing and was marked by the characteristic spoon-shapes of the forceps.

As a baby, Emily showed unusual sensitivity to noise and appeared to have great difficulty self-soothing. An anecdote revealed that she slept so lightly as a baby that the opening of a soda can a room away was sufficient to awaken her. Although she sucked her thumb at bedtime for comfort, she reportedly had difficulty separating from her parents at sleep times. She required protracted rocking to fall asleep and then would often awaken when put down. Usually unable to nap for more than 20 minutes, she did not sleep through the night regularly until she was four years old.

Nursing was easy for this mother and child; Emily took to the breast and fed well. Always within the 100th percentile for height, she grew well and thrived. Her childhood milestones were on the early side of normal: She took her first steps at 10 months and spoke before her first birthday. She weaned herself at six months and abandoned the use of a bottle at one year. Toilet training was accomplished between two and two-and-a-half years.

Emily has a brother three years younger than she is who has shown none of Emily's environmental sensitivities or school difficulties. She was very excited in advance of his birth and even impatient around his arrival. However, when her difficulties began to manifest in first grade, she appears to have taken much of her frustration and unhappiness out on her brother. Emily was very verbal about her jealousy of him and continually made comparisons whenever she thought he was favored over her. She was unkind to him and, at times, physically threatening as well. He became provocative in return, and there were some hard years in the sibling relationship.

Emily's parents have always demonstrated appropriate concern for their daughter and a capacity to put her needs first. Her parents separated when Emily was six but both parties remained cordial and focused on her needs. Her home life has been consistently supportive and nurturing. Her parents' separation did not diminish this loving environment. She has seen her father frequently and consistently since the separation, has always been close to him, and seems to have adjusted reasonably well to the separation. She spends every other weekend, alternate Sundays, and one night per week with her father.

Emily has been in the care of the same loving babysitter since she was two months old. The relationship between the sitter and Emily is warm and easy. Emily's mother works part-time so she is with the sitter several afternoons per week and occasionally at bedtime. Thus her caretakers, mother, father, and babysitter, can all be said to be provisionally "good enough" in the Winnicottian sense (Winnicott, 1965).

Emily was described as a happy and well-related child until she entered kindergarten at age five-and-a-half. Social skills came easily to her; sharing and waiting turns were not difficult to learn. As a toddler, she was active and played well with other children. Emily and her mother were part of a mother/child playgroup and she did well there. Emily has had the same best friend since both attended this toddler playgroup. They were in school together until kindergarten. The girls, now 9, are still close, with a high degree of empathy obvious between them. This early and enduring capacity for intimacy is noteworthy in light of other social issues that will be discussed.

In general, it appears that for Emily these early years were happy ones that fostered good self-esteem and social skills.

Preschool Years

Although children at this age often show difficulty making the transition from home to preschool, Emily did not. Her mother made a point of easing her transition into preschool by walking her to school with her best friend for the first two weeks. The two girls happily ran ahead of their mothers into the classroom and evinced little separation anxiety. Once in the classroom, Emily socialized well with her peers and was frequently noted for the physical affection she freely gave her teachers. Her second year preschool teacher commented that Emily appeared to use the adults in the classroom to orient herself by climbing into their laps when she was in discomfort. She would remain there for a few minutes and then resume her play. While this behavior is not atypical of the age group, Emily might be said to have employed it more frequently and with less inhibition than the other children. At this time, the issue of inappropriate affection arose with Emily. On more than one occasion her mother reported finding Emily in the lap of a stranger. Appropriate boundaries were explained to her, but she seemed to have difficulty with the concept at this age.

In preschool, the issue was principally her disorientation. When called, she frequently seemed to be daydreaming or so preoccupied with her own games that she failed to hear the summons. She never internalized the patterns and routines of a preschool day and always seemed somewhat surprised to hear that it was time for another activity even when the second activity followed the first on a daily basis.

Several times during school conferences, her parents raised their concern that Emily seemed uninterested in reading or writing, but since the school used the Montessori method and the children had little academic pressure, there was no institutional support for this concern. Instead, teachers consistently pointed out that Emily was well liked by both peers and teachers and noted that she was quite creative and cheerful. Her parents commented later that what they were seeing in their daughter at this time foreshadowed her future academic troubles, but, at the time, they couldn't have explained exactly what it was they saw, nor did the school seem to understand or help them to focus on it. Later the preschool staff were surprised to hear of Emily's academic difficulties despite her parents' early concerns. Her parents liked the preschool staff and director very much but wished they had been better able to see her difficulties at the time they were choosing a kindergarten.

Kindergarten

At five-and-a-half, Emily entered kindergarten at a private school. Her parents had selected the school because it was reputed to teach to the individual child's learning style, and her parents were already aware that her style of learning was going to require a creative approach.

Once again, Emily had no difficulty beginning her new school. She made friends easily and showed little separation anxiety despite having to use a school bus for transportation. However, her kindergarten teachers were far less tolerant of her need for their physical reassurances than her preschool teachers had been. As learning tasks began to take the place of dramatic play in the classroom with a concomitant expectation of increased autonomy and conformity to rules, her difficulties began. The introduction of academic tasks combined with the kinetic energy of 27 children was the setting into which her focusing issues emerged. Emily was the first to note that she was struggling to pay attention. She stated, "when its noisy in the classroom I can't even remember how to write my name and I KNOW how to write my name!" In the fall of her kindergarten year, the school raised concerns about her classroom functioning and recommended that Emily have a psychological evaluation.

Emily's first psychological evaluation led to a diagnosis of borderline AD/HD, anxiety disorder NOS, and possible learning disabilities. Tutoring and psychotherapy were recommended, and both began around the time of her sixth birthday. Unfortunately, these interventions did little to ameliorate her classroom difficulties.

Early that spring, the school proposed that Emily repeat kindergarten. Knowing that Emily had learned the material, her parents objected to her repeating a grade, feeling that it was Emily's growing anxiety over noise and distraction which was creating the trouble. These circumstances began to take an emotional toll as Emily's anxiety led to a budding dislike of school. She expressed this anxiety psychosomatically, complaining of sporadic headaches or stomachaches during the school week.

At this point, Emily's strengths could be seen in her warm relatedness towards others and in her creative abilities. Unfortunately, these assets did not serve her well at this time, and, in fact, increased the teachers' perception of Emily as a problem. From earliest childhood, Emily exhibited tremendous creativity; her drawing abilities far exceed those of the average child of her age. During another school conference that same year, Emily's teacher complained of her inability or unwillingness to make transitions to other assigned tasks. As evidence, the teacher showed her parents one of her drawings. Emily's desire to complete this drawing had kept her from promptly joining the class at recess. This drawing simultaneously demonstrated Emily's creativity, her ability to concentrate for an extended period of time, and the price she paid for this talent. The task was to draw narcissus bulbs sprouting in a glass bowl. Her mother recalls that one could clearly see in the drawing the shape of the three-dimensional bowl. Further, not only had Emily taught herself to draw in three dimensions, also clearly visible in the drawing was the reflection of the front of the bowl onto its back wall. It seems an irony that this creative drawing, over which Emily had obviously expended much time and energy, formed the basis of her teacher's complaint in regard to Emily's transitional difficulties. In general, Emily showed enormous talent and perseverance when any project, usually of her own design, challenged her creatively. She was reportedly able to spend two or three hours making doll clothes, for example, and expressed a strong desire to be a clothing designer.

As the school year progressed, the gap between her areas of competence and her areas of weakness widened. Emily evinced little interest in learning to read or write as her sensory difficulties became more upsetting to her and of greater concern to the teachers.

First Grade

During the winter of first grade, Emily was again evaluated, this time by a neuropsychologist. She was diagnosed with AD/HD, Predominantly Inattentive Type, Anxiety Disorder bordering on Panic Disorder, and diverse Learning Disabilities. According to the neuropsychological evaluation, she showed extreme anxiety when presented with challenging tasks and during transitions. Symptoms included shortness of breath, pounding heart, feeling unsteady, hot flushes, and stomach cramps. Clearly, Emily had begun to somatize her growing anxiety. As a result of this evaluation, a child psychiatrist prescribed Buspar, an anti-anxiety medication.

Socially, Emily began to withdraw during first grade. After kindergarten her ability and willingness to make friends in school decreased steadily. Although she greatly enjoyed parties and sleepovers on the weekends, during the week, her psychic and emotional exhaustion from the school day began to take its toll. She became distanced from her peers and her play with them became more juvenile. She continued to see her best friend, but now only on the weekends.

During the late fall of her first grade year, the school informed her parents that they felt they were no longer the appropriate setting for Emily. They suggested her parents investigate special education.

Second Grade

At seven-and-a-half, Emily was sent to a private special education school. Rather than relieve her anxiety, however, by providing her with a calmer holding environment and thus a greater psychic freedom to participate in academics, the special education classroom further harmed Emily in a number of ways.

Her mother, her therapist, and the education specialist who had been her tutor and would become her main teacher the following year consulted extensively at this time; all hoped a special education school with ten children per class would prove less distracting to Emily. In truth, however, Emily experienced the noise and disturbance created by nine other special education children as far worse than the classroom distractions in the mainstream school. As an acutely sensitive child, Emily was compromised by, and uncomfortable with, the psychic and physical chaos arising from the emotional and physical conditions of her classmates.

Her class was typical of a private special education school. It consisted of seven boys and three girls. The group appears to have included diagnoses of Oppositional Defiant Disorder, Attention Deficit Hyperactivity Disorder, and Conduct Disorder. It should be noted that all of these diagnoses involve disruption and frequent acting-out behaviors in the classroom. Her classmates distracted her, and the resulting academic failures and teachers' concerns led to classroom management techniques that seemed punitive and restrictive to her. For example, work not finished during work times led to missing recess. This appears to have caused the beginning of her depression. Her play became increasingly juvenile; increasingly she wanted to just hug and to pick up the other children. Often her affection seemed inappropriate to the other children and may have made them anxious. She demonstrated little interest in group or team games and usually declined to play them. Her teachers noted at this time that Emily preferred to spend recess among them, and usually refused to play with her peers. She complained to her mother about the other childrens' physical disabilities. It bothered her greatly at this time that she was frequently asked by the teachers to assist a disabled classmate to the bathroom. Her therapist felt that Emily's thoughts about, and fears for, her own intactness were mirrored in the other childrens' physical disabilities.

Socially, Emily was so exhausted, and then depressed, by the demands of her school day that she became unable and unwilling to socialize after the school day, or to participate in after-school activities, even with longtime friends. Participation in activities such as the arts and swimming might have helped her self-esteem but now seemed beyond her capabilities. Emily missed swimming and other beloved activities but simultaneously declined to attend, arguing that she was "too tired" and that she "didn't want to see anyone." At about this time, she told her mother that she no longer wished to be a clothing designer or an artist because she was "too stupid." By that winter, her mother noted a distinct falling off in her interest and involvement in creative projects as her depression worsened.

She argued increasingly against going to therapy through that year, and it seemed largely unproductive. She seemed unwilling or unable to bring her growing anxiety and depression into the treatment room and expressed her desire to "just play" once there. Her therapist wanted to have Emily enter analysis several times a week, but her mother felt Emily couldn't tolerate any further commitment after her draining days in school.

By winter, her anxiety and subsequent depression manifested daily in morning tears and stomachaches as she pleaded with her mother to be allowed to stay at home. In addition to ongoing struggles over school attendance, there were frequent and tearful calls from Emily at school, begging to come home. She missed a significant amount of school through this time, as her mother was forced to decide between putting her crying daughter on the bus and keeping her at home. Her mother commented at this time that Emily was always pale and had dark circles under her eyes. Both mother and daughter were exhausted by the daily struggle.

This vicious downward spiral precipitated further pharmacological recommendations on the part of the educational and psychiatric systems. The special education school psychologist first suggested Ritalin combined with an increased dosage of anti-anxiety medication, and later recommended trying a course of anti-depressants. Despite her mother's hesitation, she tried this medical approach in the hope that it would help to alleviate her daughter's suffering. Unfortunately, Emily became even more depressed on Ritalin, and it was terminated after a month. Her mother was unwilling to place her on further medication such as the recommended anti-depressants. It was then spring and the school year was ending. The treatment team began forming as her mother met repeatedly with her psychotherapist and the education specialist. Instead of trying further medication, the decision was made at that time to embark upon the treatment this article details.

ANALYTIC DISCUSSION

A Winnicottian Framework

The work of D. W. Winnicott (1965) has been extremely useful in conceptualizing the important psychodynamic issues in Emily's treatment. Applying his theories to Emily, with school as the holding environment in question, we can understand many of the key developmental issues with which Emily struggled. When Winnicott defined trauma as, "a failure of environmental provision which could result in the annihilation of the individual whose going-on-being was interrupted," he gave us a psychosocial framework in which to reexamine and redefine trauma (1965, p. 256). Speaking of impingement as "environmental distortion or deficiency" of "etiological significance," he posits that environmental interference can cause sufficient mental distress to create psychopathology (1965, p. 137). Examining which aspects of environmental stressors could be described as etiologically significant, Winnicott went on to speak of the child, delicately balanced between hereditary vulnerabilities and the environment which, "either supports, or fails and traumatizes" (1965, p. 139).

This treatment approach was founded on the belief that the emotional tone of the environment in the schools Emily attended, as well as the attitudes and judgements conveyed therein, were etiologically significant and traumatogenic in their effects. The traumata were caused by the unfortunate impact of these environmental impingements on Emily's areas of hereditary and charactological vulnerabilities, vulnerabilities which left her susceptible to the anxiety and isolation she experienced in the schools she attended.

Winnicott's sense of the failure of the environmental provision leads to the core notion of the development of the False Self (1965). For Winnicott, the False Self is the ego's response to unbearable impingements by the environment; he defines it as that which covers or hides the True Self when the exploitation of the True Self would result in its annihilation (1965). In the face of such impingement, the child develops a False Self in order to hide, and protect, the vulnerability of the True Self. When Winnicott speaks of the True Self, he refers to the aspects of the self which generate all that is spontaneous and creative in an individual; in the child, this is the inner reality (1965).

The treatment team believes this case represented a failure of the educational environment to allow the successful "going-on-being" of this child's True Self. Certainly, we can see that Emily was traumatized by her educational experiences. Her reaction to the impingements represented by the lack of support for her creative talents, or True Self, and the tremendous stress upon her vulnerabilities was twofold. She tried to defend against knowledge of her inability to meet the demands of the environment by shutting down her consciousness through reactive depression and regression, mechanisms which will be further discussed below. She also became increasingly anxious as her psyche was threatened with the annihilation of her True Self. This led to a diagnosis when her anxiety levels threatened to reach panic attacks, and, subsequently, to medication, which in this case could be perceived as the system's way of generating Emily's False Self.

Other Theoretical Contributions to Our Understanding

Following Fairbairn's concept that all humans are primarily object-seeking, we can profitably examine Emily's issues from the perspective of her Object Relationships (Fairbairn, 1952). The team believed that her functioning with respect to her objects held an important key to her psychic distress. At the time of her greatest distress, the team felt that Emily was thoroughly disappointed at school, in what Fairbairn would have described as her "need to be loved for herself" (1952). Fairbairn would say that in this state, she defended against the knowledge that the available external objects in her school were disapproving, disappointing, and possibly even sadistic by internalizing the "badness." Her own awareness of her cognitive vulnerability in the face of distraction and her subsequent low self-esteem contributed to this internalization of the punitive, or critical, voices. Instead of considering that the demands upon her might have been unreasonable in the face of her sensory issues, she internalized her perception of their negative, judgmental attitudes towards her. She was unable to experience herself as a capable individual within the school setting in which she felt so powerless. This caused her depression and low self-esteem. Despite her mother's and her therapist's urging, she was incapable of seeing herself as simply different rather than bad. She truly internalized the treatment she received and the way she had been perceived. As a sensitive child, occurrences such as discussions about Emily's vulnerabilities while she was present, her treatment by the schools she had attended, and her neurocognitive and emotional problems had all contributed to her awareness that she was different from her brother and peers. All of this intensified her depression and weakened her self-esteem. Attempts to refocus her on her positive qualities were ineffective.

An interesting side-note to this issue was her feelings about her teachers. After her experiences in first and second grade, Emily would constantly refer to her teachers as mean, and, in fact, there is some objective data in support of this. Once she left their classrooms, however, she tended to idealize them, anticipating that her new teachers would be "mean." Even when the distinction was made for her between mean teachers and those who were academically demanding but kindly, Emily seemed unable to understand. Her growing self-hatred was then projected outwards onto her new teachers. She felt she was stupid and the work was too hard. All learning had become inextricably bound up with her negative self-judgement. Although these induced beliefs seemed to have some basis in reality, Emily became stuck in the resulting harsh self-judgements. This contributed greatly to her growing unwillingness to go to school and to her psychosomatic, anxiety-related symptoms.

In kindergarten, Emily tried to use her strengths to garner needed ego support both internally and externally, as with the narcissus bowl drawing. Emily wanted to do the things at which she excelled to reinforce her ego strength in the face of the strong challenges generated by the environmental difficulties she was facing. This refers, again, to Fairbairn's notion of being loved for oneself (1952). Unfortunately, her environment failed to reward her for the efforts she made. As the school environment worsened in its failure to support her, Emily's reactions became increasingly negative but understandably self-protective. Much of her spontaneous creativity went missing and unexpressed behind the veil of unhappiness and self-hatred. Not only did she express decreasing interest in the tasks of school and greater resistance to engage in them, but her creative and dramatic play at home and with her best friend also fell off sharply. At this point, one could no longer find the cheerful Emily previously known to all under the heavy mask of the False Self.

The team feared that she had lost much of what White termed the "drive to competence," something which we, along with White, believe is normally correlated with Erikson's latency-aged task of school-based competency (Erikson, 1963; White, 1959). The drive to competence seemed adversely affected by her reactive regression. In effect, Emily's school environment failed her as a medium of normative development.

If this discussion represents an atypical way to conceive of the educational environment, the team believes it is, nonetheless, legitimate. A latency-aged child spends the majority of her waking hours in school. Erikson would say that the main task of latency revolves around achievements expected in the school environment (1963). In his words, "[the latency-aged child] now learns to win recognition by producing things" (1963, p. 259). In school, the things expected to be produced relate to the assignments given by the teacher. Autonomous production is rarely encouraged within our school system, as the anecdote involving Emily's three-dimensional production illustrates. Her creation of this drawing brought neither pleasure nor pride, for the assignment was her own creation, and the teacher was displeased with her allocation of time. This drawing used Emily's strengths in such a way as to stretch her developmentally; her creativity, autonomy, and concentration were all exercised. The resulting harm to her self-esteem lay not in the criticism of her production, but in the criticism of her developing autonomous creativity. She performed poorly at the tasks her teachers considered important and was not praised when she excelled in other areas. This deprived her of pleasure in her accomplishments. Even recreational activities after school became unbearable. To the team this represented a definitive example of latency gone awry. A remedial educational experience was deemed essential at this time, the team concluded, in order for Emily to complete the psychosocial tasks of latency. The loss of self-esteem associated with a failure to master these developmental tasks would only be further compounded by the challenges of adolescence.

Internal Object Representations

Using an object relational framework, the treatment team looked long and hard at Emily's constant need to use her teachers as both objects from whom she sought reassurance, and as external stabilizing forces in the face of a frequently overstimulating environment. We felt that this represented a possible genetic or characteristic weakness in her ability to hold onto internal objects in the face of anxiety. This distress also contributed to her high levels of anxiety when asked to work alone, as she was in the classroom and during homework time. There appeared to be a relationship between Emily's tenuously held internal objects and her inability to stay on task without guidance in the noisy classroom. The more anxious she felt, the more she needed external objects to buoy her failing internal object representations. The more her external objects failed her, the more anxious she became. The less capable she was of working within the distractions of the classroom, the worse she did academically. The worse she did academically, the lower her self-esteem and the higher her anxiety. Eventually, this vicious cycle reached crisis proportions. The combination of the repeated internal object loss, her low self-esteem, and her environmental sensitivity provided the theoretical underpinnings of the decision to create and implement this treatment plan.

It is interesting to note that her frequent waking and subsequent inability to soothe herself in infancy may show us both her early and consistent vulnerability to outside stimuli and her system's obstacles to a state of equilibrium. Her difficulty soothing herself may reflect a systemic sensitivity that resurfaced in the face of the stressors she experienced in school.

Theoretically, it appears that Emily's internal object representations were not strong enough to sustain her in the face of the growing environmental stress. Winnicott speaks of the internal object representation as that which fosters the ability to be alone in the presence of the other (1965). The capacity to be alone thus rests on the development of the good object within the psychic reality of the child. If the capacity to be alone is learned through being alone in the presence of the other, in this case, the capacity to be alone was lost through the failure of the environment to allow her to function well when she felt alone within it. We saw this in preschool when she used her teachers as anchors in time and space. We saw how the failure of the teachers to be "good-enough" objects contributed to her growing anxiety in the face of her escalating difficulties with academic tasks. We believe this was the underlying explanation of her troubles; she was unable to maintain sufficient ego strength while under these strains, and, as a result, she lost the capacity to be alone, a vulnerability we recognize from her early history around self-soothing behaviors.

When Winnicott speaks of learning the capacity to be alone in the presence of the other, he alludes to the role of the other quite specifically (1965). The job of the adult is to be present but supportive and not intrusive. In fact, the ideal object for this lesson is the mother who is well employed by her own tasks and thus present but undemanding. We know that if the environment frustrates or engenders anxiety, the child returns to mother, or a substitute object, for reassurance. But what of an environment in which this is no longer possible, one in which the teachers themselves have become a source of excessive frustration?

With increasing school difficulties also came increasing difficulty separating from home and her mother. She became easily upset by situations which called for enduring separations from home as well as from familiar, trusted, nurturing adults, as for example, in relation to the long bus ride to school each day. For Emily, at age eight, the nonpresent object seemed to have disappeared, and near panic became the psychic response.

Regression

The combination of the constant sensory distress, Emily's anxiety, and the environment's failure to provide nurturing external objects proved overwhelming to her ego. Unable to bear the threat to her self-image and previously adequate self-esteem, Emily's response was a regressive one. We conceptualized this as the False Self protecting the True Self from further ego damage through its concealment behind the mask of childishness. Her regression may be seen to represent efforts to prevent environmental failure from completely obliterating her positive self-image and self-esteem. The True Self, the artist described elsewhere, was secreted, and a regressed little girl appeared in its place.

Anna Freud said regression is not affected by the developmental stage attained; rather, it is among the most primitive of defense mechanisms and returns often in the face of trauma or threats to the ego (1965). Ego regression could be seen in Emily's statements that she wished to "be a baby again." She was quite capable of elaborating this desire, and she began to act out on it more and more as the traumatic impact of her school experience began to be felt and negative self-image issues were internalized. She regressed further during the year in special education school. She began to ask repeatedly for bottles and pacifiers. At age eight, Emily was showing her extreme psychic distress by regressing to what she unconsciously believed to have been a safer and happier time.

We view regression as a normative, and usually temporary, response to trauma. Anna Freud elucidated the fine line between temporary, and thus reversible, regressions and those which threaten permanency (1965). If the traumatic situation to which the child is responding with regression is not ameliorated, the risk arises that the regressed state will endure and may become impossible to undo. Freud (1965) notes that such regressions will deflect the drives from their age-appropriate goals. The treatment team believed Emily to be in danger of this in the face of her ongoing traumatic interactions with the educational system. Freud went on to state that it was nearly impossible to know when such regressions have or will become permanent (1965), a statement which echoes the concern that prompted the formation of the treatment plan elucidated herein. If we acknowledge that a particular regression, though at first necessary and in the service of the ego, may ultimately harm the psyche, must we not then also endeavor to identify and alleviate its cause?

Issues from Psychotherapy

Emily is a child who was unable to make good use of traditional therapy, but who is flourishing in the Winnicottian holding environment of an individualized therapeutic school setting. It is believed that her neurocognitive vulnerabilities caused her mostly intact personality and her emotional functioning to deteriorate as a result of the poor fit she repeatedly experienced within the school system. Her emotional issues were seen as secondary reactions to environmental and educational factors impacting upon neurocognitive vulnerabilities.

At the time of her greatest academic distress and greatest need for treatment, she appeared to be a poor candidate for psychotherapy. Unable to bring her issues into the treatment, Emily paradoxically appeared mostly intact when there. Her anxiety was situational; outside of school it was only apparent in her psychosomatic symptomatology and subsequent depression. It rarely appeared in her therapist's office. She protested going and had difficulty with the transitions before and after sessions; once there, however, she was usually related, calm, and happy. Her therapist was frustrated by Emily's unwillingness or inability to produce material in sessions despite its severity in school and, reactively, at home. The therapist's obvious skill and the positive nature of the therapeutic alliance between therapist and child notwithstanding, Emily mostly used her time in therapy to distract herself from her anxieties. Though her play was rich and elaborate, her defensiveness around these issues was impenetrable. Her therapist recommended three or four sessions per week after school, but her mother felt this to be impossible under the circumstances. Emily continually expressed the fact that she was too exhausted by the school day to participate in treatment, and she vehemently protested any increase in the number of sessions. She put up a fight over the once-a-week session, and, when her mother temporarily increased it to two during a period when she seemed desperately unhappy, Emily cried and refused to go. Since the therapy was supposed to be ego-supportive, there was the sense that further stress in the form of therapeutic regression was beyond Emily's coping skills at that time. Because this coincided with her behavior at home becoming seriously regressive, the lack of relief or progress in therapy was disturbing to all concerned.

The ego-dystonic nature of her regression and her tantrums over having to go to therapy or to school seemed to combine, regrettably, to ensure that she would be unable to make use of the therapy as it was. Throughout that spring, her therapist and her mother tried together to enlist Emily's participation in deepening the therapeutic alliance, but to no avail. After attending some sessions with Emily, during which her decompensation became quite alarming, her mother became unwilling to put any further pressure to attend increased sessions onto her rapidly deteriorating daughter.

Medication

One of the first decisions the treatment team agreed upon was to remove Emily from all psychotropic medications. Her mother felt that the Buspar had certainly been necessary to help Emily cope with the anxiety brought on by her failing attempt to function in the face of her school difficulties and her growing psychosomatic symptomatology; however, she now wanted her daughter off all medication. This was accomplished in June of 2000, at the conclusion of the school year, over the objections of both the school psychologist and the psychiatrist treating Emily. In fact, part of the reason for the team approach, and especially the consultations with the child analyst, was to share planning tasks and consider carefully the treatment plan and rationale to ensure that the unorthodoxy of the approach was matched by its consideration of Emily's therapeutic and educational needs.

THE TREATMENT PLAN: A HOME-TUTORING PROGRAM

As Emily's difficulties within the school environment intensified, her mother's consultations with the school psychologist, learning specialist, neuropsychologist, medicating psychiatrist, and psychotherapist all increased in both number and intensity. Her mother felt that the distress which Emily was experiencing would not be sufficiently ameliorated by medication and psychotherapy. Instead, the team of social worker and educator formed and were called upon to develop an individualized psychoeducational program. The team agreed with Emily's mother that a full-blown emotional crisis was well underway for Emily and that unless measures were taken to alleviate Emily's psychic distress and return her to a developmentally appropriate track, the results threatened to be life-affecting in the most negative fashion. In the face of Emily's inability to work even in a special education classroom, an alternative to formal education was sought.

All of Emily's school reports consistently pointed to her distractibility and inability to function in the presence of such distraction, which clearly established her emotional and neurocognitive need for a one-to-one instructional environment. This provided the second major justification for the program's design.

The decision was made to remove Emily from formal school and to create an individualized educational plan for her. We saw our job as reconstructive. The task was to retrain the psyche of a child who had learned to abhor school and who viewed learning with dread and anxiety approaching panic-attack levels. The therapeutic planning was this author's task: How to take a child with such a constellation of negative patterning and return her to the cheerfulness of her preschool days? How could we enable her to relinquish the array of defenses and symptoms which, though unsuccessful, had been steadily and systematically deployed to diminish her anxiety? Could we, in fact, return her to the peaceful and productive child she had been in time for her to enjoy a calm latency prior to the turbulence of adolescence? These were some of the questions that guided the structuring of Emily's psychoeducational treatment.

It was the intention of the home tutoring program to take a therapeutic approach to working on emotional issues in the milieu as they arose, while providing a "good enough," and certainly much improved, educational holding environment for Emily. We knew that for Emily at that time, severe anxiety accompanied nearly all academic tasks. If the program was to function as a therapeutic setting, her anxiety around learning needed to be allowed to emerge unmedicated and then be treated in and through the milieu. Her desire to regress and her tremendous need for reassuring objects were acknowledged and carefully planned for.

The treatment plan created a therapeutic environment in which her psychological issues were addressed along with her academic needs. The school environment was conceptualized as the equivalent to the therapeutic nursery in which the author had trained, where every interaction and every member of the team is psychotherapeutically informed. Winnicott's work on the holding environment was closely adhered to here.

We felt that Emily needed to reexperience the equivalent of a Winnicottian "primary maternal preoccupation" in the treatment environment of a therapeutically oriented school (1965). This, we believed, would eventually serve to ameliorate both her anxiety and her difficulty holding onto internalized object representations. Such a corrective experience was expected to aid in her recovery from the regressed state into which she was continuously thrown, or elected to return, in academic settings. Hopefully this would also help her to develop stronger good internal object representations, particularly with respect to teachers.

We made the determination that for most of the first year, and until she achieved the objectives of renewed object constancy and lowered anxiety in the face of academics, she would never be asked to function alone academically. From September to March, she worked only with a teacher by her side.

After much planning, the therapeutic individualized educational program was implemented in the fall of 2000. Both of her parents, but especially her mother, were closely involved. A well-known child analyst and Emily's occupational therapist were both extensively consulted so that all possibilities were conceptualized and planned for as well as possible. During the preceding summer, psychotherapy was appropriately terminated, happily, with little apparent sorrow or sense of loss to the child. It was felt that despite her warm feelings for her therapist, very little by way of a transference relationship had been established. The hope remained that despite Emily's inability to use traditional psychotherapy to resolve her emotional issues, the use of a therapeutic school environment would facilitate this working through. As Winnicott said, although in the context of the mother-child pair, "gradually, the ego-supportive environment is introjected and built into the individual's personality so that there comes about a capacity actually to be alone" (1965, p. 36). This was the initial primary treatment goal of this project. It was felt that everything else would follow from strong and enduring internalized good-object representations.

In September, Emily's school started in her bedroom. The decision had been to bring Emily back to her own home for schooling. It was conceptualized as a return to the safe holding environment which would encapsulate her regression and allow her psyche to regroup and regain its status in the service of normative development. Over the summer, she and her main teacher equipped her room with the conventional educational equipment for a girl in third grade. Plans were underway to secure a space a few blocks from her home, and starting in her home and then moving to the office nearby was seen as a therapeutic opportunity for recapitulating the separation and individuation issues she experienced so negatively in her transitions throughout the educational system, while simultaneously reworking the regressive impulses with which she was struggling.

The plan worked well. Emily was thrilled to be at home. She had lunch, recess, and breaks at home; however, she stayed in her room with her teachers and did her work during her scheduled school time. She never had a problem with this set-up, and her room proved remarkably soothing and surprisingly conducive to studying for her.

Her main teacher is her former tutor from kindergarten and first grade who has been involved with her education steadily since kindergarten. His work is centered in his belief that, when directed correctly, an individualized educational program has the potential to repattern a negative sense of self-esteem relative to academics. Her other teacher is a young man whose job it is to ensure that transitions are handled in ways that are therapeutic for her. He is receiving training in both education and social work and is under the dual supervision of the educational specialist and the clinical social worker. A large part of this young man's job was to help with all transitions. Indeed, we viewed him as her transitional object. He helped her transition from home to school when, in October, her school moved from her bedroom to the nearby office. With coaching and training, he began to negotiate systems with her, first on her behalf as her "mouthpiece" and later as her coach and ally. The ability to express her displeasure or her feelings of being overwhelmed verbally, instead of through nonverbal means such as somatic complaints and through regression, was a crucial therapeutic objective. He advocated for her at first, and then he helped her learn to speak for herself. Watching this duo engage with diverse environments and individuals (e.g., shop owners, therapists and extracurricular teachers), we observed her recovering self-esteem and reemerging individuation. In the beginning, there was an initial getting-acquainted period, which never takes long with this friendly and object-seeking child. She quickly came to realize that he was an ego-supportive teacher, and, rapidly overcoming her initial disbelief in the reality of such a person, she clung to him. The pair would walk down the street with her hanging from his arm. She seemed to lean into him, as if to gather strength from his size. Her mother noted that this was exactly how Emily walked with her. Thus began Emily's use of the young teacher as a supportive externalized object. Gradually, both at a symbolic level and in a more literal way, she lets go of her need to constantly cling to his hand and dances down the street in front of him. No metaphor could better illustrate her recapitulation and successful renegotiation of her separation and individuation issues.

The home tutoring program was designed to alleviate Emily's low self-esteem and lack of desire to engage in the learning process, as well as to remove the high degree of distraction posed by other children in her classroom. We felt that these goals would only be accomplished when her anxiety was reduced. We saw the provision of an external object for her to orient herself towards during academic demands as a corrective experience, permitting her to overcome her own regressive tendencies in the face of her overwhelming anxiety.

Thus the aims of the first academic year were multiple and complex but can be distilled to a few basic considerations. Primarily, the team saw its first objective as the lowering of her considerable anxiety which was causing regression and internal object loss around school attendance. Second, Emily needed to improve her self-esteem around her academic abilities as well as her willingness to try things which challenged her cognitively, neurologically, developmentally, and emotionally. The team's belief was that this would best be accomplished by educational and psychological interventions pitched to her exact academic and developmental levels. This recalls the social work caveat to "start where the client is." We followed this axiom closely. Because Emily could no longer be adequately psychically contained in a traditional educational setting, the locus of her education shifted to her bedroom. There, such regression could be treated as an adaptation rather than a pathological retreat. Academically, old material was always recapitulated before new material was introduced. This served as a reminder to her that she did, indeed, know the departure point. Her anxiety often interfered in the beginning, making her feel she didn't know material which, in fact, she had previously mastered. Needless to say, this approach was greatly facilitated by our ability to design a customized educational plan.

Frequently, it is Emily herself who indicates readiness for a new topic after acknowledging her sense of mastering material. This is akin to the way we allow our patients to guide the progress and process of psychotherapy.

Emily's day begins with exercise. For her, this serves to release some of her anticipatory anxiety and helps her settle into academics. She bikes, skates, or rollerblades to school with her younger teacher. They then spend about two hours working, always starting by recapitulating work from her main teacher the day before in order to ease her anxiety and encourage feelings of continuity and mastery. Lunch usually provides the opportunity for lessons about the negotiation of systems, the mathematics of currency, and the meaning of money, as she and her second teacher eat out in the neighborhood together. Four days a week, she spends two to three hours in the afternoon with her main teacher.

Twice a week Emily has occupational therapy, which provides vital strengthening for her weak neurological areas and help with issues such as coordination, fine motor skills, balance, and postural weaknesses.

She studies art with a well-loved former preschool teacher. The pair go to galleries, museums, and parks, talking about and creating art together. This serves both to validate her artistic talents as well as to provide time with a strong female role-model.

At 3 p.m. her academic day ends. She is free to participate in various extra-curricular activities (for example, socialization, exercise, and recreation) that provide outlets for her talents and creativity. She enjoys swimming and pottery classes and has tried yoga, stilt walking, and chorus with equal willingness and pleasure. There is no homework as this was one of her most serious secondary sources of anxiety, and the team believes she has sufficient academics from 9 to 3.

When she was told of the program being designed for her education, Emily was enthusiastic. She normally responds by idealizing change, particularly involving anything to do with her education. For her, new is going to be better. Fearful of her strong fantasies of what school was going to be like, her mother explained to her that school would still consist of lessons. She had some real difficulty with transitions as the program started, but her attitude rapidly adjusted as her new situation became real to her.

In the fall, there was a great deal of anticipatory anxiety for Emily around academics. On the first morning of school, she hid herself in her bathroom and refused to come out. In an interaction that was to prove a therapeutic turning point, her whole team was present to support and reeducate her. She was encouraged to speak out about her anxiety and her reluctance around engaging with academics. In tears, she was unable to speak and doubled over with stomach pains. Despite much encouragement, she remained mute, unable to express her fears and doubts. Finally, we formed role-play teams. The team spoke aloud for her as she was encouraged to whisper her feelings to us. Eventually, through her interpreters, she told the team that no one had listened to her when the work was too much for her so she didn't believe we would now. The team assured her that this was the entire aim of our program for her, that we wanted very much for her to tell us when the work felt too hard, when she needed a break, when she was tired, when she was fidgety. We recreated this structure only a few more times in word, though many times more in deed, before Emily once again, found her own voice. It has been an ongoing issue for her to become better able to voice her feelings and her needs, but the team is ever aware that this is the arena of her biggest emotional issues. We, therefore, listen and negotiate with and for her constantly. Emily has recently begun to be able to calmly state when tasks are too taxing or when she needs a rest. We feel that this ability to verbalize her feelings marks the single most important factor in her rapid learning of new material and the lessening of her anxiety at this time.

Her regressions have ceased in the face of an attuned and well-paced academic structure and the therapeutic milieu. Her adults are all poised to lower her anxiety by helping her to talk through what makes her nervous. Encouraging her to verbalize her discomfort with the conviction that tasks could always be explained or further broken down if necessary has alleviated much of her distress. This has led, so far, to a tremendous decrease in her anxiety levels, and a boost in her academic achievement which has exceeded the teams' expectations.

SOCIAL ISSUES

Emily's growing awareness of her differences from other children in her special education class, the social implications of her special education status, and her unwillingness to see herself as being damaged the way she perceived them to be, all contributed to the low self-esteem and isolation she experienced during her last year in school. She is acutely sensitive to her emotional environment and was quite disturbed by the demonstrations of psychic distress in her special education school. She is a highly empathic and intuitive child in this respect. It was felt that if the only environments which could be provided by the educational system contained children whose pathologies disturbed Emily so intensely, it was better for her to be alone than struggling with her issues in a typical special education classroom.

It must be noted that in the period just before the treatment program was initiated, her peer relations suffered due to her frequent regressions, which most emotionally healthy eight-year-olds cannot tolerate. She would withdraw and project this as "they don't want to play with me." She usually spent the recess period with her teachers–again an indication of both her insecurity and need to draw comfort and support from adults, and her lack of appropriate peer relationships. She saw the other children as disruptive and too loud, or as disliking her, and, therefore, chose to remain with the teachers rather than socialize. It was felt that her peer relations were unhelpful at that time in the classroom.

Better to help her to become age-appropriate with her peers, a goal which the team felt would occur simultaneously with their other goals, rather than continue to see socialization within a school-based group as paramount.

After-school activities were seen as a social arena for Emily, and the return to her neighborhood, along with the concurrent return of her psychic energy, has enabled socializing with old friends from preschool as well as new children of the neighborhood.

CONCLUSION

What have we achieved? We removed from the educational system a little girl who was highly anxious, depressed, suffering from low self-esteem and performing a year or more below grade levels. We designed a therapeutic school environment where she is the only student and is no longer asked to perform academic tasks beyond her capacity while she suffers panic at feeling unsupported and alone in a noisy classroom. We fed her a steady, manageable diet of academics and skills of daily living at a pace which she set. We worked hard therapeutically to help her lower her anxiety around learning.

As of this writing, it is late spring, and the team is evaluating the results of the first academic year. The initial results are promising. The team considers that our program has helped Emily considerably, although it is far too early to ascertain whether the results will be consolidated over time. We are eagerly awaiting the results of a recent neuropsychological evaluation to determine what can be seen in her cognitive and emotional testing. Emily has learned more than two years of reading this year and is now reading above her grade level. She is also ahead of her age levels in math and is demonstrating a love of numbers and their manipulation.

Most recently came a breakthrough which happens to every happy and healthy learner in latency: She now becomes so absorbed in a loved book that it goes everywhere with her. She is proud to relate how many pages she has read during a given interval. This truly exemplifies a return of her drive to competence and her successes with latency-aged tasks.

Recently, her skills of daily living have improved dramatically. We feel that this reflects her growing willingness to engage with the world. Her mother used to despair of Emily ever learning to read, or tell time, or understand and use money, or dial a phone. All of these skills are now hers. She is once again a related child. Her desire to be related, as well as competent, is obvious to all who see her.

Socially, she has made several new close friends this year through after-school activities. She makes friends easily and chooses to socialize with both genders and all ages of children. Not only does she no longer regress, but she also now baby-sits and takes great pleasure in being the older kid. She likes going to sleep-overs and had a group of 15 boys and girls of all ages at her recent birthday party. In as much as she only had her best friend at her birthday a year ago, the change is remarkable.

Of great significance to the treatment plan, Emily has recently begun to understand that she can work while "alone in the presence of the other" (Winnicott, 1965). Gradually, her teachers have moved from their constant position at her side during work times to sit across the room. She was quite anxious about this at first, but as she developed faith in the good intentions and reliable supportive presence of her teachers, she has relaxed and begun to work independently.

Most importantly, Emily is no longer on any medication, nor does the team believe her to be in any need of it. Those who know her best say that she has returned to the positive attitude and the compassionate and happy demeanor which marked her early childhood years.

It is beyond the scope of this article, and premature, to speak to the generalizability of this program to other children. This is the author's desire and a future goal of the team, but, at present, we are working towards consolidating Emily's gains and planning for her academic future. We are simply pleased at the turning of the course for Emily and eager to begin to examine ways in which this psychoeducational model can be further applied.

REFERENCES

American Psychiatric Association (1968). *Diagnostic and statistical manual of mental disorders, 2nd edition.* Washington, D.C.: American Psychiatric Association.

American Psychiatric Association (1994). *Diagnostic and statistical manual of mental disorders, 4th edition.* Washington, D.C.: American Psychiatric Association.

Barkley, R. A. (1998). *Attention-deficit hyperactivity disorder* (2nd Ed.). New York: The Guilford Press.

Breggin, P. (1998). *Talking back to Ritalin.* Monroe, ME: Common Courage Press.

Erikson, E. (1963). *Childhood and society.* New York: W.W. Norton and Company, Inc.

Fairbairn, W. R. D. (1952). *Psychoanalytic studies of the personality.* New York: Routledge.

Freud, A. (1966). *The ego and the mechanisms of defense.* Madison, CT: International Universities Press.

White, R. F. (1959). Motivation reconsidered: The concept of confidence. *Psychological Review, 66,* 297-333.

Winnicott, D. W. (1965). *The maturational process and the facilitating environment.* CT: International Universities Press.

About the Contributors

Irene M. Bravo, PhD, is a licensed psychologist and full-time faculty member in the doctoral program at Carolos Albizu University, Miami, Florida, where she teaches courses with an emphasis on developmental issues and psychopathology. She is also an adjunct faculty member at Florida International University and maintains a private practice in Miami, Florida. Dr. Bravo has previously published on the relation among performance evaluations, context effects, and individual differences and also on anxiety sensitivity and hypochondriasis in older adults.

Morton Chethik, MSW, completed his training as a child psychoanalyst in Cleveland, Ohio, in 1966. He was on the faculty of the Department of Psychiatry at the University of Michigan for 30 years and became Professor Emeritus in 1996. He has also been on the faculty of the Michigan Psychoanalytic Institute for the past 30 years and was founder of their Child Psychoanalytic Psychotherapy Education Program. He is the author of more than 30 articles, as well as the text *Techniques of Child Therapy: Psychodynamic Strategies,* now in its second edition. Mr. Chethik is a founding member of the editorial board of *Psychoanalytic Social Work.*

Vivian Farmery, CSW, is a psychotherapist in private practice in New York City. She is a doctoral candidate and Adjunct Professor at the Shirley M. Ehrenkranz School of Social Work at New York University and co-founder of the Center for Individualized Education.

Brenda Lovegrove Lepisto, PsyD, is a psychologist and psychoanalyst in private practice in East Lansing, Michigan. She is Adjunct Professor at Michigan State University in the College of Human Medicine and in the Department of Psychology.

Howard D. Lerner, PhD, ABPP, is Assistant Clinical Professor of Psychology in the Department of Psychiatry, University of Michigan Medical School. He is an adult, adolescent, and child psychoanalyst in private practice in Ann Arbor, Michigan. He is also on the faculty of the Michigan Psychoanalytic Institute and serves as a family consultant at the Allen Creek Preschool in Ann Arbor, Michigan.

Judith Mishne, DSW, is Full Professor and Chair of the Social Work Practice Curriculum Area at the Shirley M. Ehrenkranz School of Social Work, New York University. She maintains a part-time private practice, seeing patients and providing supervision and consultation. Dr. Mishne is the author of numerous articles and several books, including *Clinical Work with Children* and *Clinical Work with Adolescents,* and is a founding board member of *Psychoanalytic Social Work.*

Jack Novick, PhD, is a training and supervising analyst at the New York Freudian Society, a child and adolescent supervising analyst at the Michigan Psychoanalytic Institute, and Clinical Associate Professor of Psychiatry at the University of Michigan Medical School.

Kerry Kelly Novick is a child and adolescent supervising analyst at the Michigan Psychoanalytic Institute and Clinical Director of Allen Creek Preschool, Ann Arbor, Michigan.

Joseph Palombo is Founding Dean and faculty member of the Institute for Clinical Social Work, Chicago, a faculty member of the Child and Adolescent Psychotherapy Program, Chicago Institute for Psychoanalysis, and research coordinator, Rush Neurobehavioral Center. Mr. Palombo, who is a founding editorial board member of *Psychoanalytic Social Work,* has published numerous articles and book chapters, and is author of the recently published *Learning Disorders and Disorders of the Self in Children and Adolescents.* He maintains a private practice in Highland Park, Illinois.

Author Index

Subject Index

A. Ms., 15-19
AD/HD, 161,163,171,174-176
   adult, 171
adjunctive functions, 7
adolescence, 103,102 table 1,115,123
   culture conflicts of, 124-126
   developmental phase, 127,128,150
   psychoanalysis, 1, 7
adoption, 129,122,135,140,141
adult pathology, 96
affect regulator, 14,19
   mother as, 11
affection, inappropriate, 173,176
affective behavior, 72,149
affective disorders, 75,76
aggression, 71
   inability to express, 73
   role played in drug addiction, 78
alcohol, 78,97
   and drugs, 79-90
alliances, 132,150. *See* therapeutic alliance
alternative, competent, 116
ambivalent attachment, 59
ambivalent oral phase, 3,49,62,64
anaclitic depression, 51,53,54
anal stage, 49
analysis, child and adolescent, 112,
   115,116,128,177
analytic play space, 3. *See* play, play
   space
anti-anxiety medication, 177
anti-depressants, 177
anxiety, 6,78,184,186,188,190,191
anxiety disorder NOS, 174
Ashley, 161,162
Asperger's disorder, 150
attachment, 1,53-55,64,65,110
   avoidant, 59

disorganized, 100,127
infant-mother, 3,59
libidinal, 9,20
Attention Deficit/Hyperactivity Disorder. *See* AD/HD
autonomous production, 180,181
autonomy, 73,111,134,135

bad objects, 50
bipolar disorder, 74,76,82,86,88
birth trauma, 171
Blake, William, 8
borderline, 76
"brain driven" behaviors, 159
breast feeding, 50
Buspar, 176,184

castration anxiety, 51
child psychoanalysis, 2,32,33,111,
   113,186
choice, 104
Chris, 128-141
clinical social worker, 187
closed omnipotent system, 4,102 table 1,
   109-112,127-129
cocaine, 135
cognitive behavior, 72
Columbine, 80
comorbidity, 75
comparative psychology, 29
competence, 137-139,144,180,191
   lack of, 77
competent system. *See* open competence system
complementary moments, 6,147,148
   defined, 152

TO ORDER: CALL: 1-800-429-6784 / FAX: 1-800-895-0582 (outside US/Canada: + 607-771-0012) / **E-MAIL: orders@haworthpressinc.com**

Please complete the information below or tape your business card in this area.

☐ **YES**, please send me **Trauma and Cognitive Science**

—— in hard at $49.95 ISBN: 0-7890-1373-8.

—— in soft at $29.95 ISBN: 0-7890-1374-6.

- Individual orders outside US, Canada, and Mexico must be prepaid by check or credit card.
- Postage & handling: in US: $4.00 for first book; $1.50 for each additional book.
  Outside US: $5.00 for first book; $2.00 for each additional book.
- NY, MN, and OH residents: please add appropriate sales tax after postage & handling.
- Canadian residents: please add 7% GST after postage & handling. Canadian residents of Newfoundland, Nova Scotia, and New Brunswick, also add 8% for province tax. • Payment in UNESCO coupons welcome.
- If paying in Canadian dollars, use current exchange rate to convert to US dollars.
- Please allow 3-4 weeks for delivery after publication.
- Prices and discounts subject to change without notice.

Signature _____

☐ **PAYMENT ENCLOSED $** _____
(Payment must be in US or Canadian dollars by check or money order drawn on a US or Canadian bank.)

☐ **PLEASE BILL MY CREDIT CARD:**

☐ AmEx ☐ Diners Club ☐ Discover ☐ Eurocard ☐ JCB ☐ Master Card ☐ Visa

Account Number _____

Expiration Date _____

Signature _____

May we open a confidential credit card account for you for possible future purchases? ( ) Yes ( ) No

• Individual orders outside US, Canada, and Mexico must be prepaid by check or credit card.

Discounts are not available for jobbers and wholesalers.
5+ text prices are not available for 5+ text prices and not available in conjunction with any other discount. • Discount not applicable on books priced under $15.00.
Discounts are not available for jobbers and wholesalers.

☐ Check here if billing address is different from shipping address and attach purchase order and billing address information.

BILL ME LATER ($5 service charge will be added).
(Not available for individuals outside US/Canada/Mexico. Service charge is waived for jobbers/wholesalers/booksellers.)

NAME _____

INSTITUTION _____

ADDRESS _____

CITY _____

STATE _____ ZIP _____

COUNTRY _____

COUNTY (NY residents only) _____

E-MAIL _____
(type or print clearly!)

May we use your e-mail address for confirmations and other types of information? ( ) Yes ( ) No We appreciate receiving your e-mail address and fax number. Haworth would like to e-mail or fax special discount offers to you, as a preferred customer. We will never share, rent, or exchange your e-mail address or fax number. We regard such actions as an invasion of your privacy.

☐ **YES**, please send me **Trauma and Cognitive Science (ISBN: 0-7890-1374-6)** to consider on a 60-day no risk examination basis. I understand that I will receive an invoice payable within 60 days, or that if I decide to adopt the book, my invoice will be cancelled. I understand that I will be billed at the lowest price. (60-day offer available only to teaching faculty in US, Canada, and Mexico / Outside US/ Canada, a proforma invoice will be sent upon receipt of your request and must be paid in advance of shipping. A full refund will be issued with proof of adoption.)

Signature _____

Course Title(s) _____

Current Text(s) _____

Enrollment _____

Semester _____ Decision Date _____

Office Tel _____ Hours _____

This information is needed to process your examination copy order.

THE HAWORTH PRESS, INC., 10 Alice Street, Binghamton, NY 13904-1580 USA

(14) (29)   01/02   BIC02